The 30 Greatest Orchestral Works

Robert Greenberg, Ph.D.

THE
GREAT
COURSES®

PUBLISHED BY:

THE GREAT COURSES
Corporate Headquarters
4840 Westfields Boulevard, Suite 500
Chantilly, Virginia 20151-2299
Phone: 1-800-832-2412
Fax: 703-378-3819
www.thegreatcourses.com

Robert Greenberg, Ph.D.
Music Historian-in-Residence
San Francisco Performances

P rofessor Robert Greenberg was born in Brooklyn, New York, in 1954 and has lived in the San Francisco Bay Area since 1978. Professor Greenberg received a B.A. in Music, magna cum laude, from Princeton University in 1976. His principal teachers at Princeton were Edward Cone, Daniel Werts, and Carlton Gamer in composition; Claudio Spies and Paul Lansky in analysis; and Jerry Kuderna in piano. In 1984, Professor Greenberg received a Ph.D. in Music Composition, with distinction, from the University of California, Berkeley, where his principal teachers were Andrew Imbrie and Olly Wilson in composition and Richard Felciano in analysis.

Professor Greenberg has composed more than 45 works for a wide variety of instrumental and vocal ensembles. Recent performances of his works have taken place in New York; San Francisco; Chicago; Los Angeles; England; Ireland; Greece; Italy; and the Netherlands, where his *Child's Play* for String Quartet was performed at the Concertgebouw in Amsterdam.

Professor Greenberg has received numerous honors, including three Nicola de Lorenzo Composition Prizes and three Meet The Composer grants. He has received recent commissions from the Koussevitzky Music Foundation in the Library of Congress, the Alexander String Quartet, the San Francisco Contemporary Music Players, the Strata Ensemble, San Francisco Performances, and the XTET ensemble. Professor Greenberg is a board member and an artistic director of COMPOSERS, INC., a composers' collective and production organization based in San Francisco. His music is published by Fallen Leaf Press and CPP/Belwin and is recorded on the Innova label.

Professor Greenberg has performed, taught, and lectured extensively across North America and Europe. He is currently Music Historian-in-Residence with San Francisco Performances, where he has lectured and performed since 1994, and is a faculty member of the Advanced Management Program at the University of Pennsylvania's Wharton School of Business. He has served on the faculties of the University of California, Berkeley; California State University East Bay; and the San Francisco Conservatory of Music, where he chaired the Department of Music History and Literature from 1989 to 2001 and served as the director of the Adult Extension Division from 1991 to 1996.

Professor Greenberg has lectured for some of the most prestigious musical and arts organizations in the United States, including the San Francisco Symphony (where for 10 years he was host and lecturer for the symphony's nationally acclaimed Discovery Series), the Chautauqua Institute (where he was the Everett Scholar-in-Residence during the 2006 season), the Ravinia Festival, Lincoln Center for the Performing Arts, the Van Cliburn Foundation, the Nasher Sculpture Center, the Dallas Symphony Orchestra, the Hartford Symphony Orchestra, Villa Montalvo, Music@Menlo, and the University of British Columbia (where he was the Dal Grauer Lecturer in September 2006).

In addition, Professor Greenberg is a sought-after lecturer for businesses and business schools and has recently spoken for such diverse organizations as S. C. Johnson, Canadian Pacific, Deutsches Bank, the University of California/Haas School of Business Executive Seminar, the University of Chicago Graduate School of Business, Harvard Business School Publishing, Kaiser Permanente, the Strategos Institute, Quintiles Transnational, the Young Presidents' Organization, the World Presidents' Organization, and the Commonwealth Club of San Francisco. Professor Greenberg has been profiled in *The Wall Street Journal*, *Inc.* magazine, the *Times* of London, the *Los Angeles Times*, *The Christian Science Monitor*, the *San Francisco Chronicle*, the *San Jose Mercury News*, the University of California alumni magazine, *Princeton Alumni Weekly*, and *Diablo* magazine.

For many years, Professor Greenberg was the resident composer and music historian for NPR's *Weekend All Things Considered*; he presently plays that role on NPR's *Weekend Edition, Sunday* with Liane Hansen. In February

2003, Maine's *Bangor Daily News* referred to Professor Greenberg as the Elvis of music history and appreciation, an appraisal that has given him more pleasure than any other.

Professor Greenberg's other courses with The Great Courses include *How to Listen to and Understand Great Music, 3rd Edition*; *Concert Masterworks*; *Bach and the High Baroque*; *The Symphonies of Beethoven*; *How to Listen to and Understand Opera*; the *Great Masters* series; *The Operas of Mozart*; *The Life and Operas of Verdi*; *The Symphony*; *The Chamber Music of Mozart*; *Beethoven's Piano Sonatas*; *The Concerto*; *Understanding the Fundamentals of Music*; and *The Music of Richard Wagner*. ■

Table of Contents

INTRODUCTION

Professor Biography i
Course Scope 1

LECTURE GUIDES

LECTURE 1
Game Plan and Preliminaries 3

LECTURE 2
Vivaldi—*The Four Seasons* 23

LECTURE 3
Bach—Brandenburg Concerto No. 2 44

LECTURE 4
Bach—Violin Concerto in E Major 62

LECTURE 5
Haydn—Symphony No. 104 81

LECTURE 6
Mozart—Piano Concerto No. 24 in C Minor 99

LECTURE 7
Mozart—Symphony in C Major, "Jupiter" 117

LECTURE 8
Beethoven—Symphony No. 3 134

LECTURE 9
Beethoven—Piano Concerto No. 4 152

LECTURE 10
Beethoven—Symphony No. 9 170

Table of Contents

LECTURE 11
Schubert—Symphony No. 9 189

LECTURE 12
Mendelssohn—"Italian" Symphony 208

LECTURE 13
Schumann—Symphony No. 3 226

LECTURE 14
Brahms—Symphony No. 4 244

LECTURE 15
Brahms—Violin Concerto 262

LECTURE 16
Tchaikovsky—Symphony No. 4 280

SUPPLEMENTAL MATERIAL

Timeline 298
Glossary 301
Bibliography 311
Discography 322
Credits 327

The 30 Greatest Orchestral Works

Scope:

This course identifies and celebrates 30 of the greatest orchestral works in the concert repertoire. Each lecture presents learners with a historical and biographical context for each work via a guided tour of the work itself. These musical tours include both piano demonstrations of the piece's compositional structure and selected excerpts drawn from recordings.

The course is designed to serve learners as a series of expanded program notes that explores a broad range of orchestral music composed over the last 300 years: From the baroque era, the classical era, the romantic era, and the 20th century, the works featured in the course include some of the most well-known, best-loved, and most frequently performed pieces in the standard repertoire in the forms of symphonies, concertos, tone poems, symphonic poems, and suites.

By the course's end, we will understand why each featured piece is considered "great"; how each reflected, reinvented, and/or broke from contemporary musical conventions; how each reflected the individual spirit and nature of its composer; and to what extent contemporary historical circumstances affected the composition.

The works featured in the course include Johann Sebastian Bach's Brandenburg Concerto no. 2, Haydn's Symphony no. 104, Beethoven's Symphonies nos. 3 and 9, Mozart's Piano Concerto in C minor, Tchaikovsky's Violin Concerto in D major, Nikolay Rimsky-Korsakov's *Scheherazade*, Mahler's Symphony no. 5, Igor Stravinsky's *The Rite of Spring*, and other timeless works by such composers as Antonio Vivaldi, Franz Schubert, Felix Mendelssohn, Robert Schumann, Johannes Brahms, Antonín Dvořák, Sergey Rachmaninoff, Claude Debussy, Gustav Holst, Charles Ives, Aaron Copland, and Dmitri Shostakovich.

In addition to the glorious music, the course brings to life the humanity behind each composition. We will learn which of these mainstays of the repertoire was lauded at the time of its composition and which had to wait for recognition and acclaim. We also learn which fondly held conventions—musical, societal, and political—were upended by composers such as Vivaldi, Bach, Mozart, and Beethoven.

We learn that Bach's contemporaries favored Vivaldi's compositions and thought of Bach's work as an artistic dead end. We learn of Haydn's compositional thrift and revel in the originality and genius of the musical utopian Mozart, who was recognized in his own time as being outside the contemporary compositional mainstream.

The course traces the development of the different musical genres, too. For example, the course traces the evolution of the symphony from an entertainment for the privileged wealthy to one enjoyed by the wider public to the impact of Beethoven's Symphony no. 9—with its revolutionary combination of instruments and voices—on 19th-century compositions.

In addition to the historical, social, political, and cultural contexts of the music, we learn about the personal circumstances that shaped the composers' musical voices. Mental and physical illness, rejection, loss, political censure, and ostracism all play a role in the very human side of the great music we study.

The course concludes with a reflection upon the future of orchestral music, some thoughts regarding the music business, and fervent hopes for the survival of a threatened species—the modern orchestra. ∎

Game Plan and Preliminaries
Lecture 1

The goals of this first lecture are to put the course title into perspective and to explore what constitutes both an orchestra and orchestral music. Another goal is to introduce the stylistic periods and the orchestral genres that will be encountered throughout the course. In addition, we will discuss the nature of musical form and define the seven major musical forms composers either follow or from which they innovate.

In reference to the course title, the word "greatest" denotes compositions of enduring expressive content and compositional quality—works that evince their ongoing popularity by their centrality in the standard repertoire. This lecture serves as an introduction, while Lectures 2–31 are the "30 greatest." The final lecture addresses a few of the many "great orchestral works" that were not included in this course. While the order in which the works appear is, for the most part, chronological, the course itself does not require sequential viewing/listening.

By the early 1700s, the relatively large, mixed instrumental ensemble called an orchestra had come into being. At that time, composers were writing idiosyncratically orchestral music thanks to the developing concept of orchestration, which refers to how a composer assigns instruments to the melodic and accompanimental parts of a composition. The art of orchestration demands that individual instruments and/or groups of instruments enter, depart, and overlap—constantly shifting the weight and color of the musical sound as it unfolds.

The baroque era is a stylistic period that spanned from 1600 to 1750—from the birth of opera in 1600 to the death of Johann Sebastian Bach in 1750. The early baroque (1600–1650) was a musically revolutionary time in which opera appeared in Italy and evolved from a modest courtly entertainment into a hugely popular and profitable media industry. During the middle baroque (1650–1700), the compositional innovations of opera transferred to other genres of music. During the high, or late, baroque era (1700–1750),

Antonio Vivaldi, George Frederick Handel, and Johann Sebastian Bach created a transcendent body of work.

A new, more melodically direct style of music emerged in southern Italy, namely Naples, that featured what their practitioners called natural music: song-like melodies simply accompanied (a **texture** referred to as **homophony**). This new Neapolitan style rejected so-called artificial harmony, which is the intertwining of multiple, simultaneous, principal melodies (a texture known as **polyphony**). Today, what we call the **classical** style evolved from this new, more accessible, presumably natural sort of music that resonated with the spirit of the empowered individual that lay at the heart of Enlightenment doctrine.

> **After Beethoven, composers took for granted that they should express themselves in their music.**

The romantic era is a period that spanned from the death of Beethoven in 1827 to the advent of the 20th century in 1900. After Beethoven, composers took for granted that they should express themselves in their music. For some composers, the expressive imperative and their desire to be original necessitated that they go beyond the strictures of traditional **melody** and **harmony**: the so-called **tonal** system that had been the bedrock vocabulary of Western music since the 15th century.

The search for expressive originality led some composers to abandon the structures and rituals of traditional tonality around the turn of the 20th century in favor of self-created, self-referential musical languages. In general, the music of the 20th century demonstrated a sort of hyper-romanticism, in that the very musical language with which a composer spoke became contextual, or subject to the self-expressive urge. ■

The Major Musical Forms

Musical form refers to the structure of a given movement of music. Composers of a given era will generally adhere to a fairly limited number of formal procedures that are understood by a contemporary audience and, therefore, contribute mightily to rendering works comprehensible to a contemporary audience. The musical forms that are necessary for this course are as follows. With the exception of the ritornello form, all are classical-era forms.

- **ritornello**: A refrain procedure in which a theme returns in part, called a fragmentary refrain, over the course of a movement. This form is among the most common of all baroque-era instrumental procedures.

- **theme and variations**: A theme is stated at the beginning of the movement, and each subsequent section of music is perceived as a variation of that theme. Such a movement usually concludes with a coda, which informs the listener that the process of variation is over and provides a satisfying sense of conclusion.

- **minuet and trio**: A minuet—a moderate, stately three-step dance—is expressed, and then a contrasting minuet is presented in a section called the trio. Following the trio, the original minuet returns in a section called the da capo to conclude the movement.

- **scherzo**: Generally retains the structure of minuet and trio form, but eliminates the ritual repetitions of the minuet dance, which speeds up the movements.

- **rondo**: A refrain form in which a rondo theme, once stated, returns periodically after various contrasting episodes. Unlike ritornello form, the returns of a rondo theme tend to be complete.

- **sonata**: Two or more principal contrasting themes are presented, developed, and ultimately reconciled to each other.

- **double exposition**: Sonata form adapted to the needs of a concerto.

Orchestral Genres

- **solo concerto**: A multi-movement work in which a single soloist is accompanied by, and sometimes pitted against, the orchestra.

- **concerto grosso**: A multi-movement work in which multiple soloists are accompanied by, and sometimes pitted against, the orchestra.

- **symphony**: A multi-movement work composed for an orchestra.

- **symphonic poem** or **tone poem**: A single-movement orchestral work that seeks to tell some sort of extra-musical, or programmatic, story.

- **suite**: A concert work consisting of a collection of dances extracted from a longer ballet.

Important Terms

classical: Designation given to works of art of the 17th and 18th centuries, characterized by clear lines and balanced form.

harmony: The musical art (and science) of manipulating simultaneous pitches.

homophonic texture/homophony: Texture in which one melodic line predominates; all other melodic material is heard as being secondary or accompanimental.

melody: Any succession of pitches.

polyphonic texture/polyphony: Texture consisting of two or more simultaneous melody lines of equal importance.

texture: Number of melodies present and the relationship between those melodies in a given segment of music; they include monophony, polyphony (counterpoint), heterophony, and homophony.

tonal/tonality: Sense that one pitch is central to a section of music, as opposed to atonal/atonality.

Game Plan and Preliminaries
Lecture 1—Transcript

Welcome to *The 30 Greatest Orchestral Works*. This is Lecture 1, and it is entitled "Game Plan and Preliminaries."

Don't trust anything over 30. *The 30 Greatest Orchestral Works*? Is there something special about the number 30? Aside from the fact that 30 is the minimum age for a United States senator, the number of variations in Johann Sebastian Bach's *Goldberg Variations*, the number of silver pieces Judas received for betraying Jesus, Maury Wills's uniform number, the sum of the first four squares (which makes it a square pyramidal number), is there anything special about 30?

No. Simply put, I decided that 30 was the very least number of orchestral works I could survey while still maintaining some control over the size of this course. We will discuss the potential folly of making such a list; what for our purposes constitutes "great" and the criteria used to select works for this course in a moment. But first: some music! The first of our "30 greatest": the first movement of the first of Antonio Vivaldi's *The Four Seasons*, the bug-and-bird infested opening of spring.

[Musical selection: Vivaldi, *The Four Seasons*, "Spring," Movement 1.]

My friends, contemplating the music we are going to listen to and study together over these 32 lectures makes me squirmy with excitement! Works by Johann Sebastian Bach, Joseph Haydn, and Wolfgang Mozart, whose "Jupiter" symphony occupies Lecture 6. Works by Ludwig van Beethoven, Franz Schubert, Felix Mendelssohn, Robert Schumann, Johannes Brahms, Peter Tchaikovsky, and Bedřich Smetana, whose epic *Má Vlast*, meaning "My Country," occupies Lecture 18. Works by Antonin Dvořák, Nicolai Rimsky-Korsakov, Richard Strauss, Gustav Mahler, Sergey Rachmaninoff, Claude Debussy, Igor Stravinsky, Charles Ives, Gustav Holst, Aaron Copland, and Dmitri Shostakovich. Oh, be still our hearts!

Fetishes, Good and Bad

We will acknowledge up front that our contemporary fetish for making lists can potentially denigrate and trivialize those very things we choose to list. The artificiality of such lists notwithstanding, they can serve a most useful purpose: this course, for example. Over the last 350 years, tens of thousands of works have been composed for the large instrumental ensemble generically referred to as the orchestra. For the interested but inexperienced listener, the biggest question is "Where do I start?" For the more experienced listener, the question is "What works, in historical hindsight, are most representative of their time and place and their composers' greater output?" For all of us, the question is "What do we need to know about these works in order to maximize our listening experience?" This course will answer all these questions.

Hit It, Forrest: Greatest Is as Greatest Does

We will understand the word "greatest" to denote compositions of enduring expressive content and compositional quality, works that evince their ongoing popularity by their centrality in the standard repertoire. The phrase "standard repertoire" refers to works that are performed with some degree of regularity. Thus, regrettably, there are no "sleepers" here, meaning little-known works that I've tossed in to show you how very clever and repertoire-savvy I am. Such works will have to wait for a course entitled *The 30 Greatest Orchestral Sleepers.*

Neither are there any works in this course composed since 1953, a year before I was born. Depending upon your point of view, this is either a good thing or a disaster. The sad truth, however, is that orchestras and conductors have done little to cultivate a new orchestral repertoire over the last 50 years, and excepting a handful of works, what new orchestral music is performed is almost never re-performed after its premiere. Thus, this music does not qualify as being part of the "standard repertoire." I am well aware that because of this, I will be accused by some of perpetuating the "masterwork myth." I can handle that. Perhaps, at a future date, I will be able to redeem myself by creating a course entitled *The 30 Greatest post-1953 Orchestral Works*.

This first lecture will set the stage for what follows and is thus about preliminaries and goals for the course. We are presently engaged in the first of those preliminaries, which is putting the course title into perspective.

Our Remaining Goals for This Lecture

Goal No. 2: To observe the ground rules and criteria used to select the works featured in the course.

Goal No. 3: To explore what constitutes both an "orchestra" and "orchestral music," that is, music composed and arranged specifically for a performing ensemble called an orchestra.

Goal No. 4: I will offer a brief but intense primer on the stylistic periods encountered during the course, starting with the baroque era, the classical era, the romantic era, and the 20th century. (Look, I hate these period designations as much as anyone, with their pretense to clear categorization and stylistic unity; I hate my car and its internal-combustion engine as well. But I use my car because I have to, and the same is true for periodization.)

This stylistic primer will be offered as an overview, and will thus have all the nuance of blunt-force trauma. That's OK. To have some appreciation for how special—how beyond the norm—are the works of J. S. Bach, Antonio Vivaldi, Joseph Haydn, and Wolfgang Mozart, to name but a few of the composers featured in this course, we must first have some sense of what constituted their stylistic norms in the first place.

Goal No. 5: We will discuss the nature of musical form and define the seven major musical forms we will encounter during this course: ritornello form, theme and variations form, minuet and trio form, scherzo, rondo form, sonata form, and double exposition form.

Goal No. 6: We will define the orchestral genres, that is, the types of orchestral music that we will encounter during the course: the concerto grosso, the solo concerto, the symphony, the symphonic poem, the tone poem, and the suite.

The Overall "Structure" of the Course

Lectures 2 through 31 will deal with our "30 greatest," one piece per lecture. While the order in which the works appear is, for the most part, chronological, this course is not sequential: Lecture 3 is not a prerequisite to Lecture 4; Lecture 4 is not a prerequisite to Lecture 5; and so forth. Rather, each of the 30 "repertoire lectures" is a self-standing entity. I've done this so that this course might be consumed in various ways: as a single entity, Lectures 1 through 32 or as a compendium of discreet lectures, each a combination pre-concert talk and audio program note.

The 32nd and final lecture, entitled "The Ones That Got Away," will address a few of the many great orchestral works that were not included in the "big 30."

Selection Process and Criteria

My friends, it is a fact that the requisite "30 greatest" of this course could legitimately consist of Haydn's last 15 symphonies, Mozart's last three symphonies, and Beethoven's nine symphonies, fourth and fifth piano concerti, and his violin concerto. Ba-da-bing! There it is, your 30 greatest orchestral works.

But that's not what I want to accomplish with this course. My fundamental goal is to create a broad-based survey that will include three centuries of repertoire and touch upon a wide range of composers (with the added *frisson* of sparking a lively—though never acrimonious—debate on exactly which pieces should have been included in such a "top 30").

Consequently, I have had to establish some admittedly arbitrary criteria with which I could create a broad-based course entitled "The 30 Greatest Orchestral Works" and still look my colleagues in the eye and myself in the mirror. Here are those criteria.

Selection Criterion No. 1: With but one exception, no single composer is represented by more than two works in the course. The exception is Beethoven, whose orchestral music so dominates the repertoire that not to have included more than two of his works would have brought this entire project into disrepute.

Selection Criterion No. 2: The music of those composers featured in this course had to be considered on its own merits and not in reference to the music of any other composer. For example, this course includes Johannes Brahms's Symphony no. 4 but not Beethoven's Symphony no. 5. Does this mean that I consider Brahms's Fourth to be a "greater work" than Beethoven's Fifth? It does not. Neither does it mean that I consider Brahms's Symphony no. 4 to be "greater" than Brahms's Symphonies nos. 1, 2, and 3. What it does mean is that I have chosen Brahms's Fourth to represent all of Brahms's symphonies, each of which deserves to be included in this course. Some music! The rollicking and ringing opening of the third movement of Johannes Brahms's Symphony no. 4 of 1885. [**Music selection**: Brahms, Symphony No. 4 in E Minor, op. 98, Movement 3.]

Selection Criterion No. 3: All works had to be self-standing works for orchestra, which means that this course excludes opera overtures and "incidental music."

Selection Criterion No. 4: This course excludes works that I've already examined at length in my Great Course's survey, *How to Listen to and Understand Great Music*. For example, both Beethoven's Symphony no. 5 and Hector Berlioz's *Symphonie Fantastique* are examined at length in *How to Listen to and Understand Great Music* and have thus been excluded from this course. My friends, them's the breaks.

The Orchestra and What Constitutes "Orchestral" Music

The mixed instrumental group called the orchestra evolved from the instrumental ensembles that accompanied the first operas in the early 1600s. The word "orchestra" itself comes from the ancient Greek term for the semi-circular area around the lip of a stage, where the "Greek" chorus stood and chanted their commentary during a play. It was in this location, at the edge of the stage, where the instrumental ensemble sat during the performance of an opera. By the 18th century—the 1700s—this instrumental ensemble had come to be referred to by the location in which it played: the orchestra.

When the first public opera house, the Teatro San Cassio, opened its doors in Venice in 1637, the popularity of opera exploded. Ever larger audiences required larger opera houses, more sumptuous productions, and ever bigger instrumental ensembles to accompany those productions. Instruments like the flute, oboe, bassoon, and horn were modernized, that is, made "tunable," and added to the core ensemble of strings and keyboards.

By the early 1700s, a period referred to as the high baroque, the relatively large, mixed instrumental ensemble called an orchestra had come into being. Of equal import, by the early 1700s composers were writing idiosyncratically orchestral music, thanks to the developing concept of orchestration.

"Orchestration" refers to how a composer assigns instruments to the melodic and accompanimental parts of a composition. When wind and brass instruments first joined the orchestra back in the mid-1600s, what passed for orchestration was pretty crude: When they weren't being used to create some special effect, wind and brass instruments typically played along with the string parts, sacrificing their own unique character in the name of a fleshed-out string sound.

However, by the early 1700s the art of orchestration had been conceived. Wind instruments, brass instruments, and the various sections within the strings came to be grouped in ever changing combinations, combinations that sometimes played the principal melodies, sometimes counter-melodies, and sometimes simple accompaniments. This most fluid approach to the individual instruments and instrumental sections of the orchestra is what orchestration is all about. The art of orchestration assumes a fundamental principal called instrumental discontinuity, which posits that no single group of instruments plays all the time. Instead, the art of orchestration demands that individual instruments and/or groups of instruments enter, depart, and overlap—constantly shifting the weight and color of the musical sound as it unfolds. That's what the art of orchestration is all about, and as an example, we turn to the first movement of Bach's Brandenburg Concerto No. 2 of c. 1721.

The "orchestra" for which Bach composed his second Brandenburg is admittedly small by modern standards but large and brilliant by his standards. It calls for a full complement of strings—first violins, second violins, violas, 'cellos, and double bass viols (which were the direct ancestor of the modern double bass); a harpsichord; a clarino (the ancestor of what we today call a soprano or piccolo trumpet); a flute; an oboe; and a solo violin. The movement begins with a boisterous, note-filled theme played by everybody, what we call an orchestral tutti, meaning "all together." [**Musical selection**: Bach, Brandenburg Concerto no. 2 in F Major, movement 1] The flute and oboe next briefly take center stage, after which the solo violin plays a bouncing, trilling counter-melody. [**Musical selection**: Bach, Brandenburg Concerto No. 2 in F Major, movement 1.] Next, the full orchestra briefly resumes playing the opening theme. [**Musical selection**: Bach, Brandenburg Concerto No. 2 in F Major, movement 1 (continues).]

And thus a pattern is established: Various solo instruments enter and play the bouncing, trilling counter-melody, while each iteration of the counter-melody is punctuated by a bit of the opening theme as played by the full ensemble until the full ensemble brings this opening section of the movement to its conclusion.

Let's listen to the entire opening from the beginning, and let us be pre-eminently aware of the constantly shifting, discontinuous nature of the instrumental texture, as no one instrument or group of instruments predominates for more than a few seconds at a time. [**Musical selection**: Bach, Brandenburg Concerto No. 2 in F Major, Movement 1.] That, my friends, is an example of music composed specifically for the orchestral ensemble performing it—the art of orchestration in full swing!

A Brief but Intense Primer on the Stylistic Periods Encountered in the Course

The Baroque Era

The baroque era is periodized as running from 1600–1750, from the birth of opera in 1600 to the death of Johann Sebastian Bach in 1750. The early baroque [era], roughly 1600–1650, was a musically revolutionary time. Opera appeared in Italy and evolved from a modest courtly entertainment into a hugely popular and profitable media industry. Public opera was performed by a new breed of singers whose huge voices matched the exuberant emotions depicted on stage.

The middle baroque, roughly 1650–1700, saw the compositional innovations of opera transferred to other genres of music. Instrumental music emerged as a tradition unto itself, while a distinction came to be made between works composed for one player per part (works called chamber music) and multiple players per part (works called orchestral music). Genres of orchestral music evolved directly out of operatic practice, most notably the concerto and the Italian-style opera overture (which the Italians called a *sinfonia* and which would eventually evolve into the "symphony").

The high (or late) baroque, which encompasses those years between 1700 and 1750, saw Antonio Vivaldi, George Frederick Handel, and Johann Sebastian Bach create a transcendent body of work.

The Classical Era

Even as Vivaldi was composing *The Four Seasons* and Bach his Brandenburg Concerti, a new, more melodically direct style of music was emerging in southern Italy in and around the city of Naples. This more song-like and frankly more popular compositional style was, initially, cultivated by local composers in order to differentiate their operas from those of their northern colleagues by composing music that appealed directly to the tastes of local audiences.

This new Neapolitan style laid the foundations for a series of related musical styles that became increasingly popular across Europe in the 1720s and 1730s. All of these related styles featured what their practitioners called "natural" music, meaning song-like melodies simply accompanied (a texture referred to as homophony), and rejected what they called "artificial harmony," (that is, the intertwining of multiple, simultaneous, principal melodies, a texture known as "polyphony").

The French called their version of this new music the *style galant*: the "chic" style. The Germans called theirs the *Empfindsamer stil,* or the "sensitive style." Whatever we choose to call it, the rise and development of this new, more populist compositional style mirrored a changing political and social landscape, one that rejected intellectual complexity in favor of natural feeling, and artistic elitism in favor of accessibility. The new Italian style, the *style galant*, and *Empfindsamer stil* are, collectively, the early music of the Enlightenment, and together they mark a sea-change in the expressive syntax of Western music.

What today we call the classical style evolved from this new, more accessible, presumably natural sort of music, music that resonated with the spirit of the empowered individual that lay at the heart of Enlightenment doctrine. The classical style reached its artistic high-watermark in and around the Habsburg capitol of Vienna between roughly 1775 and 1800, and thus the high classical style is often referred to as the Viennese classical style. The great exponents of Viennese classicism were Joseph Haydn (who lived from 1732–1809) and Wolfgang Mozart (who lived from 1756–1791). There is no one on this planet (or any other, for that matter) whose life will not be brightened, intensified, and made more worth living by the music of Haydn and Mozart.

In support of that statement, we hear an example of Viennese classicism at its most brilliant: the opening of the fourth and final movement of Mozart's Symphony in C Major, also known as the "Jupiter," composed in 1788. [**Musical selection**: Mozart, Symphony in C Major, "Jupiter," Movement 4.]

The Age of Revolution

A consequence of the age of Enlightenment, with its philosophical emphasis on the "inalienable rights of the individual," was a growing desire on the part of the growing middle class to exercise ever more control over their own lives. Both the American Revolution (which broke out in 1775) and the French Revolution (which began 14 years later in 1789), were triggered by middle-class aspirations, needs, and concerns. When Napoleon Bonaparte came to power in 1799, it appeared as if the anti-monarchial, middle-class revolution would spread to the four corners of Europe. It did not, but Napoleon's megalomaniacal attempt to weld Europe into a single entity ruled from Paris did indeed destabilize the European status quo and opened the door for a long series of European revolutions that continued into the 20th century and found its denouement with the Russian Revolution of 1917.

The composer whose life and music has come to personify the danger and promise of the French Revolution and the Napoleonic age is Ludwig (or Louis) van Beethoven. Beethoven's Enlightenment-inspired belief in the efficacy of his personal artistic vision led him to conclude—during a period of terrible despair brought on by his progressive hearing loss—that his music had to be a vehicle for personal self-expression. Believing thus, Beethoven created a body of work that subscribed to no particular stylistic or compositional norm beyond his own desire to be original and true to his own muse. His Ninth Symphony of 1824 is to music what the United States Bill of Rights is to American culture: a quintessential Enlightenment document that celebrates and asserts the fundamental rights of the individual in society.

The symphony is capped by Beethoven's Fourth Movement setting of Friedrich Schiller's poem *Lied an die Freude* ("Song—or 'Ode' to Joy"):

> Oh joy, thou lovely spark of God,
> Daughter of Elysium
> we enter, drunk with fire,
> immortal goddess, thy holy shrine.
> Thy magic does again unite
> what custom has torn apart;
> all men shall be brothers,
> where thy gentle wing is spread.

[**Musical selection**: Beethoven, Symphony No. 9 in D Minor, Movement 4.]

Beethoven's Ninth Symphony is the only work in this course in which we will hear voices, something we will discuss at length in Lecture 10.

The Romantic Era

The romantic era is periodized as running from the death of Beethoven in 1827 to the advent of the 20th century in 1900. (Yes, an unruly number of years, especially if we consider that the 20th century didn't technically begin until 1901. Again, we will work with what we have.)

The word "romantic" in this application does not relate to love or affection. Rather, it was used in the 19th century to identify something remote, mysterious, sublime, boundless, and beyond the everyday; in contemporary surf-speak, something far out. The intrinsic "far-outness" of much 19th- music manifested itself in various ways, but it all boiled down to one fundamental artistic premise. In the post-Beethoven, increasingly me- oriented 19th-century musical environment, composers took for granted that they should express themselves to pretty much whatever degree they chose in their music.

For some composers, the expressive imperative and their desire to be original necessitated that they go beyond—sometimes far beyond—the strictures of traditional melody and harmony: the so-called tonal system that had been the bedrock vocabulary of Western music since the 15th century. Such departures from traditional practice—like stepping into a batter's box wielding not a Louisville Slugger but a feather duster—could be *über*-shocking. Composers as far apart on the musical spectrum as Richard Wagner (whom many considered to be a radical revolutionary) and Johannes Brahms (whom many considered to be a conservative traditionalist) each experimented with harmonic and melodic materials that left traditional practice in the dust.

The 20th Century

The search for expressive originality led some composers to abandon the structures and rituals of traditional tonality around the turn of the 20th century in favor of self-created, self-referential musical languages.

For example, in his seminal work, *The Rite of Spring* of 1912, the St. Petersburg native Igor Stravinsky elevated pure rhythm—visceral, primal, and more-often-than-not irregularly accented rhythm—to a level theretofore occupied by thematic melody. [**Musical selection**: Stravinsky, *The Rite of Spring*, Dance of the Adolescents.]

Speaking generally but not inaccurately, the music of the 20th century demonstrated a sort of hyper-romanticism, in that the very musical language with which a composer spoke became contextual, that is, subject to the self-expressive urge. And while this fetish for originality continues unabated here in the 21st century, its roots can be traced back to the 18th century and the Enlightenment, with its philosophical emphasis on the importance of the individual and the individual's right to revel in his or her own life.

Musical Form

Musical form refers to the structure of a given movement of music. Composers of a given era will generally adhere to a fairly limited number of formal procedures, procedures which—like the structure of a baseball game—are understood by a contemporary audience and therefore contribute mightily to rendering works comprehensible to a contemporary audience.

A passing knowledge of these formal procedures, these architectural templates, is especially important when dealing with instrumental music. By its very nature, instrumental music is the most abstract of all the arts. It has no physical substance, and lacking words, instrumental music must "explain itself," its reason to be, through a complex combination of emotion, metaphor, analog, and intellect. Instrumental musical forms, then, are ritual (if elastic) formal structures that create expectations—conscious and unconscious—that a composer can (and will) manipulate during the course of a movement. The major musical forms we will encounter during this course are as follows.

Ritornello Form

Ritornello form is among the most common of all baroque-era instrumental procedures. Ritornello means literally, "little return," and that's what Ritornello form is, a refrain procedure, where a theme, the ritornello theme, returns in part as a fragmentary refrain over the course of a movement.

There are five classical era formal procedures with which we must be familiar. Despite the fact that they're known as the classical-era forms, many composers continued to use them through the 20th century. Here are the classical-era forms, presented in order of increasing complexity.

theme and variations form movement: A theme and variations form movement is one in which a theme—the more tuneful and memorable the better—is stated at the beginning of the movement. Each subsequent section of the movement is perceived as a variation of that theme. The variations can be as simple as changing the accompaniment or as complex as embellishing the theme beyond easy recognition. There is no fixed number of variations. A composer can (and will) provide as many (or as few) as she sees fit. Such a movement will usually conclude with a section of music called a coda, which informs the listener that the ongoing process of variation is *finis* and provides a satisfying sense of conclusion.

minuet and trio form: The minuet and trio grew out of a baroque dance form of the same name. In such a movement, a minuet—a moderate, stately three-step dance—is stated. A contrasting minuet is then presented in a section called the trio. Following the trio, the original minuet returns in a section called the da capo to conclude the movement.

The "bad boy from Bonn," Ludwig van Beethoven, had no use for the formulas and aristocratic pretensions of the minuet. Fairly early in his career, he began calling his minuet-like movements scherzos, which means "I'm joking," as in "the joke is on the minuet." In his scherzi, Beethoven generally retained the triple meter of the minuet and the large scale A-B-A structure of minuet and trio form. But Beethoven did away with the ritual repetitions of the minuet dance and so sped up his movements that any reference to a stately dance of moderate tempo is usually completely lost.

rondo form: Like ritornello form, rondo form is a refrain form, in which a rondo theme, once stated, returns periodically after various contrasting episodes. However, the difference between the two is that while the returns of a ritornello theme tend to be fragmentary, the returns of a rondo theme tend to be complete.

sonata form: A sonata form movement is one in which two or more principal contrasting themes are presented, developed, and ultimately reconciled to each other. The opening section of a sonata form movement—during which the multiple, contrasting themes are introduced—is called the exposition. In performance, sonata form expositions are usually repeated verbatim, the better to know and recognize the themes. Materials from the exposition are then developed in a section called the development, after which the themes return in their original order (but with important changes) in a section called the recapitulation. A coda will usually bring such a movement to its conclusion. We will encounter more sonata form movements in this course than any other, from Haydn's Symphony no. 104 of 1795 in Lecture 5 to Shostakovich's Symphony No. 10 of 1953 in Lecture 31.

double exposition form: Double exposition form is the sonata form adapted to the needs of a concerto. Instead of the exposition repeat typical of sonata form, a double exposition form movement will feature two separately composed expositions played back to back. In the first exposition, the orchestral exposition, the orchestra plays the themes. In the second exposition, the solo exposition, the soloist gets to play the themes.

Orchestral Genres

concerto: Once upon a time, during the Renaissance and early baroque era, the word "concerto" could refer to any piece of music in which instruments played together—in concert—with one another. However, by the 1680s, the word had come to designate three different types of orchestral music, of which we are concerned with two: the solo concerto and the concerto grosso.

solo concerto: A solo concerto is a multi-movement work in which a single soloist is accompanied by—and sometimes pitted against—the orchestra.

concerto grosso: A concerto grosso (meaning a " big or large concerto") is a multi-movement work in which multiple soloists are accompanied by—and sometimes pitted against—the orchestra (Handy terms: In a concerto grosso, the soloists are referred to as the concertino, meaning the "little ensemble," and the orchestra is referred to as the ripieno, meaning the "full ensemble." When everyone plays together, concertino and ripieno, it is referred to as the tutti.)

Symphony

A symphony is a multi-movement work composed for an orchestra. The first self-standing symphonies were composed in Vienna in the 1740s.

Symphonic Poem

A symphonic poem is a single-movement orchestral work that seeks to tell some sort of extra-musical, or programmatic story. The term was coined in the late 1840s by the pianist/composer Franz Liszt.

Tone Poem

A tone poem is the same thing as a symphonic poem. The term was coined in the 1880s by the composer Richard Strauss, who did not want his works identified with those of Franz Liszt!

Suite

A suite is a concert work consisting of a collection of dances extracted from a longer ballet. The concert versions of Tchaikovsky's *The Nutcracker*, Stravinsky's *The Firebird*, and Aaron Copland's *Appalachian Spring* are all such suites. Copland's *Appalachian Spring* will occupy Lecture 29.

Thus armed and ready, we proceed!

Thank you.

Vivaldi—*The Four Seasons*
Lecture 2

Taken as a whole, Vivaldi's *The Four Seasons* is about humankind's relationship to nature. Musically, the cycle demonstrates a satisfying degree of contrasts and balances. In both "Spring" and "Autumn," nature is idealized and depicted as benign. Alternately, in "Summer" and "Winter," nature is depicted as a terrifying force. Both "Spring" and "Autumn" deal with collective communities celebrating nature's kindness: birds, nymphs, shepherds, and villagers. However, "Summer" and "Winter" focus much more on the individual, and his struggle to survive the elements.

The four, three-**movement** violin concerti known collectively as *The Four Seasons* stand today, along with Handel's *Messiah*, as the most famous works composed during the baroque era. Composed in 1720 by Antonia Vivaldi, *The Four Seasons* is scored for solo violin—a string orchestra consisting of first and second violins, violas, and 'cellos—and what is called a continuo part—typically a harpsichord, which reinforces the bass line as it plunks out the harmonies. Each violin concerto within *The Four Seasons* is based on a poem—a sonnet—extolling one of the four seasons and, consequently, is program music—music that describes and illustrates a literary story.

Vivaldi, born in Venice in 1678, was trained as both a violinist and a priest. He was known as *il prieto rosso*, or "the red priest," because of his bright red hair. While he composed 49 operas in the ornate Venetian style, Vivaldi is best remembered for his concerti—over 500 in number. Just under half of Vivaldi's concerti are for solo violin and orchestra, and most, if not all, of them were performed at a Venetian convent/orphanage/conservatory of music called the *Pio Ospedale della Pietà* (the "Devout Hospital [Orphanage] of Mercy"), or *Pietà* for short. For 37 years, Vivaldi was the violin master, conductor, composer, and dean of music at the *Pietà*.

Antonio studied violin with his father, a barber and professional musician (string player), and displayed remarkable precocity as both a violinist and composer. However, as the eldest son of a poor household, it was expected that he would join the priesthood, and he was ordained a priest in March of 1703. He joined the faculty of the *Pietà* as *maestro di violino* (master of the violin) in September of 1703, and after about a year, the Venetian publishing house of *Sala* issued his opus 1, a set of **trio sonatas**: works for two violins, 'cello, and continuo. In 1711, Vivaldi's set of 12 concerti was published as opus 3 and is generally considered to be the most influential music publication of the first half of the 18th century. By 1718, the 40-year-old Vivaldi's career had taken off, and he became very successful.

As will be the case in all four of the concerti that comprise *The Four Seasons*, the first movement of "Spring" is cast in ritornello form.

Concerto No. 1 in E Major, "La Primavera" ("Spring")
Movements 1, 2, and 3

As will be the case in all four of the concerti that comprise *The Four Seasons*, the first movement of "Spring" is cast in ritornello form. Part of the zest of the first **theme** is its outdoor rusticity, as evidenced by the steady, droning, bagpipe-like accompaniment in the 'cellos. The solo violin depicts the extra-musical details described by the sonnet, and in doing so, features the extended violin techniques for which Vivaldi was so famous.

The second movement is scored for the solo violin, orchestral violins, and viola only—no 'cellos and no harpsichord continuo. Beyond the murmuring, lyric mood of the music there are, in truth, no explicit programmatic references in this second movement. At best, this music is impressionistic, or evocative of a mood rather than a specific picture. The fast third movement is likewise more impressionistic than programmatically explicit. The movement is labeled as being a rustic dance, with long-held accompanimental drones creating, again, a bagpipe-like effect.

Concerto No. 2 in G Minor, "L'estate" ("Summer")
Movements 1, 2, and 3

The overwhelmingly bright mood depicted in "Spring" does not exist in "Summer," which presents an altogether less idealistic and grittier seasonal depiction. In this movement's ritornello theme, quiet, drooping, isolated **motives** depict rather convincingly the oppressive, miasmic heat of the Venetian summer. The climax of the movement is the advent of a storm, which is so dramatically dominating that Vivaldi concluded the movement with it rather than returning to the exhausted ritornello theme.

In the second movement of "Spring," a growling bit of thunder interrupts things every few **measures**, and after a few such interruptions, this movement begins to sound a bit absurd. In the third movement, bad weather remains the issue. The entire movement is a nonstop riff on this stormy weather, with a series of particularly virtuosic passages for the solo violin. The last of these solo passages is followed by the conclusion of the movement.

Concerto No. 3 in F Major, "L'autunno" ("Autumn")
Movements 1, 2, and 3

"Autumn" returns to the Arcadian mood of "Spring," while the last of the seasons—"Winter"—will be dominated by the sort of meteorological extremes that made "Summer" such a dramatic downer. The ritornello theme that exists in this movement is among the most famous melodies Vivaldi ever composed. The solo violin-dominated episodes that alternate with the ritornello theme depict merry partygoers, as referenced in the sonnet. The movement ends as it began—with the ritornello theme—and clearly, a good time has been had by all.

The contented, feel-good nature of the first movement continues through the remainder of the concerto. The second movement picks up where the first left off, with the partygoers having dozed off. The dreamy inactivity of the second movement comes to an end with the hustle and bustle of a hunt, as referenced by the sonnet that represents the third movement.

The theme of the third movement is appropriately upbeat. The artful simplicity of this theme is a product of careful compositional calculation: A compact melodic idea is repeated almost verbatim three times over a bagpipe-like drone, all of which assures that this music will have a direct, almost folk-like quality to it. It is just this melodic directness and mock thematic simplicity that has made "Autumn," like "Spring," an audience favorite.

Vivaldi's Orchestral Works

The concerti of Antonio Vivaldi are the capstone of the Italian baroque instrumental style and constitute—in number and quality—one of the greatest bodies of work ever composed. While Vivaldi's compositional style continued to evolve over the course of his career, several generalizations can be made about his concerti.

- Vivaldi institutionalized the three-movement, "fast-slow-fast" scheme of movements.

- Vivaldi's first movements are almost always cast in ritornello form.

- Vivaldi was a first-class tunesmith and his themes—busy and ornate though they are—set a new standard for dramatic expression and sheer memorability.

- Vivaldi's solo parts are more brilliant and virtuosic than any composed in his time. His solo parts reflect the dual influence of his own virtuosity as a violinist as well as the vocal virtuosity that was characteristic of contemporary Venetian opera.

Putting all of this together, Vivaldi's concerti exhibit a degree of contrast and dramatic thrust that raised the expressive orchestral bar to an entirely new level. Along with the concerti of his contemporary Johann Sebastian Bach, Vivaldi's are the earliest orchestral works performed today as part of the standard repertoire.

Concerto No. 4 in F Minor, "L'inverno" ("Winter")
Movements 1, 2, and 3

The fourth and final of the seasons, "Winter," is programmatically and compositionally the most complex of the set. The ritornello theme that drives the first movement has more of a special effects construct than a thematic melody. Twitching, rising, repeated **dissonances** build toward a trembling, shivering climax as the solo violin cuts loose with a slashing line labeled "*orrido vento*," which means "horrid wind."

The second movement, with its momentary warmth by the fire, is perhaps the most memorable slow movement in *The Four Seasons*. The solo violin sings a warm and contented song, accompanied by **pizzicato** (meaning "plucked") orchestral violins that depict the raindrops outside, sustained violas, and a solo 'cello.

The opening of the third movement is nothing less than comic theater. The careful, mincing footsteps of someone treading on ice are depicted by the solo violin. According to the score, after a series of theatrical slips and slides, the individual falls down. The movement concludes brilliantly as the Sirocco—the warm, Saharan desert wind—collides with the Boreas, "the cold north wind." The storm that follows concludes the movement, the concerto, and the set. ■

Important Terms

dissonance: A musical entity or state of instability that seeks resolution to consonance, a point of rest.

measure: Metric unit; space between two bar lines.

motive: Brief succession of pitches from which a melody grows through the processes of repetition, sequence, and transformation.

movement: Independent section within a larger work.

pizzicato: Plucking, rather than bowing, a stringed instrument.

theme: Primary musical subject matter in a given section of music.

trio sonata: Baroque-era genre of chamber music consisting of two soprano instruments, a bass instrument, and a chord-producing instrument (called the continuo). The most common trio sonata instrumentation was two violins, a 'cello, and a harpsichord.

Vivaldi—*The Four Seasons*
Lecture 2—Transcript

Welcome back to *The 30 Great Orchestral Works*. This is Lecture 2, and it is entitled "Vivaldi—*The Four Seasons*."

The Particulars

The four, three-movement violin concerti known collectively as *The Four Seasons* stand today, along with Handel's *Messiah*, as the most famous works to have been composed during the baroque era.

Vivaldi never bothered writing dates on his manuscripts. *The Four Seasons* was first published in 1725 as part of Vivaldi's opera ottava (op. 8), which is a collection of 12 concerti of which the "*Seasons*" are nos. 1 through 4. Modern scholarship has revealed that the concerti of op. 8 were likely composed between 1718 and 1720. Thus the date of composition for *The Four Seasons* is now given as 1720, when Vivaldi was 42 years old.

Vivaldi dedicated the 12 concerti of op. 8, including *The Four Seasons*, to a Bohemian count named Wenzel von Morzin. Vivaldi, who was living in his native Venice at the time he composed *The Four Seasons*, mailed the concerti to the count, presumably to be premiered by the count's own orchestra. At the same time, Vivaldi was also under contract to the *Ospedale della Pietà* (an institution about which we'll speak much more later in this lecture) to compose concerti for performance at the *Pietà*.

Well, Vivaldi had no qualms about using the same pieces to serve two purposes. Point in fact, Antonio Vivaldi had few qualms about anything. So it appears that *The Four Seasons*, which was paid for and dedicated to "Lord Wenzel Count von Morzin," was actually first performed in Venice at the *Ospedale della Pietà* with Vivaldi himself as violin soloist. *The Four Seasons* is scored for solo violin, a string orchestra consisting of first and second violins, violas, and 'cellos, and what is called a continuo part, typically a harpsichord, which reinforces the bass line as it plunks out the harmonies.

The Red Priest

Every now and then a composer comes along who by dint of his genius and dedication to a single genre becomes the gold-standard by which other composers' works are measured for generations. What Joseph Haydn did for the string quartet and symphony in the late 18th century, so Antonio Vivaldi did for the concerto in the early 18th century. He took the genre as it existed to his time and developed it in such a way as to become, according to musicologist Arthur Hutchings, "indisputably, the most influential composer in the history of the baroque concerto."

Vivaldi was born in Venice in 1678. He was trained as both a violinist and a priest and was known as *il prieto rosso* ("The Red Priest") because of his bright red hair. And while he composed 49 operas in the ornate Venetian style, Vivaldi is best remembered for his concerti, over 500 in number.

Just under half of Vivaldi's concerti are for solo violin and orchestra, and modern scholarship has confirmed that most—if not all of them—were performed at a Venetian convent-slash-orphanage-slash-conservatory of music called the *Pio Ospedale della Pietà* (the "Devout Hospital [Orphanage] of Mercy"), or "*Pietà*" for short.

In a seaport town like Venice—filled with sailors, tourists, and prostitutes—unwanted children were an unfortunate (and numerous) reality. Venice had four orphanages for girls: the *Pietà*, the *Incurabili*, the *Mendicanti*, and the *Ospedaletto*. The girls at the orphanages were taught trades, and no trade was more important or popular in Venice than music. By the 17th century, these four orphanages operated the city's most important schools of music, where the standards were so high that the nobility sent their own daughters there to study. Concerts held at the orphanages generated a significant amount of income and no less an authority than H. C. Robbins Landon states that by Vivaldi's time, "the center of musical activity in Venice had moved away from [the Basilica of] San Marco to the orphanages."

In 1739, Charles de Brosses described the concert scene in Venice:

> A transcending music here is that of the [orphanages]. There are four of them, made up of bastard or orphaned girls. They are trained solely to excel in music. They perform, and each concert is given by about 40 girls. I swear to you that nothing is so charming as to see a young and pretty nun in her white robe, with a bouquet of pomegranate flowers over her ear, leading the orchestra with all the grace and precision imaginable. The orphanage I go most often to is that of the *Pietà*, where one is best entertained.

The *Pietà* was founded in 1346 and was situated on the *Riva degli Schiavoni*, just a few dozen yards away from the basilica San Marco. By 1700, its music staff included a choir director, an organist, and teachers for violin, viola, oboe, bassoon, flute, 'cello, horn, and timpani. For 37 years, the violin master, conductor, composer, and sometime general superintendent (or dean) of music at the *Pietà* was the violinist, composer, and priest Antonio Vivaldi.

Vivaldi's Concerti

The concerti of Antonio Vivaldi are the capstone of the Italian baroque instrumental style, and constitute, in number and quality, one of the greatest bodies of work ever composed by anybody. While Vivaldi's compositional style continued to evolve over the course of his career, there are a number of generalizations we can make about his concerti.

No. 1: Vivaldi institutionalized the three-movement, "fast-slow-fast" scheme of movements. No. 2: Vivaldi's first movements are almost always cast in ritornello form. No. 3: Vivaldi was a first-class tunesmith and his themes, busy and ornate though they are, set a new standard for dramatic expression and sheer memorability! No. 4: Vivaldi's solo parts are more brilliant and virtuosic than any composed to his time. His solo parts reflect the dual influence of his own virtuosity as a violinist as well as the vocal virtuosity that was characteristic of contemporary Venetian opera.

Putting all of this together, Vivaldi's concerti exhibit a degree of contrast and dramatic thrust that raised the expressive orchestral bar to an entirely new level. Along with the concerti of his contemporary Johann Sebastian Bach, Vivaldi's are the earliest orchestral works performed today as part of the standard repertoire.

The Four Seasons

The Four Seasons consists of four separate, three-movement violin concerti. Each concerto is based on a poem, a sonnet, extolling one of the four seasons. Consequently, *The Four Seasons* are program music, music that describes and illustrates a literary story. Our examination will observe the programmatic content of each concerto, and will focus, in particular, on the four first movement ritornello form movements, which are among the most expressively and dramatically substantial movements of orchestral music composed to their time.

Concerto No. 1 in E Major, *La Primavera: Spring*, Movement 1

Here is the portion of the sonnet on which this first movement is based:

> Spring has arrived and merrily
> The birds hail her with happy song.
> And, meanwhile, at the breath of the Zephyrs
> The streams flow with a sweet murmur.
> Thunder and lightning, chosen to proclaim her,
> Come covering the sky with a black mantle,
> And then, when these fall silent, the little birds
> Return once more to their melodious incantation.

For our information, we haven't a clue who wrote the sonnets on which *The Four Seasons* is based. Frankly, they are awful, which supports the claim made by some that they were cobbled together by Vivaldi and/or by a collaborator only after the music was composed. According to one Vivaldi scholar, the sonnets are: "a botched job that suffices."

As will be the case in all four of the concerti that comprise *The Four Seasons*, the first movement of *Spring* is cast in ritornello form. Typical of Vivaldi, the opening Ritornello melody, which represents spring in all its glory, is as memorable as your first kiss. Vivaldi scholar Paul Everett points out that, "For Vivaldi, the first ritornello is the movement's essence: a zest to be encapsulated immediately, irrespective of what happens afterwards."

Part of the "zest" of the first theme is its out-of-doors rusticity, as evidenced by the steady droning bag-pipe-like accompaniment in the 'cellos. Let's hear this first appearance of the ritornello theme, played by the *tutti* (by everybody), the violin soloist and orchestra. Quoth the sonnet: "Spring has arrived." [**Piano demonstration**: Vivaldi, *The Four Seasons*, "Spring," movement 1, opening ritornello.] It will be the job of the solo violin to depict the extra-musical details described by the sonnet, and in doing so will feature the sorts of "extended violin techniques" for which Vivaldi was so famous.

The first contrasting episode is labeled in the score as *Il canto degli uccelli*, "the song of the birds." This episode paints these words from the sonnet: "and merrily the birds hail spring with happy song." Let's hear this first solo episode, in which the "song of the birds" is played by the solo violin and echoed by the orchestral violins. This avian episode will be followed by an abbreviated version of the ritornello theme, played by everybody. [**Musical selection**: Vivaldi, *The Four Seasons*, "Spring," movement 1.]

The next episode, played by everybody, illustrates the next two lines of the sonnet: "And, meanwhile, at the breath of the Zephyrs, the streams flow with a sweet murmur." That "murmuring" is initially depicted by quietly undulating violins and is labeled in the score by Vivaldi as *scorrono il fonti*, "trickling of the springs." Once again, this episode is followed by a fragmentary playing of the ritornello theme. [**Musical selection**: Vivaldi, *The Four Seasons*, "Spring," movement 1.]

It's time for the storm described by the lines: "thunder and lightning come covering the sky with a black mantle." Brilliant and virtuosic arpeggios in the solo violin depict the lightning and the downpour of rain, heard over a rumbling accompaniment provided by the orchestra. The storm is followed by a fragmentary return—in minor—of the ritornello theme. [**Musical selection**: Vivaldi, *The Four Seasons*, "Spring," movement 1.]

The storm is over, and according to the sonnet, "the little birds return once more to their melodious incantation." My friends, let's hear the remainder of the movement, which consists of these elements: the return of the birds, a fragmentary appearance of the ritornello theme, a cadenza (or solo) for the solo violin, and finally, a last and almost complete appearance of the ritornello theme. [**Musical selection**: Vivaldi, *The Four Seasons*, "Spring," movement 1.]

A Couple of Observations

The dramatic degree of contrast between the ritornello theme and the intervening episodes is typical of Vivaldi's ritornello form movements. Also typical is Vivaldi's fragmentary treatment of the ritornello theme as it returns across the span of a movement; only rarely is the theme restated in its entirety. This very flexible approach to thematic restatements gives Vivaldi's ritornello form movements a tremendous degree of dynamism and fluidity. It's no wonder Vivaldi's concerti so inspired Johann Sebastian Bach, whose own proclivities as a musical dramatist found a kindred spirit in Vivaldi.

Movement 2

The portion of the sonnet on which the second movement is based goes as follows:

> And so, on the pleasant, flowery meadow,
> To the welcome murmuring of fronds and trees,
> The goatherd sleeps with his trusty dog beside him.

This movement is scored for the solo violin, orchestral violins, and viola only; no 'cellos and no harpsichord continuo. According to the score, the first and second violins depict the murmur of the fronds and plants. [**Piano demonstration**: Plays violins 1 and 2, measures 1–2.] According to the score, the leisurely lyric melody played by the violin solo represents "The sleeping goatherd." [**Piano demonstration**: Plays solo violin, measures 2–5.] Finally, according to the score, the viola part represents *il cane che grida*, "the barking dog." Let's hear the opening of the movement. [**Music selection**: Vivaldi, *The Four Seasons*, "Spring," movement 2.]

Do you hear a "barking dog"? No, neither do I. This is a case of don't believe everything you read: Beyond the murmuring lyric mood of the music there are, in truth, no explicit programmatic references in this second movement. At best—and this is something we can say about all the slow movements of *The Four* Season—we'd observe that this music is impressionistic, evocative of a mood rather than a specific picture.

Movement 3

The fast third movement is likewise more impressionistic than programmatically explicit. The portion of the sonnet on which this movement is based reads as follows:

> To the festive sound of a shepherd's bagpipe,
> Nymphs and shepherd's dance beneath the beloved sky
> At the joyful appearance of spring.

The movement is labeled as being a "rustic dance," and that's precisely what it is, with long-held accompanimental drones creating, once again, a bagpipe-like effect. [**Music selection**: Vivaldi, *The Four Seasons*, "Spring," Movement 3.]

Concerto No. 2 in G Minor, *L'Estate:* Summer, Movement 1

The overwhelmingly bright mood depicted in *Spring* is nowhere to be found in *Summer*, which presents an altogether less idealistic and more gritty seasonal depiction. Here's the portion of the sonnet Vivaldi sets in his first movement ritornello form:

> Beneath the harsh season inflamed by the sun,
> Man languishes, the flock languishes, and the pine tree burns;
> The Cuckoo unleashes its voice and, as soon as it is heard,
> The turtle dove sings and the goldfinch too.
> Sweet Zephyrus blows, but Boreas [the Greek god of the cold
>   north wind]
> Picks a fight with his neighbor;

> And the shepherd weeps, for he fears
> A fierce storm looming, and with it, his fate.

The ritornello theme that dominates this first movement of *Summer* could not be more different than the one that began *Spring*. The theme is marked "*Languidezza per il caldo*"—"Exhausted by the heat"—and exhausted it is, characterized almost as much by silence as it is by sound. Quiet, drooping, isolated motives depict rather convincingly the oppressive, miasmic heat of the Venetian summer. [**Music selection**: Vivaldi, *The Four Seasons*, "Summer," Movement 1.] The first of the birdcall episodes evoked by the sonnet demands real virtuosity from the violin soloist. Here's the first of those episodes, labeled "The cuckoo." [**Music selection**: Vivaldi, *The Four Seasons*, "Summer," Movement 1.]

My friends, that's one rockin' cuckoo. The climax of this movement is the advent of the storm. Unlike the relatively benign, "April showers bring May flowers" squall we heard back in *Spring*, this summer storm is a nasty one. So dramatically dominating is this storm that Vivaldi concludes the movement with it, rather than return to the "exhausted" ritornello theme. Here's the tempestuous conclusion of the movement. [**Music selection**: Vivaldi, *The Four Seasons*, "Summer," movement 1.]

Movement 2

The sonnet:

> The fear of lightning and fierce thunder
> And the furious swarm of flies and wasps
> Deprives the shepherd's weary limbs of rest.

Like the "barking dog" of the second movement of *Spring*, the "flies and wasps" here are portrayed by an accompanimental figure that is easily mistaken for an accompanimental figure. The fear of the shepherd is ably depicted by a weepy solo violin. Every few measures a growling bit of thunder interrupts things, and after a few such interruptions this movement begins to sound really silly to me. We listen from the beginning through the first of these "thunderous interruptions." [**Music selection**: Vivaldi, *The Four Seasons*, "Summer," movement 2]

Movement 3

Bad weather remains the issue. The sonnet continues:

> Oh, unfortunately the shepherd's fears are only too true!
> The sky thunders, flares, and with hailstones
> "*Tronca il capo*"—severs the heads of the ripe crop of grain.

The entire movement is a non-stop riff on this stormy weather thing, with a series of particularly virtuosic passages for the solo violin. We hear the last of these solo passages followed by the conclusion of the movement.

[**Music selection**: Vivaldi, *The Four Seasons*, "Summer," movement 3.]

Antonia Lucio Vivaldi, Man and Musician

Antonio Vivaldi was an egomaniacal, opportunistic, thin-skinned, greedy, often outrageously dishonest wheeler-dealer. Thankfully, we don't have to live with him, just listen to his music. According to the Vivaldi scholar John Talbot:

> Antonio Vivaldi was unconventional. His vanity was notorious: He boasted constantly of his fame and patrons, and of his fluency in composing, asserting that he could compose a concerto in all its parts more quickly than it could be copied. In many cases these claims are clearly exaggerated. Along with his vanity went an extreme sensitivity to criticism. His preoccupation with money was excessive by any standards; it is a subject that surfaces continually in his letters. Yet the sheer zest of the man compells admiration.

Vivaldi's father was both a barber and a professional musician (a string player), which reminds us all of the advice wisely dispensed to young musicians, which is "everybody needs a day gig."

Antonio studied violin with his father and displayed remarkable precocity as both a violinist and as a composer. However, as the eldest son of a poor household, it was expected that he would join the priesthood, and this he did, receiving the first of the so-called minor orders, that of *Ostario* ("Porter") at the age of 15.

Vivaldi was ordained a priest 10 years later, in March of 1703. He joined the faculty of the *Ospedale della Pietà* as *maestro di violino* ("master of the violin") in September of 1703, and thus began a relationship with the *Pietà* that would continue for 35 years.

About a year after Vivaldi took up his position at the *Pietà* the Venetian publishing house of *Sala* issued his op. 1, a set of trio sonatas: works for two violins, 'cello, and continuo. A series of major publications followed. Vivaldi's set of 12 concerti published as op. 3 in 1711 is generally considered to be the most influential music publication of the first half of the 18th century. (That is not an overstatement. Roughly 340 miles to the north, the court organist of the Saxon city of Weimar—one Johann Sebastian Bach—read through Vivaldi's op. 3 concerti and was so taken by what he saw that he arranged two of them for solo harpsichord, three for solo organ, and one for four harpsichords and orchestra. By doing so, Bach absorbed Vivaldi's musical voice the way the blob absorbed all those people in the movie theater, and made it his own.)

By 1718, the 40-year-old Vivaldi's career had taken off. He composed operas for houses across Italy followed while, at the same time, he continued to compose concerti for the *Pietà*. These were Vivaldi's "salad days," during which he made a lot of money. Vivaldi was a natural born entrepreneur. The 12 concerti that make up his op. 8—which includes *The Four Seasons*—is a case in point. He entitled the entire set of 12 concerti "*Il Cimento dell'armonia e dell'inventione*," which translates "The Contest of Harmony and of Invention."

"The Contest of Harmony and of Invention"

In Vivaldi's time, this would have meant "The Contest between Learned Craft and Intuitive Imagination," a title that was pure marketing savvy. The Vivaldi scholar Paul Everett points out that:

> In the competitive world of concerto publishing a set with a name stood a greater chance of attracting attention than one advertised simply as "Concerti." A title full of tantalizing promise had the additional advantage of implying that the music was extraordinary and well-worth buying.

Yes, a title like "*The Four Seasons.*"

Concerto No. 3 in F Major, *L'Autunno*: Autumn, Movement 1

Autumn returns to the Arcadian mood of *Spring*, while the last of the *Seasons*—winter—will be dominated by the sort of meteorological extremes that made *Summer* such a dramatic downer.

The autumnal sonnet goes as follows:

> The peasant celebrates in song and dance
> The sweet pleasure of the rich harvest
> And, fired by Bacchus's liquor,
> Many end their enjoyment in slumber.

Sounds like our kind of party. The ritornello theme that represents the villagers song and dance is among the most famous melodies Vivaldi ever composed. [**Music selection**: Vivaldi, *The Four Seasons*, "Autumn," movement 1.]

The stumbling, bumbling, and often falling down solo violin-dominated episodes that alternate with this ritornello theme depict the increasingly inebriated party-goers, who eventually doze off in an episode labeled "*L'Ubriaco che dorme*"—"The sleeping drunkard." The movement ends as it began, with the ritornello theme; clearly, a good time has been had by all.

Movements 2 and 3

The contented, feel-good nature of the first movement continues through the remainder of the concerto. The second movement picks up where the first left off, with the villagers having abandoned themselves "to the great pleasure of sweetest slumber."

The dreamy inactivity of the second movement comes to an end with the hustle and bustle of the third movement "hunt."

The sonnet:

> At the new dawn the hunters set out on the hunt
> With horns, guns, and dogs.
> The wild beast flees, and they follow its track;
> Already bewildered, and wearied by the great noise
> Of the guns and dogs, and wounded,
> The beast tries weakly to escape, but, overwhelmed, dies.

OK. It's not a poem that PETA would condone, but since everyone but the beast has a good time, the theme of this ritornello form movement is appropriately up-beat. [**Music selection**: Vivaldi, *The Four Seasons*, "Autumn," movement 3.] he artful simplicity of this theme is a product of careful compositional calculation: a compact melodic idea is repeated almost verbatim three times over a bagpipe-like drone, all of which assures that this music will have a direct, almost folk-like quality to it. It is just this melodic directness and mock thematic simplicity that has made "Autumn" (like "Spring") an audience favorite. The fourth and final of the *Seasons*, "Winter," is programmatically and compositionally the most complex of the set, meaning the least "popular" of the set. Well, you know what? Popularity can be overrated.

Concerto No. 4 in F Minor, *L'Inverno*: Winter

The sonnet on which *Winter* is based is by far the most personal of the set; there's no doubt that whoever wrote this sonnet did not like the winter. I'll read the entire sonnet, indicating which lines apply to which movements.

Movement 1

> To shiver, frozen, among icy snows,
> At the harsh wind's chill breath;
> To run, stamping one's feet at every moment;
> With one's teeth chattering on account of the excessive cold;

Movement 2

> To pass the days calm and contented by the fireside
> While the rain outside drenches a hundred others;

Movement 3

> To walk on the ice, and with slow steps
> To move about cautiously for fear of falling;
> To go fast, slip, and fall to the ground;
> To go on the ice again and run fast
> Until the ice cracks and breaks open;
> To hear, as they whistle through the iron gates,
> Sirocco, Boreas, and all the winds at war.
> This is winter, but of a kind to bring joy.

"But of a kind to bring joy"! Right! After 13 lines of whining, that last-ditch, last-line attempt to put to put a positive spin on winter sounds just a tad insincere!

Let's sample a bit of each movement.

Movement 1

The ritornello theme that drives this first movement is more a special effects construct than a thematic melody. Twitching, rising, repeated dissonances build toward a trembling, shivering climax, as the solo violin cuts loose with a slashing line labeled "*Orrido Vento*": "Horrid Wind." Let's hear the ritornello theme and the chill violinistic wind that follows it. [**Music selection**: Vivaldi, *The Four Seasons*, "Winter," movement 1.]

Movement 2

Movement 2, with its momentary warmth by the fire, is perhaps the most memorable slow movement in *The Four Seasons*. The solo violin sings a warm and contented song, accompanied by pizzicato (meaning "plucked") orchestral violins that depict the raindrops outside (a standard operatic device for depicting rain), accompanied as well by sustained violas and a solo 'cello. [**Music selection**: Vivaldi, *The Four Seasons*, "Winter," Movement 2.]

Movement 3

The opening of the third movement is nothing less than comic theater. The careful, mincing footsteps of someone treading on ice are depicted by the solo violin, "walking slowly and fearfully" according to the score. [**Music selection**: Vivaldi, *The Four Seasons*, "Winter," Movement 3.] According to the score, the "walker" makes "a bold turn"; a mistake as it turns out, because after a series of theatrical slips and slides, he falls down and goes boom! (The score indicates "*Cader a terra*": "Falling to the ground!"). [**Music selection**: Vivaldi, *The Four Seasons*, "Winter," Movement 3.]

The movement concludes brilliantly as the Sirocco—the warm, Saharan desert wind (represented by a quotation from the first movement ritornello theme of *Summer*; a very nice touch)—collides with the Boreas, "the cold north wind." Let's hear the storm that follows and with it, the conclusion of the movement, the concerto, and the set. [**Music selection**: Vivaldi, *The Four Seasons*, "Winter," Movement 3.]

Conclusions

Taken as a whole, Vivaldi's *The Four Seasons* is about humankind's relationship to nature. Musically, the cycle demonstrates a most satisfying degree of contrasts and balances. In both *Spring* and *Autumn*, nature is idealized and depicted as benign. Alternately, in *Summer* and *Winter*, nature is depicted as a terrifying force.

Both *Spring* and *Autumn* deal with collective communities celebrating nature's kindness: birds, nymphs, shepherds, and villagers. However,

Summer and *Winter* focus much more on the individual, and his struggle to survive the elements.

Vivaldi's published concerti, including *The Four Seasons*, were stupendously popular in his lifetime. For a time, he had both fame and fortune. Unfortunately, fame is fleeting and fortune gets spent. In 1741, the 63-year-old Vivaldi, having gone bankrupt in Venice, decided to revive his flagging fortunes in Vienna. On July 28, 1741, a month to the day after having arrived in Vienna, Vivaldi died in Vienna. The cause of death was listed as "internal inflammation," which could have been anything.

Vivaldi was buried in the cemetery of the public hospital, the *Bügerspital*. At his last rites six choirboys—one of whom was the nine-year-old Joseph Haydn—sang his Requiem Mass. The cemetery was abandoned and built over sometime in the late 18th century. No trace of Vivaldi's grave remains; to this day his bones lie somewhere beneath the city of Vienna.

Back in Venice, Pietro Gradinego's obituary of Vivaldi concluded with these words:

"[So we mark the death of] Abbé Lord Antonio Vivaldi, incomparable virtuoso on the violin, known as the Red Priest, much esteemed for his compositions and concerti, who earned more than 50,000 ducats in his life, but his disorderly prodigality caused him to die a pauper in Vienna."

Bummer of an epitaph.

Thank you.

Bach—Brandenburg Concerto No. 2
Lecture 3

Bach's Brandenburg Concerto no. 2, like pretty much everything Bach composed, expanded the formal, melodic, harmonic, and expressive frameworks that were his baroque inheritance. It is this expansion of the musical language that prompts Bach scholar Martin Geck to write: "Bach assumes a pivotal role in history. He sums up what went before him and, at the same time, lays the foundation for important developments that will come after him. In Bach, the universalism of the baroque merges into modern idealism."

Johann Sebastian Bach spent the bulk of his professional life as a musical functionary of the Lutheran Church and at war with the authorities for whom he worked. His dream job lasted for only six years; he was the victim of budget cuts, disillusionment, and personal estrangement. Bach was born on March 31, 1685, and died on July 28, 1750. During his life, he held a total of six professional positions: a court musician in the chapel of Duke Johann Ernst, organist at St. Boniface's Church, organist at the Church of St. Blasius, court organist and concertmaster at the ducal court, Kapellmeister (music director) of Anhalt-Cöthen, and finally, cantor (liturgical music director) at the St. Thomas School. Bach held this last position for the remaining 27 years of his life.

In early 1719, Bach traveled to Berlin to commission the construction of a new, state-of-the-art harpsichord for the Cöthen court. It was during this trip that Bach met and played for Margrave Christian Ludwig of Brandenburg, the youngest son of the elector of Brandenburg, Friedrich Wilhelm. In 1721, Bach sent the margrave an artistic resume: six concerti that Bach clearly felt offered a cross-section of his skills as a court composer. The concerti Bach sent were filed and forgotten until their rediscovery in the 1870s, when they were collectively dubbed the *Brandenburg Concertos* by the Bach scholar and biographer Philipp Spitta.

Brandenburg Concerto No. 2 in F Major

The Brandenburg Concerto no. 2 is a concerto grosso, which means that it is a large concerto that features multiple soloists. The Brandenburg no. 2 includes four soloists: a clarino, a flute, an oboe, and a violin. A concerto grosso features two performing ensembles in one: a group of soloists—called the concertino, meaning the "little ensemble"—and the ripieno, meaning the "orchestra." A passage in which the concertino and ripieno play together is called a tutti, meaning literally "all together."

The ripieno of Bach's Brandenburg no. 2 consists of a string orchestra—first and second violins, violas, 'cellos, violone (or bass viol, the ancestor of today's double bass), and a harpsichord. The brilliant, celebratory nature of the Brandenburg no. 2 has much to do with its treble-dominated concertino: trumpet, flute, oboe, and violin. Never before—or since—has this particular set of solo instruments been used in a concerto grosso.

Johann Sebastian Bach (1685–1750) held a total of six professional positions during his lifetime.

Movement 1

This first movement ritornello form might have been inspired by the ritornello movements of Vivaldi, but in terms of its length, complexity, and sheer invention, it is superior to its models. The theme is a vigorous, memorable, though typically busy baroque-styled melody, and it concludes with a **closed cadence**—a musical punctuation mark equivalent to a period—that effectively separates it from what comes next.

The ritornello theme is cast in four distinct phrases, which we will call phrases *a*, *b*, *a¹*, and *b¹*. Phrases *a* and *a¹* have a jolly, dance-like bounce to them; phrases *b* and *b¹* consist almost entirely of fast, running 16th **notes**. The chattering bass line heard beneath phrase *a* is strictly a background element when we first hear it. Given that our ears are focused on the ritornello theme unfolding above it, we probably don't even notice it. However, that chattering bass line will soon enough rise from the accompaniment to become a thematic element itself and will be played by each solo instrument during the course of the movement.

Bach introduces the solo instruments—one at a time—with a brief, trilling melody that offers a considerable contrast to the foot-stomping heaviness of the ritornello theme. Since this little theme will only be played by the solo instruments, we will refer to it as the solo theme. Following the movement opening statement of the ritornello theme, the solo violin enters with the solo theme, immediately after which the opening phrase *a* of the ritornello theme is again played by the tutti.

Next it's the solo oboe's turn to play the solo theme, which is again followed by phrase *a* of the ritornello theme. The solo flute next plays the solo theme, followed once again by the opening phrase of the ritornello theme. Lastly, the trumpet plays the solo theme, and the ritornello theme picks up where it left off, followed by the remainder of the theme (phrases *b*, *a¹*, and *b¹*) plays and then a closed cadence.

This first large section of the movement—part 1 of the movement— is expository, meaning that it features thematic music: the ritornello theme itself, the chattering bass line that rises from the bass to become a surface element, and the solo theme. Part 1 is a brilliant and idiosyncratic interpretation of ritornello form, an approach dictated by the brilliant and idiosyncratic set of solo instruments Bach employs in the concertino.

There are six large parts to this first movement, and each of the subsequent five parts concludes with the final two phrases of the ritornello theme— *a¹* and *b¹*—played by the tutti and followed by a closed cadence. These (and other) appearances of the ritornello theme are fragmentary and are used to punctuate developmental episodes dominated by the instruments of the concertino—episodes during which we are witness to all sorts of phrase extensions, polyphonic overlapping of voices, and new **key** areas.

Part 2 is dominated by the trumpet. It begins with a very high version of the solo theme played by the trumpet, continues with a lengthy episode that features the trumpet, and concludes with the final two phrases of the ritornello theme set in the key of D **minor** that is dominated by the trumpet. Part 3 of the movement features the entire concertino, as the solo instruments emphatically play phrases a and a^1 of the ritornello theme.

The Brandenburg Concerto no. 2 is a concerto grosso, which means that it is a large concerto that features multiple soloists.

In part 4, the concertino plays the solo theme and then phrase a of the ritornello theme until, once again, the tutti performs the section-ending statement of the last two phrases of the ritornello theme, now in the key of G minor. In part 5, the instruments of the concertino are paired in various ways and again conclude with the final phrases of the ritornello theme, now in the key of A minor. The sixth and final part of the movement is recapitulatory: It is based entirely on the ritornello theme, and it begins and ends in the **home key**, or the **tonic** key, of F **major**.

The harmonic leap between the conclusion of part 5 (in the key of A minor) and the beginning of part 6 (in the home key of F major) features one of Bach's favorite devices: a pivot that uses common tones to transit a large harmonic distance in a virtually short amount of time. Immediately after the A minor harmony at the conclusion of part 5, without transition or preparation, Bach begins the ritornello theme back in the home key of F major. This device works because an A minor harmony and an F major harmony have two of their three **pitches** in common. Bach uses those common tones as a hinge to swing instantly from A minor to the ritornello theme in F major.

Movement 2
The second movement is scored for the solo flute, oboe, and solo violin, accompanied only by a single 'cello and the harpsichord. For reasons both practical and musical, the trumpet does not appear in this movement. Given the incredible rigors of the first and third movements of this concerto, a rest is both a physical necessity and an act of mercy. On the musical side is the

expressive message of the movement. Set in D minor, it is a sublime and lyric bit of night music—a nocturne—particularly notable for the gentle intertwining of the solo flute, oboe, and violin. The trumpet—with its piercing, brilliant sound—would dominate the other instruments and disrupt the shadowy, expressive mood of the movement.

Movement 3

Presumably well rested, the trumpet returns as the lead instrumental voice in the third movement **fugue**, which is a multi-voiced, or polyphonic, formal process in which a theme—called the fugue **subject**—is introduced and then restated in various voices and in various keys. The first large section of a fugue is called the exposition, during which each constituent "voice" enters in turn with the subject. There are four such voice entries in this movement, one for each instrument of the concertino (trumpet, oboe, violin, and flute).

The accompaniment here is provided by the **basso continuo**, which is a single 'cello and a harpsichord. The ripieno—the orchestral strings—are not active participants in the unfolding of the fugue. This third movement is about the bright, brilliant, treble-dominated timbral colors of the concertino, while the ripieno is reduced to the role of deep-background accompanist.

The fugue subject consists of two parts: the first called the head and the second the tail. The head is vigorous and dancelike, while the tail consists of a running series of 16th notes. The head and tail of the fugue subject should sound familiar because phrases *a* and *b* of the first movement ritornello theme have almost exactly the same rhythmic and harmonic profile. This sort of macro-relationship between outer movements is something we generally will not observe until the mature music of Beethoven—music composed more than 50 years after Bach died. ∎

Important Terms

basso continuo: Those instruments in a baroque-era ensemble (typically a chord-producing instrument and a bass instrument) whose job it was to articulate with unerring clarity the bass line and play the harmonic progressions built atop the bass line.

closed cadence: Equivalent to a period or an exclamation mark; such a cadence ends on the tonic and gives a sense of rest and resolution.

fugue: Important baroque musical procedure in which a theme (or subject) is developed by means of various contrapuntal techniques.

home key: Main key of a movement or composition.

key: Collection of pitches that relate to a specific major or minor mode.

major: Modern term for Ionian mode; characterized by an intervallic profile of whole tone–whole tone–semitone–whole tone–whole tone–whole tone–semitone (symbolized as: T–T–S | T–T–T–S).

minor: Modern term for Aeolian mode; characterized by an intervallic profile of whole tone–semitone–whole tone–whole tone–semitone–whole tone–whole tone (symbolized as T–S–T | T–S–T–T).

note: A sound with three properties: a single, sing-able fundamental frequency; timbre; and duration.

pitch: A sound with two properties: a single, sing-able fundamental frequency and timbre.

subject: The theme of a fugue.

tonic: Home pitch and chord of a piece of tonal music. Think of the term as being derived from "tonal center" (tonic). For example, if a movement is in C, the pitch C is the tonic pitch, and the harmony built on C is the tonic chord.

Bach—Brandenburg Concerto No. 2
Lecture 3—Transcript

We return to *The 30 Greatest Orchestral Works*. This is Lecture 3, and it is entitled "Bach—Brandenburg Concerto No. 2."

Bach's Jobs

My friends, Johann Sebastian Bach's professional life stands as an object lesson for all those good people who never quite get (or keep) the job they really deserve.

Bach spent the bulk of his professional life as a musical functionary of the Lutheran Church and at war with the authorities for whom he worked. His dream job—the one he hoped would be his for life—lasted for only six years, the victim of budget cuts, disillusionment, and personal estrangement. Yes, that sounds like my life as well. Johann Sebastian Bach was born on March 31, 1685, and died on July 28, 1750. All told, Bach held a total of six professional positions.

Position 1: In January of 1703, the 17-year-old Bach took a job as a court musician in the chapel of Duke Johann Ernst in the central-German city of Weimar. Bach hated the job and quit seven months later.

Position 2: In August 1703, the now 18-year-old Bach took up the post of organist at St. Boniface's Church in the central-German city of Arnstadt. Among other incidents, Bach got into a public brawl with a music student named Johann Heinrich Geyersbach and took an unauthorized leave-of-absence for several months, about which the authorities were most unhappy. Bach told them to stick it, and then he quit.

Position 3: In 1706, Bach took the job as organist at the Church of St. Blasius in the central-German town of Mühlhausen. It was a good job in a fairly large town, but Bach's professional reputation was on the rise, so when he was offered a position as court organist and concertmaster at the ducal court back in Weimar, it was sayonara Mühlhausen.

Position 4: Welcome back to Weimar! Bach stayed in Weimar from 1708 to 1717. It was in Weimar that Bach had a chance to study the latest scores by the leading Italian composers. In particular, he was knocked out by the concerti of a red-haired Venetian priest named Antonio Vivaldi. Bach was intrigued by the dramatic possibilities inherent to concerto ritornello form, with its contrast and alternation between solo instruments and the full orchestra.

Bach's nine year tenure at Weimar was an eternity for him. Eventually, he ceased to get along with anybody, tried to quit, and was thrown in jail for trying to quit. ("Herr Bach: this is 1717! Musicians do not quit their jobs at a ducal court!") After cooling his heels in the Weimar hoosegow for a month, he was released on December 2, 1717, with a notice of "unfavorable discharge."

Position 5: The dream job. Bach was hired as Kapellmeister (that is, music director) of Anhalt-Cöthen by Prince Leopold, a 21-year-old music freak who had inherited his little principate a year before, in 1716. Prince Leopold was a Reformist, which meant that only the simplest religious songs were sung in his chapel. However, the Prince loved music, and spent a large fortune (too large, as it turned out) hiring many of the best musicians in central Europe to play in his court orchestra. What this meant for Bach was that he was freed from church duties to compose secular, that is, nonreligious, music for some of the best musicians in Europe. Among the works he completed in Cöthen are the "six concerti for diverse instruments" today known as the Brandenburg Concerti as well as the Violin Concerto in E Major.

Sadly, the bloom came off the Cöthen rose. Prince Leopold's finances started to nose-dive, Bach's wife Barbara—the mother of his first seven children—suddenly died, and the prince himself married a princess who did not care for music or Bach. Bach sadly began looking for a new job.

Position 6: Bach was appointed cantor (liturgical music director) at the St. Thomas School in the central German city of Leipzig. Among his many other duties was music director for the four principal churches in town. It was an admittedly prestigious job in a major commercial center, although we must note that Bach was Leipzig's fourth choice for the job, and only after it had been turned down by Georg Philipp Telemann, Christoph Graupner, and Johann Friedrich Fasch (yes, who?) did the Leipzig authorities deign to offer the position to Bach, who, after all, did not have a university degree but did have a reputation for being difficult to work with.

Bach held this position for the remaining 27 years of his life, until 1750, by which time he had come to be considered an epic pain in the tuchas by the majority of the many ecclesiastic and municipal authorities who were collectively his "bosses." Did they appreciate what they had in Bach? Apparently not.

The "Naming and Assembly" of the *Brandenburg Concerti*

In early 1719, Bach traveled to Berlin in order to commission the construction of a new, state-of-the-art harpsichord for the Cöthen court from a respected builder named Michael Mietke. It was during the course of this trip that Bach met and played for the margrave of Brandenburg, Christian Ludwig, the youngest son of the elector of Brandenburg, Friedrich Wilhelm, and half-brother of the recently deceased Prussian King Friedrich I.

Two years later, in 1721, Bach decided that his days at Cöthen were numbered. He began casting about for a new job, and among the first things he did was to write his old pal the margrave of Brandenburg to offer him his services. Along with a gaggingly obsequious cover letter, Bach sent the margrave an artistic resume: six concerti, works that Bach clearly felt offered a cross-section of his skills as a court composer.

Alas, the margrave had but a small orchestra at his disposal, besides which his musical tastes ran towards the more up-to-date, Italian-styled music of Handel than to that of the more "academic" Bach. The concerti Bach sent were never performed in Berlin and were filed and forgotten until their rediscovery in the 19th century. It was in the 1870s that they were collectively dubbed the *Brandenburg Concerti* by the Bach scholar and biographer Philipp Spitta.

(A parenthetical comment. We must be eternally grateful that Bach did send these six concerti to the margrave; that they were filed and forgotten; and that when they were rediscovered in the Brandenburg archives, it was at a time when they could be appreciated and not used as kindling or fish wrapping, because Bach sent the margrave his original and only copies. A total of nine concerti have come down to us from Bach's Cöthen years: the six Brandenburgs, the violin concerti in E major and A minor, and the concerto in D minor for two violins. Given Bach's proclivity to systematically compose in a single genre for an extended period of time, we can safely assume that he composed more concerti than the nine that have survived. Let's hear it for the safety of the Brandenburg State archives!)

Understatements

In his cover letter to the margrave, Bach described the six so-called Brandenburg Concerti as "Concertos with Several Instruments" because each concerto is scored for a different ensemble. That subtitle of "Concertos for Several Instruments" has come to be considered one of the great understatements of all time. Writes Bach scholar Christoph Wolff:

> [In the Brandenburgs], Bach makes use, in a systematic manner, of the widest imaginable spectrum of orchestral instruments. The modest title does not begin to suggest the degree of innovation exhibited in the daring [instrumental] combinations, as Bach once again enters uncharted territory. Every one of the six concertos set a precedent in its scoring, and every one was to remain without parallel.

The Particulars

We do not know when the concerto now known as Brandenburg 2 was first performed. Here's what we do know. Musical performances were an integral part of court life at Cöthen. The Concerto in F Major (that is, "Brandenburg 2") would have been performed as part of a courtly entertainment sometime between 1718 and 1720.

We also know that the first performance of Brandenburg 2 would have been a good performance, because Bach was a rehearsal nut. One of the first things he did on taking up the position of Kapellmeister at Cöthen was to relocate the rehearsals of the court orchestra to his own house in the city. The players were happy about this because they all lived in town and didn't have to waste their time schlepping out to the prince's castle. Bach was happy because he could exercise more control over rehearsal time. A colleague of Bach's, the Cantor at Cöthen's St. Jacobi Church, marveled at the rigor of Bach's rehearsal schedule: "The princely [orchestra] in this town, which week in [and] week out holds its rehearsals, makes an example that even the most famous virtuosi rehearse and exercise their things together beforehand."

We also know the names of at least a few of the performers who would have participated in the premiere of Brandenburg 2, most notably the trumpet virtuoso Johann Ludwig Schreiber. Schreiber played an instrument called a clarino, a valveless soprano trumpet consisting of about 7½ feet of tightly coiled brass tubing with a small, shallow metal mouthpiece at one end and a flared bell at the other. In order to play all the pitches of the chromatic collection on such an instrument, a player has to overblow into its third and fourth octaves (into a register called the clarino) while covering and uncovering small holes drilled at nodal points in the instrument's tubing.

If this sounds difficult you don't know the half of it! To play Bach's part on a modern valved trumpet is hard enough; to play it on a clarino is near impossible, an act of such daunting physical challenge as to induce nosebleeds, hernias, and hemorrhoids, at best, and strokes—I kid you not— at worst. It's hard to believe that Bach could ever have conceived the gut-busting trumpet part of the Brandenburg 2 without Schreiber's presence and Bach's knowledge that Schreiber would play the part in performance.

Indeed, the clarino is the signature instrument of Bach's Brandenburg 2. Despite the fact that the trumpet is just one of four solo instruments featured in the concerto, it is the star of the concerto. Its sound is just too brilliant, the virtuosity of its part is just too great, for us to hear it as anything less than the first among equals. Here's how the third and final movement begins. [**Musical selection**: Bach, Brandenburg Concerto No. 2 in F Major, movement 3.]

The Brandenburg Concerto No. 2 in F Major: Instrumentation

The Brandenburg 2 is a concerto grosso, which means a "big" or "large" concerto. What is big about a concerto grosso is the number of soloists: a concerto grosso will feature multiple soloists. In the case of the Brandenburg 2, this means four soloists: a clarino, a flute, an oboe, and a violin. (By the way, despite the fact that Bach specifies that the flute part be played by a flauto—by a flute—many original instrument performances will use a recorder instead, as does our recording. We can live with this.)

A concerto grosso, then, features two performing ensembles in one: a group of soloists, called the *concertino* (meaning the "little ensemble") and the *ripieno*, meaning the "orchestra." A passage in which everyone plays together—*concertino* and *ripieno*, soloists and orchestra, is called a tutti, meaning literally "all together": the whole enchilada.

The *ripieno* of Bach's Brandenburg 2 consists of a string orchestra—first and second violins, violas, 'cellos, violone (or bass viol, the ancestor of today's double bass), and, in addition, a harpsichord. When first performed at the Cöthen Court, Bach would have played either viola or harpsichord and Prince Leopold—himself a decent musician—would have played a bass viol.

The brilliant, celebratory nature of the Brandenburg 2 has much to do with its treble-dominated concertino: trumpet, flute, oboe and violin. Never before or since has this particular set of solo instruments been used in a concerto grosso.

Movement 1: Ritornello Form

This first movement ritornello form might have been "inspired" by the ritornello movements of Vivaldi, but in terms of its length, complexity, and sheer invention, it leaves its models in the dust.

Let's hear the ritornello theme as it begins the movement, played by the tutti. For now, let's be aware of the following two points: One, the theme is a vigorous, memorable, though typically "busy" baroque-styled melody and two, it concludes with a closed cadence—a musical punctuation mark equivalent to a period—that effectively separates it from what comes next. [**Musical selection**: Bach, Brandenburg Concerto No. 2 in F Major, movement 1 (ritornello theme).] The ritornello theme is cast in four distinct phrases, which we will call phrases *a*, *b*, *a¹*, and *b¹*. Phrases *a* and *a¹* have a jolly, dance-like bounce to them; phrases *b* and *b¹* consist almost entirely of fast, running 16th notes. [**Piano demonstration**: Playing phrases *a*, *b*, *a¹*, and *b¹*.] Let's hear the ritornello theme again. I'll identify the phrases as they roll by: phrases *a*, *b*, *a¹*, and *b¹*. [**Musical selection**: Bach, Brandenburg Concerto No. 2 in F Major, movement 1.] The next melodic idea we need to be aware of is the chattering bass line heard beneath phrase "a." It sounds like this. [**Piano demonstration**: Playing chattering bass line.] Let's hear that again. [**Piano demonstration**: Playing chattering bass line.]

When we first hear that chattering bass line under phrase "a," it is strictly a background element. Given that our ears are focused on the ritornello theme unfolding above it, we probably don't even notice it. [**Musical selection**: Bach, Brandenburg Concerto No. 2 in F Major, movement 1, ritornello theme *a*.] But Johann Sebastian Bach never wastes a note or squanders a melody. That chattering bass line will soon enough rise from the accompaniment to become a thematic element unto itself and will be played by each solo instrument during the course of the movement. For example, some 40 seconds into the movement, the chattering bass line leaps to stage front when it is played by the trumpet. Once again, here's the chattering bass line. [**Piano demonstration**: Playing chattering bass line.] And here's what it sounds like when the trumpet first plays it. [**Musical selection**: Bach, Brandenburg Concerto No. 2 in F Major, movement 1.]

So not only does the ritornello theme contain four thematic phrases, but its accompaniment will also become a thematic element during the course of the movement! We're not done yet, because there's still another thematic entity we need to be aware of. Bach introduces the solo instruments— one at a time—with a brief, trilling melody that offers up a considerable contrast to the foot-stomping heaviness of the ritornello theme. Since this little theme will only be played by the solo instruments, we will refer to it—cleverly, I think—as the solo theme. Here's what it sounds like. [**Piano demonstration**.]

Following the movement opening statement of the ritornello theme, the solo violin enters with that solo theme, immediately after which the opening phrase *a* of the ritornello theme is again played by the tutti. [**Musical selection**: Bach, Brandenburg Concerto No. 2 in F Major, movement 1, solo theme.] Next it's the solo oboe's turn to play the solo theme, which is—again—followed phrase *a* of the ritornello theme. [**Musical selection**: Bach, Brandenburg Concerto No. 2 in F Major, movement 1, solo theme.]

The solo flute/recorder next plays solo theme, followed—once again—by the opening phrase of the ritornello theme. [**Musical selection**: Bach, Brandenburg Concerto No. 2 in F Major, movement 1, solo theme.] (An observation: the quick cross-cutting back-and-forth between the solo theme and ritornello theme, between solo instruments and tutti is—to my ears—so modern in its impact that I wonder if Bach was watching music videos when he wasn't listening to Vivaldi!)

Last but not least, the trumpet takes its spin with the solo theme after which Bach brings this first large section of the movement to its conclusion. He does this not by playing the ritornello theme in its entirety, but rather, by finishing it. Think about it: We've just heard the opening phrase of the ritornello theme three times as it punctuated the appearances of the solo theme. So after the trumpet plays the solo theme, the ritornello theme picks up where it left off, and we hear the remainder of the theme: phrases *b*, *a¹*, and *b¹*. Let's hear it: the solo theme as played by the trumpet followed by the remainder of the ritornello theme and a closed cadence. [**Musical selection**: Bach, Brandenburg Concerto No. 2 in F Major, movement 1, solo theme.]

This first large section of the movement—"Part 1" of the movement—is expository, meaning that it features thematic music: the ritornello theme itself, the chattering bass line that rises from the bass to become a surface element, and the solo theme. From the beginning: [**Musical selection**: Bach, Brandenburg Concerto No. 2 in F Major, movement 1, ritornello form, part 1.] In a word: sensational. This is not your Italian grandfather's ritornello form, but rather a brilliant and idiosyncratic interpretation of ritornello form, an approach dictated by the brilliant and idiosyncratic set of solo instruments Bach employs in the concertino.

There are five additional large parts to this first movement, making a total of six. Each of these subsequent five parts concludes with the final two phrases of the ritornello theme—a^l and b^l—played by the tutti and followed by a closed cadence. These other appearances of the Ritornello Theme are fragmentary and are used to punctuate developmental episodes dominated by the instruments of the concertino, episodes during which we are witness to all sorts of phrase extensions, polyphonic overlapping of voices, and new key areas. Let us listen to these five additional parts one at a time.

Part 2 is dominated by the trumpet. It begins with a stratospherically high version of solo theme played by the trumpet. It continues with a lengthy episode that features the trumpet and concludes with the final two phrases of the ritornello theme set in the key of D minor dominated by the trumpet! [**Musical selection**: Bach, Brandenburg Concerto No. 2 in F Major, movement 1, part 2.] Part 3 of the movement features the entire concertino, as the solo instruments go to town on phrases a and a^l of the ritornello theme. [**Musical selection**: Bach, Brandenburg Concerto No. 2 in F Major, movement 1, part 3.]

Part 4 sees the concertino first work its way through the solo theme and then phrase a of the ritornello theme until, once again, the tutti performs the section-ending statement of the last two phrases of the ritornello theme, now in the key of G minor, part 4. [**Musical selection**: Bach, Brandenburg Concerto No. 2 in F Major, movement 1, part 4.] Part 5 sees the instruments of the concertino paired in various ways and again concludes with the final phrases of the ritornello theme, now in the dark and distant key of A minor. [**Musical selection**: Bach, Brandenburg Concerto No. 2 in F Major, movement 1, part 5.]

The sixth and final part of the movement is recapitulatory. It is based entirely on the ritornello theme, and it begins and ends in the home key—the tonic key—of F major. Let's hear this concluding part of the movement, after which we'll discuss one more little detail before moving on. [**Musical selection**: Bach, Brandenburg Concerto No. 2 in F Major, movement 1, part 6.]

The harmonic leap between the conclusion of part 5 (in the key of A minor) and the beginning of part 6 (in the home key of F major) features one of Bach's favorite devices: a pivot that uses common tones to transit a large harmonic distance in a virtual blink of an eye. Here's how part 5 ends, on an A minor chord. [**Piano demonstration.**] Immediately after that A minor harmony, without transition or preparation, Bach begins the ritornello theme back in the home key of f major. [**Piano demonstration.**] Let's hear them together. [**Piano demonstration.**]

Why does that work? Why does that sound okay? Because it does sound OK! Here's why. An A minor harmony consists of these three pitches: an A, a C, and an E. [**Piano demonstration.**] An F major harmony consists of these three pitches: F, A, and C. [**Piano demonstration.**]

An A minor harmony and an F major harmony have two of their three pitches in common: A and C. Well, Bach pivots off of those common tones and uses them as a hinge to swing instantly from A minor to the ritornello theme in F major. [**Piano demonstration.**] Let's hear that joint, that hinge, that common tone pivot as performed by "the band." [**Musical selection:** Bach, Brandenburg Concerto No. 2 in F Major, movement 1, parts 5–6.] That pivot, my friends, is as slick as Brylcream on a doorknob.

Movement 2

The second movement is scored for the solo flute, oboe, and solo violin, accompanied only by a single 'cello and the harpsichord. For reasons both practical and musical, the trumpet does not appear in this movement. On the "practical" side: leather-lunged and steel-lipped though he may be, the trumpet player cannot be expected to play as continuously as the other instruments of the ensemble. Given the incredible rigors of the first and third movements of this concerto, a rest is both a physical necessity and an act of mercy.

On the "musical side" is the expressive message of the movement. Set in D Minor, it is a sublime and lyric bit of "night music"—a nocturne—particularly notable for the gentle intertwining of the solo flute, oboe, and violin. The trumpet—with its piercing, brilliant sound—would not just dominate the other instruments; it would also disrupt (if not outright destroy) the shadowy expressive mood of the movement as well. Let's hear the opening of this second movement. [**Musical selection**: Bach, Brandenburg Concerto No. 2 in F Major, movement 2.]

Movement 3

Presumably well rested, the trumpet returns as the lead instrumental voice in the third movement fugue. [**Musical selection**: Bach, Brandenburg Concerto No. 2 in F Major, movement 3.] A fugue is a multi-voiced (that is, polyphonic) formal process in which a theme—called the fugue subject— is introduced and then restated in various voices and in various keys. The first large section of a fugue is called the exposition, during which each constituent voice enters in turn with the subject. There are four such voice entries here in this movement, one for each instrument of the concertino.

Let's hear the exposition. The order of the voice entries is: trumpet, oboe, violin, and flute. [**Musical selection**: Bach, Brandenburg Concerto No. 2 in F Major, movement 3.] The accompaniment here is provided by the "basso continuo": a single 'cello and a harpsichord. The ripieno—the orchestral strings—are not active participants in the unfolding of this third movement fugue. In fact, the orchestral strings do not play at all until the 47th measure of this 139 measure movement. Musicologist Malcolm Boyd goes so far as to suggest that: "The orchestral strings could be omitted [entirely] without any real loss to the fabric of the music." The point is well taken: This third movement is "about" the bright, brilliant, treble-dominated timbral colors of the concertino, while the ripieno—the orchestral compliment—is reduced to the role of deep-background accompanist.

One last point before we bring this lecture to its conclusion. The fugue subject consists of two parts, the first called the "head" and the second the "tail." The head is vigorous and dancelike. [**Piano demonstration**.] The tail consists of a running series of 16th notes. [**Piano demonstration**.] If the head and tail of the fugue subject sound familiar, they should, because phrases *a* and *b* of the first movement ritornello theme have almost exactly the same rhythmic and harmonic profile. Listen! Once again, here's the third movement fugue subject. [**Musical selection**: Bach, Brandenburg Concerto

No. 2 in F Major, movement 3.] And now the opening two phrases of the first movement ritornello theme. [**Musical selection**: Bach, Brandenburg Concerto No. 2 in F Major, movement 1, ritornello theme *a* and *b*.]

These first and third movement themes are just different enough to be different, but alike enough to be closely related, siblings, perhaps even fraternal twins. This sort of macro-relationship between outer movements is something we generally will not observe until the mature music of Beethoven: music composed more than 50 years after Bach died.

Conclusion

Bach's Brandenburg Concerto No. 2, like pretty much everything Bach composed, expanded the formal, melodic, harmonic, and expressive "frameworks" that were his baroque inheritance. It is exactly this sort of expansion of the musical language that prompts Bach scholar Martin Geck to write, with 20-20 hindsight of course, that:

> Bach assumes a pivotal role in history. He sums up what went before him and at the same time lays the foundation for important developments that will come after him. In Bach, the universalism of the baroque merges into modern idealism.

Thank you.

Bach—Violin Concerto in E Major
Lecture 4

Bach took the alternation of solo and tutti of the Italian concerto and transformed it into something far more complex and original. It is ironic but typical that those very things we prize most in Bach's concerti— their extraordinary originality and attendant complexity of craft and invention—are the things that made them controversial in their own time. The message is clear: Compose what you desire to compose, and let time decide what is of lasting value.

In May of 1723, Johann Sebastian Bach was appointed director of religious music at the St. Thomas School in the central German city of Leipzig. Bach spent the remainder of the 1720s composing a mind-boggling repertoire of masterworks for the churches of Leipzig. In March of 1729, he took over the directorship of Leipzig's prestigious *Collegium Musicum*, a secular-music performance organization. By the mid-1730s, Bach's estrangement from the religious musical institutions he presumably directed had become clear, and in November of 1736, Bach finally managed to persuade August III, king of Poland and elector of Saxony to appoint him royal court composer.

In May of 1737, six months after Bach's appointment, an article appeared in a journal called *The Critical Musician*. Published in Hamburg and edited by a Leipzig-born writer and musician named Johann Adolph Scheibe, the article attacked Bach's music and musical aesthetic. In his defense of Bach published in 1738, Johann Abraham Birnbaum, a lecturer in rhetoric at Leipzig University, addressed Scheibe's claims. Both men were correct in their own way. Scheibe was speaking for his generation during the time of the Enlightenment. However, in Birnbaum's defense, Bach's music has stood the test of time and has even become a genre unto itself.

Violin Concerto in E Major
While we do not know exactly when Bach composed his Violin Concerto in E Major, we do know that it was composed while he was Kapellmeister— court musical director—for the principality of Cöthen in central Germany,

a position he held from 1717 to 1723. At some point between 1729 and 1731, Bach revised the Concerto in E Major for performance by Leipzig's *Collegium Musicum* while he was the director there. The concerto as we know it today is almost certainly this revised "Leipzig" version.

Bach's concerti—most, if not all, of which were initially composed at Cöthen between 1717 and 1720—are built along the lines of what is called the Vivaldi model: a three-movement template in which the first movement is a fast ritornello form movement, the second movement is slow, and the third movement is upbeat and might be a ritornello form, a fugue, or a dance. While the influence of Vivaldi's concerti on Bach's must rightly be acknowledged, Bach's concerti reach far beyond Vivaldi's model. Bach's concerti are longer, more melodically interesting, more harmonically and structurally complex, more brilliant, and more profound than anything that came before him.

However, unlike today's audiences—who perceive Bach as the apex of the high baroque—most of Bach's contemporaries perceived Vivaldi and his Italian colleagues as the apex and Bach's music as an academic offshoot and artistic dead end. We now recognize that Bach was a true universalist—someone who synthesized in his own work a continent's worth of national styles and 300 years of compositional techniques.

Movement 1
This first movement is a textbook example of Bach's compositional transcendence. Typical of the Vivaldi concerto model, the movement is cast in ritornello form. However, Bach's movement transcends entirely its model in terms of the length and complexity of his ritornello theme, the compositional methods by which he manipulates the theme, the musical substance of his solo part, his unrivalled harmonic imagination, and the manner in which he creates a large-scale A–B–A (statement-departure-return) structure that transcends the small-scale episodes characteristic of ritornello form.

Bach's lengthy and elaborate theme is set in four phrases. The first phrase, phrase *a*, is melodically and harmonically straightforward. It begins by spelling out the tonic **triad** of E major, and then it spends time in an E major triad. It concludes with two turn-like motives, the second heard lower than the first; the repetitions of a motive at different pitch levels like these is called a **sequence**. The second thematic phrase, phrase *b*, features a downward sequence consisting of repeated notes and arpeggios. Phrase *c* features another downward sequence, this one based on the turn-like motive that concluded phrase *a*. The closing, or cadential, phrase *d* is the most motivically varied of the bunch, summarizing what has come before it by featuring the repeated notes of phrase *b* as well as the turn-like motive heard in phrases *a* and *c*.

While the influence of Vivaldi's concerti on Bach's must rightly be acknowledged, Bach's concerti reach far beyond Vivaldi's model.

One of the many things that set Bach apart from his contemporaries was his ability to create large-scale narrative structures out of the typically small-scale, episodic nature of baroque-era **musical forms**. For example, concerto ritornello form is a refrain-type musical form in which a ritornello theme is stated and then returns periodically in fragments. In between these fragmentary restatements of the ritornello theme are episodes dominated by the soloist that may (or may not) be based on the ritornello theme. The constant shifting of emphasis and the fragmentary returns to the ritornello theme do not create a large-scale sense of departure and return so much as a constant shift between two poles. However, in this movement, Bach does create a large-scale A–B–A narrative out of the otherwise fragmentary and episodic nature of ritornello form.

The first large section of the movement, which we will label as A, consists of three versions of the ritornello theme, each of which is in a major key. Because of the overwhelmingly thematic content of this first large section of music, we perceive it as being expository in nature. The second large section of the movement, section B, is much more fragmentary and episodic than the opening A section and is set in predominately minor keys. Because of its fragmentary, episodic character, we perceive this passage as being developmental in nature. The third large section of the movement is a literal repeat of the opening A section.

What makes the B section sound different is the more fragmentary treatment of the ritornello theme as well as its relatively unstable and predominantly minor-**mode** harmonic underpinning. Bach manages to create a sense of thematic coherency in the A sections, despite the nature of a fragmented ritornello theme, by inserting solo episodes between the phrases of the theme, a process called gapping in which gaps are created between the phrases of the theme that are then filled with solo episodes.

Movement 2
In its structural originality and expressive power, this second movement **adagio** is a full equal to the first movement. A passacaglia is a baroque variations procedure in which the theme is a brief bass line, called the ground bass, and/or the harmonies stacked above that ground bass. In a passacaglia, the ground bass is repeated over and over again beneath the continuously changing material above it.

Bach's treatment of passacaglia form in the second movement is as novel as his treatment of ritornello form in the first movement. Just as he did with the first movement ritornello theme, Bach gaps the ground bass and inserts solo material within those gaps. He creates a large-scale A–B–A form in the second movement—with the middle section, B, taking on the more fragmentary and harmonically unstable character of a development.

As we would expect in a passacaglia, the first section of the movement presents the ground bass without accompaniment, played here by the 'cellos. Soulful, lyric, and set in C-**sharp** minor, the ground bass is six measures long. Then, the solo violin enters, floating above the ground bass, which—because of its gaps—is now 8 measures long. The more developmental middle section of the movement begins with the ground bass dropping out entirely. In its place, the solo violin weaves an exquisite melody around harmonic elements extracted from the ground bass.

The third and final section of the movement is recapitulatory and consists of two parts. In the first part, the solo violin floats above the ground bass, which has now been expanded to nine measures in length. In the second part of this third section, the ground bass returns as we heard it at the beginning of the movement. This third section is an ethereally beautiful and utterly idiosyncratic movement.

Movement 3
After the formal and expressive complexities of the first two movements, the dance-like and structurally straightforward rondo pleases our musical palates. The movement is cast in rondo form, which Bach rarely used. Like ritornello form, rondo form is a refrain form in which the rondo theme returns after various contrasting episodes. Unlike ritornello form, in which the ritornello theme typically returns in fragments, a rondo theme will typically return in its entirety each time we hear it. Where ritornello form is primarily about its solo episodes—punctuated by fragments of the ritornello theme—a rondo form movement is primarily about the rondo theme, which is punctuated by the contrasting episodes.

During the course of the third movement, the rondo theme will be heard, verbatim, a total of five times. Thus, the overall structure of the movement is transparent. However, while the formal structure of the movement might be straightforward, the nature of the solo episodes between the reiterations of the rondo theme is not. There are four solo episodes, and they become increasingly virtuosic as the movement unfolds.

The first of these solo episodes is simple enough: It consists of a steady stream of 16th notes. At 16 measures in length, this episode is exactly as long as the rondo theme itself. By the time we reach the fourth and final contrasting episode, the virtuosity level of the solo violin part has risen substantially. At 32 measures in length, this final solo episode is double the length of any other section of the movement; it features a brilliant solo violin, the most active accompaniment, and the greatest rhythmic and harmonic variety in the movement. This final solo episode brings the rondo to its climax, followed by the final statement of the rondo theme and the conclusion of the concerto. ■

adagio: Slow.

mode: A type of pitch collection (or scale).

musical form: The manner in which a given movement of music is structured.

sequence: Successive repetitions of a motive at different pitches; compositional technique for extending melodic ideas.

sharp: Accidental (sign/symbol) placed to the left of a note, indicating that the pitch should be raised by a semitone.

triad: A chord consisting of three different pitches built from some combination of major and/or minor thirds.

Bach—Violin Concerto in E Major
Lecture 4—Transcript

Welcome back to *The 30 Greatest Orchestral Works*. This is Lecture 4, and it is entitled "Bach—Violin Concerto in E Major."

Bach Under Fire

In May of 1723, Johann Sebastian Bach was appointed director of religious music at the St. Thomas School in the central German city of Leipzig. The school was part of the St. Thomas Lutheran Church, and among Bach's many duties was music director for the Church of St. Thomas as well as the other three principal churches in Leipzig.

Bach spent the remainder of the 1720s composing a mind-boggling repertoire of masterworks for the churches of Leipzig, including at least three complete annual cycles of church cantatas. These are one-act operas performed at Sunday services, works based on that particular week's prescribed Bible reading. All together, including cantatas composed earlier in his career, Bach composed a total of seven annual cycles: a cantata a week—an opera a week, give or take—for seven years. Mind-boggling.

By the late 1720s, Bach desperately wanted to branch out. To that end, in March of 1729, he took over the directorship of Leipzig's prestigious *Collegium Musicum*, a secular-music performance organization founded by his old chum Georg Philipp Telemann back in 1701. The *Collegium* performed once a week at Zimmerman's Coffee House in Leipzig (a venue sadly destroyed during World War II) and was made up of members of the community as well as students from Leipzig University.

By the mid-1730s, Bach's estrangement from the religious musical institutions he presumably directed had become clear to everybody, in particular his various ecclesiastic "superiors," who hadn't a clue as to how they should deal with their rogue music director.

In November of 1736—after three years of finagling—Bach finally managed to persuade August III, "King of Poland, Grand Duke of Lithuania, and Elector of Saxony" to appoint him Royal Court Composer. It was an honorary title; the "royal court" was in Dresden; Bach was in Leipzig; and there's no evidence that Bach's appointment led to any royal commissions. However, it did give Bach some visibility outside of Leipzig and no small amount of political leverage in Leipzig; according to Christoph Wolff: "The Dresden court title seems [initially] to have had its desired effect of protecting Bach from further unpleasantness in Leipzig." Yes. "Further unpleasantness." Unfortunately, "further unpleasantness" was right around the corner.

On May 14, 1737, just six months after Bach's appointment as "Royal Court Composer," an article appeared in a journal called *The Critical Musician*. Published in Hamburg and edited by a Leipzig born writer and musician named Johann Adolph Scheibe, the article attacked Bach's music and musical aesthetic. (By the way, it did not attack Bach by name, but everybody who was anybody knew precisely who the article referred to.) When it was revealed that Scheibe—whom Bach knew personally—had written the article, Bach's wig went through the roof.

Scheibe was born in 1708. He was a 29-year-old whippersnapper when he wrote and published his article. It is a generational screed, the work of a young, Enlightenment-inspired *artiste* arguing in favor of a new, more up-to-date musical aesthetic; the patricide of a younger generation attempting to validate itself at the expense of its elders.

We read Scheibe's piece, paraphrased in brief part:

> Herr ___ is the most prominent among the musicians in ___. He is an extraordinary artist on the clavier and on the organ. I have heard this great man play a number of times; one is astonished at his skill.
>
> This great man would be the wonder of entire nations, had [his music] a more pleasing character, and if he did not deprive his pieces of all naturalness through excessive and confusing ornamentation, and obscure their beauty with a surfeit of artistic effects. He demands that singers execute with their voices what he

can play on the clavier. But such a thing is impossible. [Instead], he deprives his pieces of harmonic beauty and makes his singers inaudible. His bombastic ornamentation has led him from a natural style to an artificial one; and while one admires his extraordinary technique, it is exerted in vain because it clashes with nature.

Ouch, baby. Ouch.

Now, given the opportunity, Scheibe would probably have copped a plea and claimed that he meant no disrespect beyond declaring—in the name of progress—that Bach's time was past. In this, Scheibe could also, if he chose to, invoke "confirmation through anonymous association" by claiming that "I'm not the only one who feels this way!"

Much as we hate when people say that, it was, in Scheibe's case, true: He did indeed represent the thinking of many young German composers of the time, including Bach's own sons!

Of course, not everybody thought that Bach was an anachronism; Bach-the-composer was held in the highest esteem by some very important contemporary musicians, including Georg Philipp Telemann, the music director of the city of Hamburg (and the godfather of Bach's son Carl Philipp Emanuel) and the famed music theorist, composer (and close friend of Handel's) Johann Mattheson.

So—in its time and its place—did Scheibe's criticism have any merit? Well, the fact is, even Bach's defenders had to admit that aspects of his music appeared to be overly complicated and mired in the past. For example, on March 5, 1739, the music scholar (and Bach-devotee) Lorenz Mizler wrote in his newsletter-slash-blog the *MusikalISche Bibliothek* that:

> Herr Telemann and Herr [Carl Heinrich] Graun are excellent composers, and Herr Bach has produced equally excellent works. But when Herr Bach sometimes scores the middle voices more fully than others, he is taking his cue from the musical styles of 20 and 25 years past.

In his defense of Bach, published in 1738, Johann Abraham Birnbaum, a lecturer in rhetoric at Leipzig University, addressed Scheibe's claim that Bach's music went "counter to nature."

> Art improves nature's better condition. Many things are supplied by nature in a misshapen form, which only [become] beautiful when art has shaped them. Thus art lends nature the beauty it sometimes lacks and increases the beauty it possesses. The greater the artistry, the more brilliantly shines the "natural" beauty thus brought forth. Accordingly, it is impossible that the greatest art could obscure the beauty of anything.

So, who was "right"? Bach's critic, Adolph Scheibe, or his defender, Abraham Birnbaum? They were, each in his own way, correct, although Birnbaum was a lot more correct than Scheibe. Scheibe was speaking only locally, for his generation and his time, a time when a sea-change was underway in Western history that today we call the Enlightenment. In its "apparent" complexity and reliance on "old" musical structures—like ritornello form and fugue—Bach's music seemed to be out of touch with the spirit of "natural directness" so prized by "Enlightened" aesthetes.

Conversely, Johann Abraham Birnbaum was speaking for all times and all generations. We would observe the obvious: Bach's music has not just stood the test of time, but has become a genre unto itself: a body of work the breadth, depth, and scope of which has actually merged with and become a force of nature unto itself, art at its greatest, most beautiful, and most profound.

Johann Sebastian Bach, Violin Concerto in E Major (c. 1717–1720): The Particulars

While we do not know exactly when Bach composed his Violin Concerto in E Major, we do know that it was composed while he was Kapellmeister (court musical director) for the principality of Cöthen in central Germany, a position he held from 1717 to 1723.

In 1723, Bach became music director for the churches and city of Leipzig. Six years later, in 1729, he took over the directorship of Leipzig's *Collegium Musicum*. At some point between 1729 and 1731, Bach took the opportunity to revise the Concerto in E Major for performance by the *Collegium*. The concerto as we know it today is almost certainly this revised, "Leipzig" version.

Johann Sebastian Bach was a man of many talents, and it is very possible that Bach himself performed as violin soloist during the *Collegium* performances of his violin concerto. According to Bach's son Carl Philipp Emanuel, Bach "was happier directing an orchestra from the violin than from the harpsichord." No doubt, Johann Sebastian Bach had mad skills.

Bach and the Concerto

Bach's concerti—most (if not all) of which were initially composed at Cöthen between 1717 and 1720—are built along the lines of what is called "the Vivaldi model," a three movement template in which the first movement is a fast ritornello (meaning "refrain") form movement; a slow second movement; and an upbeat third movement that might be a ritornello form, a fugue, or a dance.

Bach was powerfully attracted to concerto composition, with its inherent contrast between the forces of the orchestra and the soloist (in the case of a solo concerto) or soloists (in the case of a concerto grosso). And while the influence of Vivaldi's concerti on Bach's must rightly be acknowledged, Bach's concerti go as far beyond Vivaldi's model as a Mercedes S-class does a Fiat. It's a fact: Bach's genius was not satisfied with creating works that stayed within the yellow lines of pre-existing frameworks, of composing music the likes of which already existed. So Bach expanded the frameworks. His concerti are longer, more melodically interesting, more harmonically and structurally complex, more brilliant and profound than anything that came before him; frankly, by an order of magnitude. No wonder so many of Bach's contemporaries had trouble understanding his music. Unlike today's audiences, who perceive Bach as the apex of the high baroque, most of Bach's contemporaries perceived Vivaldi and his Italian colleagues as the apex and Bach's music as an academic offshoot, an artistic dead end.

We now recognize that Bach was a true universalist, someone who synthesized in his own work a continent's worth of national styles and 300 years of compositional techniques. As an example of Bach's universal art, we turn to his Concerto for Violin in E Major. According to the great Bach scholar, organist, philosopher, and physician Albert Schweitzer, it is a work characterized by "unconquerable *joie de vivre*."

Movement 1: Ritornello Form

This first movement is a textbook example of Bach's compositional transcendence. Typical of the Vivaldi concerto model, the movement is cast in ritornello form. This means that a theme—the ritornello theme, played by the tutti (meaning the soloist and the orchestra)—will return in fragments after various contrasting episodes featuring the violin soloist.

However, Bach's movement transcends entirely its model in terms of, one, the length and complexity of his ritornello theme; two, the compositional methods by which he manipulates the theme; three, the musical substance of his solo part (in which nothing is ever done for mere virtuosic effect); four, his unrivalled harmonic imagination; and five, by the manner in which Bach manages to create a large-scale A-B-A (statement-departure-return) structure that transcends the small-scale episodes characteristic ritornello form.

The Ritornello Theme

Bach's lengthy and elaborate theme is set in four phrases. Let's first hear the ritornello theme in its entirety, after which we'll discuss the phrases one by one. [**Musical selection**: Bach, Violin Concerto in E Major, movement 1, ritornello theme.] That theme is filled with enough small melodic ideas—or "motives"—to power both a small city and the remainder of this movement. The first phrase of the theme is melodically and harmonically straightforward. It begins by spelling out the tonic triad of E major. [**Piano demonstration**.] It then noodles around a bit on an E major triad. [**Piano demonstration**.] And concludes with two turn-like motives, the second heard lower than the first. [**Piano demonstration**.]

(For our information, we call the repetitions of a motive at different pitch levels a sequence. We just heard a sequence at the end of phrase one, when the turn-like motive was repeated at a lower pitch level. Here is that sequence, again. [**Piano demonstration**.] Let's hear this first phrase—which we shall now call phrase *a*—in its entirety [**Piano demonstration**.] The second thematic phrase, phrase *b*, features a downwards sequence consisting of repeated notes and arpeggios. [**Piano demonstration**.] Phrase *c* features another downwards sequence; this one based on the turn-motive that concluded phrase *a*. Here's phrase *c*. [**Piano demonstration**.]

The closing or cadential phrase *d* is the most motivically varied of the bunch, summarizing what has come before it by featuring the repeated notes of phrase *b* as well as the turn-like motive heard in phrases *a* and *c*. Here's that closing phrase. [**Piano demonstration**: Playing phrase *d*.] Once again, let's hear the entire ritornello theme as played by the tutti, by the orchestra and the violin soloist. [**Musical selection**: Bach, Violin Concerto in E Major, movement 1, ritornello theme.]

Structural Alchemy

One of the many things that set Bach-the-composer apart from his contemporaries was his ability to create large-scale narrative structures out of the typically small-scale, episodic nature of baroque-era instrumental forms. For example, concerto ritornello form is a refrain-type musical form in which a ritornello theme is stated and then returns periodically in fragments. In between these fragmentary restatements of the ritornello theme are episodes dominated by the soloist that may (or may not) be based on the ritornello theme. The overall effect is kaleidoscopic, but not narrative; the constant shifting of emphasis and the fragmentary returns to the ritornello theme do not create a large-scale sense of departure and return so much as a constant shift between two poles.

However, in this movement, Bach does indeed create a large-scale A-B-A, statement-departure-return narrative out of the otherwise fragmentary and episodic nature of ritornello form. Here's how he does it. The first large section of the movement, which we will schematicize as large case A, consists of three versions of the ritornello theme, including the opening version we just heard. Each of these three versions of the ritornello theme is in a major key. Because of the overwhelmingly thematic content of this first large section of music, we perceive it as being expository in nature.

The second large section of the movement, which we will "schematicize" as B, is much more fragmentary and episodic than the opening A section. This chunk of music is set in predominately minor keys. Because of its fragmentary, episodic character, we perceive this passage as being developmental in nature.

The third large section of the movement is a literal repeat of the opening A section. With the advent of this third large section, beginning, as it does with a complete playing of the ritornello theme back in the home key of E major, it sounds as if we have "arrived," as if we have "returned" from some contrasting place. But it's all smoke and mirrors; thematically, we never left; thematically, the music never "goes" anywhere: The B section is built from the same thematic motives as the A sections. What makes the B section "sound different" is the more fragmentary treatment of the ritornello theme as well as its relatively unstable and predominantly minor-mode harmonic underpinning.

Okay. Here's a really good question: How does Bach manage to create a sense of thematic coherency in the A sections when we know that ritornello form is about fragmenting a theme and using the fragments to punctuate solo episodes? He does it by gapping the theme! Yes, I'll explain!

In lieu of fragmenting the ritornello theme in the A sections, Bach inserts solo episodes between the phrases of the theme, a process called "gapping." Gaps are created between the phrases of the theme, gaps that are then "filled" with solo episodes. For example, following the opening statement of the ritornello theme and a brief, three-measure declaration by the solo violin—"Here I am!"—Bach delivers the first of his "gapped" versions of the ritornello theme. It begins with phrase *a* played by the tutti. [**Musical selection**: Bach, Violin Concerto in E Major, movement 1.] The solo violin now enters, "filling in the gap" between the phrases of the ritornello theme by playing, first, arpeggios drawn from phrase *b* and then a series of turn-like motives drawn from phrase *a*. [**Musical selection**: Bach, Violin Concerto in E Major, movement 1.] The ritornello theme now resumes as the tutti plays the second half of phrase *a* once again, which is followed by another solo violin episode. [**Musical selection**: Bach, Violin Concerto in E Major, movement 1.] Picking up exactly where it left off, the tutti next plays phrases *b*, *c*, and the first half of phrase *d* of the ritornello theme. [**Musical selection**: Bach, Violin Concerto in E Major, movement 1.]

The solo violin again squeezes itself into the gap, now playing material drawn from phrase *d*. Finally, the tutti re-enters and brings phrase *d* and this gapped version of the ritornello theme to its conclusion. [**Musical selection**: Bach, Violin Concerto in E Major, movement 1.] Bach immediately offers up another gapped version of the ritornello theme, which brings the first large part of the movement to its conclusion. Let's hear it: the second gapped version of the ritornello theme. [**Musical selection**: Bach, Violin Concerto in E Major, movement 1.]

Part B of the movement now begins with an abrupt and unexpected shift to the key of C-sharp minor. The developmental character of this second large part of the movement is made immediately apparent by the lengthy solo episode with which it begins. [**Musical selection**: Bach, Violin Concerto in E Major, movement 1.] This developmental second part of the movement concludes with a dazzling, contrapuntal passage for the solo violin, followed by an extended version of phrase *c* played by the tutti and capped by a brief but heart-breaking cadenza for the solo violin. Let's hear this concluding music, starting with the contrapuntal passage for solo violin. [**Musical selection**: Bach, Violin Concerto in E Major, movement 1.]

This second large part of the movement concludes darkly in the key of G-sharp minor, expressively and harmonically light years away from the bright and energized opening of the movement in E major. We rightly wonder during the dismal pause we just heard—where is this music headed? I'll tell you where it's headed: right back to E major. Let's listen from the melancholy solo violin cadenza through the opening of the return to part "A," the return to the ritornello theme in the key of E major. [**Musical selection**: Bach, Violin Concerto in E Major, movement 1.] Whoa. What an incredible harmonic and expressive leap! From a musical point of view Bach's harmonic leap works because it represents something called a "pivot modulation." A pivot modulation is a sudden change of key achieved through common tones. To whit: Following the melancholy solo violin cadenza, the music settles on a forlorn G-sharp minor chord. [**Piano demonstration**.]

That G minor chord consists of three different pitches: a G-sharp, a B, and a D-sharp. The harmony then suddenly pivots—shifts—to an E major chord. [**Piano demonstration**.] And I would point out that an E major chord consists of three different pitches: an E, a G-sharp, and a B. Thus, a G-sharp minor chord [**Piano demonstration**.] and an E major chord [**Piano demonstration**.] have two pitches in common: They each contain a G-sharp and a B. Using those two common tones, Bach pivots from one key to the next; the common tones become a musical hinge that allows the harmonic door to swing from one place to another without any break in the musical continuity. Let's hear the pivot again. [**Musical selection**: Bach, Violin Concerto in E Major, movement 1.] Its shocking expressive effect notwithstanding, that transition is harmonically as smooth as snail slime on a peeled onion.

Movement 2: *Passacaglia*

In its structural originality and expressive power, this second movement Adagio is a full equal to the first movement. A passacaglia is a baroque variations procedure. In a passacaglia, the theme is a brief bass line (called the "ground bass") and/or the harmonies stacked above that ground bass. In a passacaglia, the ground bass is repeated over and over again beneath the continuously changing material above it. (Think of it as baroque boogie-woogie, if you will.)

Bach's treatment of passacaglia form here in the second movement is as novel as his treatment of ritornello form in the first movement. Just as he did with the first movement ritornello theme, Bach "gaps" the ground bass and inserts solo material within those gaps. Just as he did in the first movement ritornello form, Bach creates a large-scale, A-B-A form here in the second movement, with the middle section—B—taking on the more fragmentary and harmonically unstable character of a development.

As we would expect in a passacaglia, the first section of the movement presents the ground bass without accompaniment, played here by the 'cellos. Soulful, lyric, and set in C-sharp minor, the ground bass is six measures long. [**Musical selection**: Bach, Violin Concerto in E Major, movement 2.] The solo violin now enters, floating above the ground bass which, because of its gaps, is now eight measures long. [**Musical selection**: Bach, Violin Concerto in E Major, movement 2.]

The more developmental middle section of the movement begins with the ground bass dropping out entirely. In its place, the solo violin weaves an exquisite melody around harmonic elements extracted from the ground bass. Here's the beginning of the developmental, middle section of this second movement. [**Musical selection**: Bach, Violin Concerto in E Major, movement 2.]

The third and final section of the movement is recapitulatory and consists of two parts. The first part sees the solo violin float above the ground bass, which has now been expanded to nine measures in length. The second part of this third section brings us full circle, as the ground bass returns as we heard it at the beginning of the movement. Here, in its entirety, is the third and final section of the movement. [**Musical selection**: Bach, Violin Concerto in E Major, movement 2.]

This is an ethereally beautiful and utterly idiosyncratic movement. The violinist Yehudi Menuhin tells a wonderful story about practicing it as a youngster: "I saw myself mentally as a peacemaker cutting Gordian knots, settling neurotic quarrels in an instant, saw mankind abandoning its entrenchments and embracing one another for my sake."

Movement 3: Rondo Form

After the formal and expressive complexities of the first two movements, the dance-like and structurally straightforward rondo strikes our musical palates like a perfectly chilled bottle of Château d'Yquem after a heavy meal. The movement is cast in rondo form, which Bach rarely used. Like ritornello form, rondo form is a refrain form that sees the rondo theme return after various contrasting episodes. Unlike the ritornello form, in which the ritornello theme typically returns in fragments, a rondo theme will typically return in its entirety each time we hear it.

As a result, rondo form exhibits an entirely different emphasis than ritornello form. Where ritornello form is primarily about its solo episodes (which are punctuated by fragments of the ritornello theme), a rondo form movement is primarily about the rondo theme (which is punctuated by the contrasting episodes). Here's Bach's dancing, vaguely rustic and in all ways popular-sounding, 16-measure-long rondo theme. [**Musical selection**: Bach, Violin Concerto in E Major, movement 3.] This wonderful tune will be heard, verbatim, a total of five times during the course of the movement. Thus, the overall structure of the movement will be as transparent as a freshly Windexed pane of glass.

However, while the formal structure of the movement might be straightforward, the nature of the solo episodes sandwiched between the reiterations of the rondo theme is not. There are four solo episodes, and they become increasingly virtuosic as the movement unfolds.

The first of these solo episodes is simple enough: It consists of a steady stream of 16th notes. At 16 measures in length, this episode is exactly as long as the rondo theme itself. Here's the first contrasting episode. [**Musical selection**: Bach, Violin Concerto in E Major, movement 3.] By the time we reach the fourth and final contrasting episode, the virtuosity level of the solo violin part has gone through the roof! At 32 measures in length, this final solo episode is double the length of any other section of the movement. It features the most brilliant solo violin writing, the most active accompaniment, and the greatest rhythmic and harmonic variety in the movement, and thus brings the rondo to its climax. Let's hear this fourth and final solo episode, followed by the final statement of the rondo theme and the conclusion of the concerto. [**Musical selection**: Bach, Violin Concerto in E Major, movement 3.]

Conclusions

The eminent musicologist Claude Palisca writes: "[Though] Bach leaned greatly upon Vivaldi for the forms and types of [his concerti], in vastness of conception and complexity of thematic and contrapuntal relationships, [Bach's concerti] surpass the work of any of the Italians."

Indeed they do. Bach took the alternation of solo and tutti of the Italian concerto and transformed it into something far more complex and original. It is ironic, but oh so typical, that those very things we prize most in Bach's concerti—their extraordinary originality and attendant complexity of craft and invention—are just those things that made them controversial in their own time. The message here is clear: Compose what you must, and let time decide what is of lasting value.

Thank you.

Haydn—Symphony No. 104
Lecture 5

Along with Ludwig van Beethoven, Haydn was the thriftiest composer of the late 18th and early 19th centuries. Haydn's three-movement, 11-minute-long Symphony no. 1 of 1759 is an updated version of an early-18th-century Italian opera overture. Composed 36 years later, Haydn's Symphony no. 104, which is cast in four movements that together run a full 30 minutes in length, looks forward—in its spirit and mood—to the beginning of the 19th century.

Franz Joseph Haydn was born on March 31, 1732, in the eastern Austrian town of Rohrau, close to the Hungarian border. Haydn was the second of twelve children born to Mathias Haydn—who was a wheelwright—and Anna Maria Koller Haydn. As a small child, he had an excellent singing voice. With the hopes that he would someday join the clergy, Haydn's parents sent him away to study music at the age of six. Two years later—in March or April of 1740—Haydn became a choirboy at St. Stephen's Cathedral in Vienna. The music young Joseph sang as a choirboy formed the foundation of his musical ear and education.

When Haydn's voice broke, he was unceremoniously booted out of the choir at St. Stephen's Cathedral. Because he was determined not to join the priesthood but, rather, to make a career in music, Haydn moved into a small attic room above the wealthy widow Princess Maria Octavia Esterházy. The princess's two sons, Prince Paul Anton Esterházy and Prince Nikolaus, were destined to become Haydn's employers for about 29 years; Haydn served as assistant Kapellmeister (and later, first Kapellmeister) in Prince Paul's musical establishment.

In 1758, Haydn was hired as the Kapellmeister for Count Karl Joseph Franz von Morzin and composed, among other works, his first symphonies. In 1790, Johann Peter Salomon, a German-born violinist, composer, conductor, and concert producer working out of London, offered to pay Haydn to move to London for a few years to compose an opera, six symphonies, and some smaller works. In total, Haydn agreed to two separate London residencies in which he composed twelve symphonies—which were the last symphonies he composed—that are collectively known as Haydn's *London Symphonies* and are each a masterwork.

Symphony No. 104 in D Major, "London"

Haydn's First Symphony was composed in 1759 for Count Morzin's orchestra and was 11 minutes in length. It is a modest work cast in three movements built along the lines of a baroque-era Italian opera **overture**. By the time Haydn composed his Symphony no. 104 in 1795, what is now referred to as the

Franz Joseph Haydn (1732–1809) pioneered the Viennese classical style with his Symphony no. 104, which was composed in 1795.

Viennese classical style—with its balance of melodic fluidity and beauty, formal clarity, and emotional restraint—was fully developed with Haydn being its essential proponent. In the 36 years between Haydn's first and final symphonies, the genre of symphony had transformed from being an entertainment for aristocrats to a public entertainment. For Haydn, this meant composing symphonies that struck a balance between intellect and feeling—between high rhythmic energy and gentle lyricism.

Movement 1

The first movement opens with a solemn introduction that begins with a magisterial fanfare played in what is called an **orchestral unison**, meaning that all the instruments of the orchestra simultaneously play the same pitches—in this case, D–D–D–A, D–D–D–A, the bottom and top pitches of a D **chord**. However, the orchestra does not play the middle pitch of the chord, the one that would tell us whether this music is set in D major (as the symphony advertises itself) or D minor. This tonal ambiguity is resolved in the third measure of the introduction, when we hear an F-**natural** played along with the D and A—at which point we realize that we are, at least for now, in D minor. This appearance of D minor—dark and dramatic, when we expected the light and brilliance of D major—imparts tremendous expressive depth to the music in D major that will eventually follow.

In 1758, Haydn was hired as the Kapellmeister for Count Karl Joseph Franz von Morzin and composed, among other works, his first symphonies.

Marked "**allegro**"—meaning "fast"—the sonata form begins with the first theme. It is lyric, elegant, and compact, consisting of two thematic phrases which we will refer to as phrases a and a^1. This theme, in D major, takes on the character of a contrasting element, following the dark-toned introduction. The shadow cast by the key of D minor in the introduction imbues the first theme with an expressive depth that it would not have otherwise had.

A lengthy, high-octane modulating bridge follows that bridges the distance between themes 1 and 2, using music that is melodically fragmented and, therefore, is not perceived as being thematic. It also **modulates**, or changes key, in preparation for theme 2. The **cadence** immediately follows, and about halfway through the cadence material, Haydn introduces a cadence theme: an optional melody that will be associated with conclusions. Haydn's cadence theme—set in the new key of A major—is followed by a loud and vigorous passage that brings the exposition to its conclusion.

In a typical sonata form exposition, themes 1 and 2 will contrast by being different melodies and by being in different keys. However, in this movement, only the key is different; it is set in the new, contrasting key of A major. In fact, it is the same as theme 1, set in the new key area presumably reserved for theme 2. In this sonata form exposition, there are a few reasons Haydn chose not to include a contrasting second theme: The introduction provides all the thematic contrast Haydn requires for the movement, the optional inclusion of a cadence theme provides all the contrast he required for the body of the exposition, and the theme's recognizability factor is maximized because he intends to build almost the entire development section from a single, utterly inauspicious aspect of theme 1.

The first development section contains a motive-rich melody. The most memorable of its motives—and therefore the one we'd most expect to hear developed—is its opening. The next most memorable motive is the one that brings the theme to its conclusion. Among the least memorable elements of the theme are the four repeated notes sitting in the middle of motive three, which sound like filler but supply the requirements for the development section.

In a sonata form recapitulation, the principal themes (typically two) will be heard in the same key—the home key. If Haydn did that in this movement, we would hear the same theme played twice in the same key, which would be boring and obvious. So, following the initial recapitulation of theme 1 in D major, Haydn offers what amounts to a second development section, which is based on the repeated notes of motive 3 and motive 1 of the theme. The cadence follows and brings the movement to its conclusion.

Movements 2 and 3
The second movement is a moderately paced two-step dance of great elegance and style. The third movement is set in minuet and trio form. There is no more predictable ritual in the music of the classical era than the presence of a minuet and trio form movement as a middle movement in a four-movement work, with its moderate **tempo**, **triple meter**, large-scale A–B–A form, and ritual phrase repetitions. Therefore, it remains a miracle of Western art that Joseph Haydn continuously turned the clichéd genre of minuet and trio into something special. With effervescent, bubbly phrase endings, the music of the third movement has a "champagne" feel.

Movement 4
The fourth movement opens with the sort of rustic, countryside-type dance music that Haydn often used in his finales. Its rural flavor is doubly reinforced by the bagpipe-like drone that accompanies the theme's first appearance. While theme 1 dominates the movement, theme 2 is brilliant and celebratory. Even as theme 2 first appears in the first violins, theme 1 is played by the winds and second violins. Theme 3 is a cadence theme and is sustained and quiet; it offers just about the only moment of respite in this otherwise upbeat exposition. Haydn uses an extended version of this cadence theme to conclude the development section and to transition into theme 1 at

the beginning of the recapitulation, followed by the remainder of the last movement of Haydn's last symphony. ∎

allegro: Fast.

cadence: A harmonic or melodic formula that occurs at the end of a phrase, section, or composition and conveys a momentary or permanent conclusion—in other words, a musical punctuation mark.

chord: Simultaneous sounding of three or more different pitches.

modulation: The process of changing key during the course of a piece of music.

natural: Accidental (sign/symbol) placed to the left of a note, indicating that the note should not be sharpened or flattened; a white key on a keyboard.

orchestral unison: A technique by which multiple instruments simultaneously play the same pitch but in different registers (ranges).

overture: Music preceding an opera or play, often played as an independent concert piece.

tempo: Relative speed of a passage of music.

triple meter: Metrical pattern having three beats to a measure.

Haydn—Symphony No. 104
Lecture 5—Transcript

Welcome back to *The 30 Greatest Orchestral Works*. This is Lecture 5, and it is entitled "Haydn—Symphony No. 104."

It is a tired but still entirely relevant fact that had Joseph Haydn died at the same age as Wolfgang Mozart—35 years and 11 months—we would have no reason to remember him, because the music for which we do remember him was all composed after his 36th birthday. Consequently, we will not generally hear the phrases "Joseph Haydn" and "early bloomer" used in the same sentence except to point out how inappropriate is such a combination.

Now this is not to say that Haydn was lacking in talent. However, different people manifest their talents at different times of their lives depending upon their circumstances and genetic coding. Haydn's journey from his working-class roots to the pinnacle of late-18th-century Euro-music was a long and difficult one, a journey marked by incredible perseverance and hard work, leavened by one of the most good-humored and endearing personalities to ever put pen to manuscript paper.

Many years later, looking back at his years of struggle and self-education, Haydn told his biographer Albert Dies: "Young people can learn from my example that something can come out of nothing. What I am is all the result of the direst need."

Early Life

Franz Joseph Haydn was born on March 31, 1732, in the eastern Austrian town of Rohrau, close to the Hungarian border. Haydn was the second of 12 children born to Mathias Haydn—who was a wheelwright—and Anna Maria Koller Haydn. Haydn grew up in a working-class home notable, as he later remembered, for its "neatness, industry, and order." As a small child he had an excellent singing voice, and with the hopes that he would someday join the clergy, Haydn's parents sent him away to study music at the age of six. Two years later, in March or April of 1740, the now 8-year-old Haydn became a choirboy at St. Stephen's Cathedral in Vienna.

The music young Joseph sang as a choirboy at St. Stephens formed the foundation of his musical ear and education. (Haydn later claimed that he had learned much more from hearing music than from studying it.) Certainly, it was not the instruction he received at St. Stephens School, which was cursory, bordering-on-nonexistent. According to Albert Christoph Dies, whose 1810 biography of Haydn was based on a series of interviews conducted with Haydn over the course of three years:

> As soon as Joseph in his newly achieved status [as choirboy] had received as much instruction as he needed to fulfill his duties as choirboy, the instruction came to a complete standstill. He did learn a little Latin. Everything else went by the board, and one might venture to say that he lost the 10 youthful years best suited to study.

When Haydn's voice broke, he was unceremoniously booted out of the choir at St. Stephens. And while the sources disagree as to precisely when this happened, one thing they all agree on is that Haydn was determined not to join the priesthood but, rather, to make a career in music. To that end, Haydn found "a miserable little attic room without a stove" in a building known as the "Michaelerhaus." (For our information, the "Michaelerhaus" is still there on Vienna's Michaeler Square, next to St. Michael's Church and opposite the entrance to the Hofburg. The plaque memorializing Haydn's residence in the building is right under the "Kohlmarkt" street sign affixed to its wall.)

It was at the Michaelerhaus that Haydn "Innocent of the comforts of life, divided his whole time among the giving of lessons, the study of his art, and performing. He played for money in serenades and in the orchestras, and he was industrious in the practice of composition."

Nasty though his accommodations were, Haydn chose his address very well. Living on the first floor beneath him was the dowager (meaning "rich widow") Princess Maria Octavia Esterházy. The princess's two sons—Prince Paul Anton Esterházy and Prince Nikolaus Esterházy—were destined to become Haydn's employers for some 29 years. On the third floor of the Michaelerhaus lived Pietro Metastasio, the official poet and opera librettist for the Habsburg Court, a man of tremendous fame and influence. Both Princess Esterházy and Pietro Metastasio were to play key roles in Haydn's discovery and future employment. Having said that, for Haydn, his future success was disguised as hard work, and work hard he did. Later in life Haydn is quoted as having said:

> Proper teachers I have never had. I always started right away with the practical side, first in singing and in playing instruments, later in composition. I listened more than I studied, but I heard the finest music in all forms, and of this there was much in Vienna. Oh, so much! I listened attentively and tried to turn to good account what most impressed me. Thus little by little my knowledge and ability were developed.

Haydn obtained his first full-time job in 1758, when he was 26, when he was hired as the Kapellmeister (the music director) for a Bohemian Count named Karl Joseph Franz von Morzin. It was for Count Morzin's court that Haydn composed, among other works, his first symphonies.

Unfortunately, within a few years financial problems forced Count Morzin to disband his orchestra. (Oh, my friends, I would wager to say that very few of us have ever been forced by financial circumstances to "let the orchestra go." Oh, the problems faced by 18th-century nobility!)

Anyway, Count Morzin's financial pain turned out to be Haydn's professional gain. During his three-year stint with Count Morzin, Haydn had gone from being a composer of promise to a genuine professional. As a composer, he had learned how to handle the instruments of the orchestra. As a conductor, he had learned how to lead an orchestra. And of equal importance, he had learned how to handle the men who played in his orchestra. Haydn's natural-born tact and good humor—and the fact that he never forgot own his working-class roots—held him in good stead with the men of the orchestra. Small, wiry, spry, badly scarred by smallpox and boasting a schnozzle that by its size and shape would have been at home in a Picasso painting, Haydn never lost his working-class appearance, either. It was all to his advantage when dealing with his fellow musicians.

Thanks to a recommendation from Haydn's former downstairs neighbor—the dowager Princess Maria Octavia Esterházy—he was hired by her son,

Prince Paul Anton Esterházy, to serve as assistant Kapellmeister (and later, first Kapellmeister) in his musical establishment.

The Esterházy

My friends, there is big money. Then there is old money. Then there is big, old money. Big old money means big attitude and big-time connections; folks who do not live in the same world as you and I. Think the Rockefellers, the Rothschilds, the Vanderbilts, the Du Ponts, the Al Sauds, and the Windsors. To this golden list we would add the Esterházy family, who were among the great landowner-magnates of central Europe and one of the richest families in all of Europe from the 17th century until the mid-20th century.

The Esterházys were big, old money, in whose employ Haydn spent 29 years. Donald Grout and Claude Palisca describe Haydn's relationship with the family and its impact on his musical development:

> In the service of Paul Anton and his brother Nicholas, who succeeded to the title in 1762, Haydn passed nearly 30 years under circumstances ideal for his development as a composer. [Starting in] 1766, Prince Nicholas lived for most of the year on his country estate of Esterhaza, the palace and grounds of which had been constructed to rival the splendor of the French court at Versailles. Haydn was obligated to compose whatever music the prince demanded, to conduct the performances, to train and supervise all the musical personnel, and to keep the instruments in repair. He built up the orchestra from 10 to about 25 players; all the principal musicians were recruited from the best talent available in Austria, Italy, and elsewhere. Two operas and two long concerts were presented each week. In addition, there were special operas and concerts for notable visitors, as well as almost daily chamber music in the prince's private apartments, in which the prince himself usually joined.

Although [the palace of] the Esterhaza was isolated, the constant stream of distinguished guests and artists, together with occasional trips to Vienna, enabled Haydn to keep abreast of current developments in the world of music. He had the inestimable advantages of a devoted, highly skilled band of musicians, and a patron whose understanding and enthusiasm were an inspiration. As Haydn [himself] once said:

> My prince was pleased with all my work. As conductor of an orchestra I could make experiments, observe what strengthened and what weakened an effect and thereupon improve, substitute, omit, and try new things. I was cut off from the world, there was no one around me to mislead or harass me, and so I was forced to become original.

By the time Prince Nicholas Esterházy died in 1790, Haydn was the most popular composer in all of Europe. He was released from his duties and took up residence in Vienna. The world beat a path to his door, and after 29 years in the employ of the same family, the 58-year-old Haydn was thrilled to entertain offers from abroad. And a great offer was not long in coming.

Late in 1790, a stranger appeared at Haydn's door and introduced himself with these words: "I am Salomon of London and have come to fetch you. Tomorrow we will arrange an accord." Johann Peter Salomon he was and arrange a sweet, sweet deal he did.

Salomon was a German-born violinist, composer, conductor and concert producer who had been working out of London since the early 1780s. It was agreed that Haydn would move to London for one or two years. Haydn would be paid 300 pounds to compose an opera that would be produced at the Kings Theater. Haydn was to receive another 300 pounds to compose six symphonies, and an additional 200 pounds for the copyrights to them. Haydn was to receive yet another 200 pounds to write 20 smaller works, to be performed at 20 concerts. He was also guaranteed another 200 pounds for performing at a benefit concert, to benefit Haydn himself. (My friends, are you getting this all down?) As a down payment, Salomon paid Haydn 5000 florins (that is, 5000 gold pieces) on the spot. This down payment alone being equal to 6½ years of Haydn's salary with the Esterházys. Sweet.

A long story short: Haydn's most excellent English adventure from January 1791 to July 1792 was such a smash that he returned for a second residency between February 1794 and August 1795, during which he composed six more symphonies. In total, then, Haydn composed 12 symphonies during his two London residencies, six during the first stay and six during the second.

Haydn's "London Symphonies"

These 12 symphonies—which were the last symphonies Haydn composed—are collectively known as Haydn's "London Symphonies." They are each and every one a masterwork, each deserving to be among the *The 30 Greatest Orchestral Works*. I've selected Haydn's final symphony, no. 104 for reasons and symmetry: We are also going to focus on Mozart's final symphony, the "Jupiter," of 1788, and Beethoven's final symphony as well, his Symphony no. 9 of 1824.

(Here's a bit of trivia that links all three of these "final symphonies" and their composers. It was Johann Peter Salomon who brought Haydn to London and was thus responsible for the creation of Haydn's Symphony no. 104. It was the same Johann Peter Salomon who is believed to have given Mozart's C Major Symphony its nickname of "Jupiter." Finally, Salomon was born in 1745 in the German city of Bonn at Bonngasse 515 [today it's Bongasse 20]. Twenty-five years later, in 1770, Ludwig van Beethoven was born in exactly the same building. How 'bout them apples?)

Haydn's first Symphony was composed back in 1759 for Count Morzin's smallish orchestra of 16 players. At 11 minutes in total length, it is a modest work cast in three movement built along the lines—as were virtually all the symphonies of that time—of a baroque-era Italian opera overture.

By the time Haydn composed his Symphony no. 104, 36 years later, everything had changed. What is now referred to as the Viennese classical style, with its balance of melodic fluidity and beauty, formal clarity and emotional restraint was, by 1795, fully developed, with Joseph Haydn being its essential proponent. The ideals of the Enlightenment had progressed from a set of philosophic principles to hard social and political reality with the advent of the Age of Revolution: the American Revolution occurred between 1775 and 1782, and the French Revolution, which had begun in 1789, was finally winding down in 1795, at precisely the time Haydn composed his Symphony no. 104.

In the 36 years between Haydn's first and final symphonies, the genre of symphony itself had gone from being an entertainment for aristocrats to a public entertainment, one embraced by both aristocratic and middle-class audiences. Haydn's Symphony no. 1 was written to be performed for the pleasure of one man—Count Karl Joseph Franz von Morzin—in his own home. Haydn's last 12 symphonies—the "London Symphonies"—were by Haydn's own admission meant to appeal to what he perceived as a generalized "English" taste. For Haydn, that meant composing symphonies that struck a balance between intellect and feeling, between high rhythmic energy and gentle lyricism; music that Haydn believed would appeal to both aristocratic and middle-class English listeners. As it turned out, what Haydn achieved in his London Symphonies was the capstone of what he had always sought to achieve in his music: an extraordinary, dare we say perfect balance between head and heart, between dance and song!

Haydn's three-movement, 11 minute-long Symphony No. 1 of 1759 is an updated version of an early 18th century Italian opera overture. Haydn's Symphony no. 104, which is scored for an orchestra double the size of his first and is cast in four spectacular movements that together run a full half-hour in length, looks forward—in its spirit and mood—to the beginning of the 19th century.

Symphony No. 104 in D Major (1795)

As we have already observed, Haydn's final 12 symphonies are collectively know as the "London Symphonies." Under the heading of "slightly confusing," Haydn's Symphony no. 104 also bears the moniker of "London." My friends, we can handle this.

Movement 1: Sonata Form with Introduction

The first movement opens with a solemn introduction that begins with a magisterial fanfare played by the entire orchestra. [**Music selection**: Haydn, Symphony no. 104 in D major, movement 1, introduction.] This fanfare-like opening is performed by what is called an "orchestral unison," meaning that all the instruments of the orchestra simultaneously play the same pitches, in this case D-D-D-A, D-D-D-A, the bottom and top pitches of a D chord. [**Piano demonstration.**]

However, the orchestra does not play the middle pitch of the chord, the one that would tell us whether this music is set in D major (as the symphony advertises itself) or D minor. Here's what it would have sounded like if that middle pitch had been filled in in D major. [**Piano demonstration.**] And here's what it would have sounded like if it had been filled in in D minor. [**Piano demonstration.**] The major is bright; the minor is dark. This bit of tonal ambiguity is only resolved in the third measure of the introduction, when we hear an F-natural played along with the "D" and the "A," at which point we realize, to our shock, that we are, at least for now—not in D major as the symphony advertises itself—but in D minor! [**Piano demonstration.**] This appearance of D minor—dark and dramatic, when we expected the light and brilliance of D major—imparts tremendous expressive depth to the music in D major that will eventually follow. Before we get to that music in D major, let's hear the remainder of the introduction, characterized, as it is, by "sighing," descending motives and further fanfare. [**Music selection**: Haydn, Symphony No. 104 in D major, movement 1.]

Theme 1

Thrifty! Along with Ludwig van Beethoven (who was, for a brief and not particularly shining period, a student of Haydn's) Haydn was the thriftiest composer of the late 18th and early 19th centuries. His thematic ideas are portraits in pith, precisely as long as they need to be, with nary a wasted note. His development sections and cadential units get maximum mileage out of his thematic ideas. His music never overstays its welcome but rather almost always seems to end exactly when it should. Haydn's music is a classic case (pun intended) of "less is more," and nowhere is that more true than here, in the first movement of his final symphony.

Marked "*allegro*," meaning "fast," the sonata form proper now begins with theme 1. It is lyric, elegant, and compact, consisting of two thematic phrases which we will refer to as phrases *a* and *a¹*. Let's hear the theme.

[**Music selection**: Haydn, Symphony No. 104 in D Major, movement 1.] More than just a "pretty face" in D major, this theme takes on the character of an arrival, of a contrasting element, following—as it does—the dark-toned introduction.

It is a fact: The shadow cast by the key of D minor in the introduction imbues theme 1 with an expressive depth that it would not have otherwise had. A lengthy, high-octane modulating bridge follows. As we would expect from a passage that functions as a modulating bridge, this one "bridges" the distance between themes 1 and 2 using music that is melodically fragmented and therefore is not itself perceived as being thematic, and it modulates—while it changes key—in preparation for theme 2. A general statement: In a sonata form exposition, themes 1 and 2 will contrast in two ways: one, they will be different melodies. Two, they will be in different in different keys. However, in this movement, only one of those statements is true. Let's hear what purports to be theme 2, set in the new, contrasting key of A major. [**Music selection**: Haydn, Symphony No. 104 in D major, movement 1.] Dang but that sounds a lot like theme 1. In fact, it is theme 1, set in the new key area presumably reserved for theme 2.

We'll discuss why Haydn chose not to come up with a contrasting theme in a moment, but first, let's finish discussing this first large section of the movement: the exposition. The cadence or closing material immediately follows the excerpt we just heard. About halfway through the cadence material Haydn introduces a cadence theme, an optional melody that will be associated with conclusions. Haydn's cadence theme, set in the new key of A major, is followed by a loud and vigorous passage that brings the exposition to its conclusion. Let's hear the second half of the cadence material, starting with the cadence theme through the end of the exposition. [**Music selection**: Haydn, Symphony No. 104 in D Major, movement 1.]

We address the question: why, in this sonata form exposition, did Haydn choose not to include a contrasting second theme? OK. Here are two answers we will not accept: one, because he felt like it; and two, because he was having a bad compositional day.

I would suggest three acceptable reasons: one, the introduction—big, stark, and set in D minor—provides all the thematic contrast Haydn requires for the movement. Two, the (optional) inclusion of a cadence theme provides, for Haydn, all the contrast he required for the body of the exposition. Finally, as he intends to build almost the entire development section from a single, utterly inauspicious aspect of theme 1, he wanted to maximize the theme's "recognizability quotient."

This is so typical of Haydn, to take what seems to be the least important part of a melody and elevate to a level of principal importance during the course of a development section. Here's theme 1. [**Piano demonstration**.]

That, my friends, is a motive-rich melody. I'd suggest the most memorable of its motives—and therefore the one we'd most expect to hear developed—is its opening. [**Piano demonstration**.] The next most memorable motive is the one that brings the theme to its conclusion. [**Piano demonstration**.] Among the least memorable elements of the theme are the four repeated notes sitting in the middle of motive three. Here's motive 3. [**Piano demonstration**.] And here's the tail-end of motive 3, with its four repeated notes; they sound like filler, really, just marking time until something different happens. [**Piano demonstration**.]

Inauspicious filler, though it may be, that repeated-note idea will supply the grist for the development section. And a killer development section it is, as all the drama and harmonic darkness of the introduction are now given the opportunity to step forward and make their presence felt once again. Let's hear it. [**Music selection**: Haydn, Symphony No. 104 in D Major, movement 1.] Well that's just fabulous! So is what happens next in the recapitulation.

In a sonata form recapitulation, the principal themes, typically two in number, will be heard in the same key, in the home key. If Haydn did that in this movement, we would hear the same theme played twice in the same key. That would be boring and obvious and Haydn is never boring and obvious. So, following the initial recapitulation of theme 1 in D major, Haydn offers us what amounts to a second development section, this one based on the repeated notes of motive 3 and motive one of the theme. [**Piano demonstration**.] Let's hear the remainder of the movement, starting with the onset of the recapitulation and theme 1. [**Music selection**: Haydn, Symphony No. 104 in D Major, movement 1.] Superb!

Movement 2

The second movement is a moderately paced two-step dance of great elegance and style. [**Music selection**: Haydn, Symphony No. 104 in D Major, movement 2.]

Movement 3: Minuet and Trio Form

My friends, there is no more predictable ritual in the music of the classical era than the presence of a minuet and trio form movement as a middle movement in four movement work, with its moderate tempo and triple meter, its large-scale A-B-A form and its ritual phrase repetitions. So it remains one of the ongoing miracles of Western art that Joseph Haydn, over and over again, continued to turn the clichéd genre of minuet into something truly special and very much his own.

My friends, long before Lawrence Welk hoisted his accordion and became the king of champagne music, Joseph Haydn made himself the emperor of champagne music with this bubbling, effervescent third movement minuet and trio. Let's hear the opening minuet section in its entirety, and let's be particularly aware of the trilling, bubbly phrase-endings that give this music its "champagne" feel. [**Music selection**: Haydn, Symphony No. 104 in D Major, movement 3.]

Movement 4: Sonata Form

This fourth movement opens with the sort of rustic, countryside-type dance tune that Haydn just loved to use in his finales. Its rural flavor is doubly reinforced by the bagpipe-like drone that accompanies the theme's first appearance. Let's hear this bouncing and most bucolic first theme as it begins the movement. [**Music selection**: Haydn, Symphony No. 104 in D Major, movement 4.]

Different sources claim different origins of this theme. According to Edward Downes in his *Guide to Symphonic Music*, the theme is a Croatian folksong entitled *Oj Jelena*, which, according to Downs, "was sung not only by members of the Croatian colony in Haydn's one-time residence of Eisenstadt, but with minor variations throughout Croatia, Serbia, and Carniola."

According to Haydn's contemporary Charlotte Papendiek, who was the "assistant keeper of the wardrobe and reader to her majesty Queen Charlotte of England," Haydn's theme was meant to imitate London fish mongers crying "Live Cod." According to Haydn biographer Karl Geiringer: "In the finale the composer employs [a] subject based on the old English street song *Hot Cross Buns*."

Musicologist A. Peter Brown rejects all of these assertions, implying (though never stating) that the tune is of Haydn's own creation. (In this the good professor indulges in what I call "assertion through negation," a rather distasteful technique by which one avoids taking a stand and thus steers clear of criticism while still demolishing the claims of others.) Whatever its source, theme 1 dominates the movement. Having said that, there are two other themes with which we should be aware.

Theme 2 is brilliant and celebratory and sounds like this. [**Piano demonstration**.] Even as theme 2 first appears in the first violins, theme 1 is played by the winds and second violins. Let's hear this stunning bit of non-imitative counterpoint. [**Music selection**: Haydn, Symphony No. 104 in D Major, movement 4.]

Theme 3 is a cadence theme, a theme associated with the closing of large sections of music. Haydn's cadence theme here is sustained and quiet, and offers just about the only moment of respite in this otherwise rock 'n' roll exposition. Let's hear the cadence theme and the conclusion of the exposition that follows. [**Music selection**: Haydn, Symphony No. 104 in D Major, movement 4.]

Haydn uses an extended version of this cadence theme to conclude the development section and ease his way back into theme 1 at the beginning of the recapitulation. It is, according to Michael Steinberg: "The most mysterious and surprising transition into a recapitulation that ever occurred to him." Let's hear this mysterious transition back to the recapitulation and from there, the remainder of this last movement of Haydn's last symphony. [**Music selection**: Haydn, Symphony No. 104 in D Major, movement 4.]

The English adored Haydn. The music writer Charles Burney was at the Haymarket Theater on the evening of May 4, 1795, where he heard the premiere of this Symphony in D Major as well as a performance of Haydn's Symphony No. 100 in G Major. In a letter written a few days later, Burney described the symphonies as works "such as were never heard before; of what Apollo and the Muses compose we can only judge by such productions as these." Haydn was delighted with the premiere as well, but for different reasons. He wrote in his diary: "The whole company was thoroughly pleased, and so was I. I made 4000 gulden on this evening: such a thing is possible only in England."

Conclusion

Haydn's symphonies are the first large body of orchestral music by a single composer to become standard repertoire. At a time when audiences were accustomed to hearing new works at every sitting, Haydn's symphonies demanded and received repeat performances. According to musicologist A. Peter Brown, it was thanks to Haydn's symphonies that: "The demand for new [orchestral] repertoire was broken, as a canon of first-rate compositions became, through repeated hearings, imprinted in the minds of the public."

Thank you.

Mozart—Piano Concerto No. 24 in C Minor
Lecture 6

The classical style—of which we today consider Wolfgang Mozart to be a leading exponent—was a style of music that was principally characterized by lyric, engaging, accessible thematic melody. Mozart was a musical utopian: a composer of such lyric, dramatic, and technical gifts that his music transcends the stylistic rituals and clichés of classicism. If Mozart is indeed the greatest composer of concerti, then his Piano Concerto in C Minor must be considered among a handful of the most extraordinary concerti ever composed.

Wolfgang Mozart was born in the Austro-Bavarian city of Salzburg on January 27, 1756, and was one of the most accomplished child prodigies of all time. The instrument Mozart learned to play as a child was the harpsichord, which is a mechanical harp whose strings are plucked by picks activated from a keyboard. While piano technology developed tremendously during Mozart's lifetime, the piano was still a relatively small, lightweight and light-sounding instrument compared to the modern grand pianos of the 1860s. It was in 1782 that Mozart began performing exclusively on pianos. From a quantitative and qualitative point of view, Mozart was the greatest composer of concerti who has yet to live.

Composed between 1781 and 1791, Mozart's 17 Viennese piano concerti are a very special body of work: a concentration of masterworks in a single genre composed over a relatively brief period of time with few equals in the history of Western music. Mozart's Piano Concerto in C Minor is the 14th of his 17 Viennese piano concerti and was completed on March 24, 1786, about a month after he completed his operatic masterwork *The Marriage of Figaro*. As in much of the music he composed after moving to Vienna in 1781, the Piano Concerto in C Minor delivered to the public what it expected while satisfying Mozart's self-expressive urge, which was moving beyond public taste and beginning to trump the standards of what we today consider the classical style.

Piano Concerto No. 24 in C Minor

In Mozart's Piano Concerto in C Minor of 1786, the orchestra is a full, symphonic ensemble consisting of two flutes, two oboes, two clarinets, two bassoons, two horns, two trumpets, timpani, and a full string complement. Because the pianos of Mozart's time were small and tinny sounding, he employed lighter orchestral textures while the piano plays so that the orchestra does not drown out the piano. However, when the piano is not playing, the C minor orchestral passages have a symphonic impact and expressive gravity for a concerto. From an expressive and orchestral point of view, Mozart's Concerto in C Minor was a work that had a profound influence on a young composer named Ludwig van Beethoven, who began composing his first piano concerto a few years later.

Movement 1

Typical of Mozart's concerti, this first movement is cast in double exposition form, which is an adaptation of sonata form to the particular dramatic requirements of the concerto. A typical sonata form movement has four main

At the time of Mozart's birth, the piano was only beginning to become advanced enough to compete with the harpsichord as a musical instrument.

sections: **exposition, development, recapitulation,** and **coda**. It is in the exposition that the principal themes (usually two in number) are introduced. Sonata form expositions are typically repeated in their entirety to express the contrasting themes and key areas. The development section is the action sequence, during which the themes are fragmented—or metamorphosed, or overlapped—in a predominately unstable harmonic environment. In the recapitulation, the themes return in their original order, though with the second theme now in the same key as the first. The coda is a closing section of music that brings the movement to its conclusion.

Mozart's double exposition form movements differ from sonata form in a number of ways, of which we will identify two. Instead of repeating the exposition, there are two separately composed expositions. In the first, called the orchestral exposition, the orchestra plays the themes. In the second, called the solo exposition, the soloist plays the themes. The second difference is that a third theme will typically be introduced and played only by the solo instrument, a theme generally referred to as the solo theme. These compositional elements represent a structural template, and the way in which Mozart manipulates or disregards these expectations will contribute to the expressive message and impact of a given movement.

In the first movement of his Piano Concerto in C Minor, Mozart disregards these expectations: The orchestral exposition introduces only one theme—a craggy, dissonant, non-classical melody. During the course of the orchestral exposition, there are moments when we think we might be hearing a second theme, but each such passage is a diversion. Lacking thematic contrast, the orchestral exposition is not so much an argument as it is an introduction, an overture, for the solo piano.

The piano enters 100 measures into the movement with a sighing and reflective solo. The piano's voice is that of a character who acknowledges—bravely but sadly—that it is about to enter a world in which it will attempt to maintain its lyric equilibrium in the face of the dark and dissonant harmonic environment around it. This is made clear the moment the piano concludes its entrance solo and the orchestra boldly and insistently reenters with the opening of theme 1. Rather than be drawn into an argument with the huge orchestra, the piano instead quiets things down by reflecting on theme 1 and then launches into a brisk, scalar passage that enlivens the mood as it heads for the brighter harmonic world of E-**flat** major.

The piano takes over the moment with this key shift to E-flat major—a mood shift from dark angst to quiet good cheer—and is now prepared to introduce a contrasting theme, which is played first by the solo piano and then by the winds. Buoyed by the lyric beauty of theme 2, the piano blazes through a dazzling episode, deftly accompanied by a flute, oboe, clarinet, bassoon, and very quiet strings. Overlapping with the piano's conclusion, a solo oboe begins what is the third and final theme: a gentle, exquisite melody that descends lightly. The theme's first phrase is played by the winds, and its second phrase is played and embellished by the piano. The C minor darkness that began the movement seems, for now, a distant memory.

Wolfgang Mozart was born in the Austro-Bavarian city of Salzburg on January 27, 1756, and was one of the most accomplished child prodigies of all time.

The new, contrasting key of E-flat major predominates for the remainder of this solo exposition. However, the comparatively compact development section will swing the music back toward the dark harmonic side, after which the recapitulation will emphatically express the key—and dark mood—of C minor. The coda begins with one last tutti iteration of theme 1, after which the movement concludes on a very special harmony called a cadential six-four chord.

Movement 2

This exquisite second movement played larghetto, meaning slowly, is as structurally straightforward as the first movement is idiosyncratic. A gentle, singing theme in E-flat major acts as a refrain, which occurs three times across the span of the movement. This theme alternates with two contrasting episodes, the first of which is set in C minor and the second in A-flat major, after which a coda brings the movement to its conclusion.

The rondo theme is introduced by the piano, and the two contrasting episodes both begin with wind instruments alone. Mozart had a special affinity for the sound and combination of wind instruments, which breathe in a manner very much like the human voice. By scoring this concerto for large orchestra, Mozart had a full wind choir at his disposal. His use of the winds imbues this second movement with a vocality that is very operatic in sound and feel.

Movement 3

Mozart's theme is marked allegretto, meaning moderately fast. The orchestra introduces the theme, while the role of varying it will fall principally to the piano. Six variations of the theme follow.

- In variation 1, the solo piano gently embellishes the theme over a quiet string accompaniment.

- Variation 2 is a dialogue between the wind choir and the solo piano.

- In variation 3, the theme becomes a ferocious march to war, initiated by the solo piano.

- Variation 4 features a jaunty version of the theme set in A-flat major, played initially by the winds.

- Variation 5 opens with a sinuous and **chromatic** version of the theme in the solo piano, set back in C minor.

- Set in C major, variation 6 constitutes the last light expressive moment in the concerto and is initiated by the winds.

The lengthy coda, set back in C minor, begins with the theme played by the orchestral violins for the first time since the beginning of the movement. The coda includes a brief **cadenza**, a passage played exclusively by the solo instrument in a concerto, that concludes the movement—and the concerto. ■

cadenza: Passage for solo instrument in an orchestral work, usually a concerto, designed to showcase the player's skills.

chromatic: A pitch that lies outside of whatever key area presently anchors a passage.

coda: The closing few measures of a composition; usually not a part of the main theme groups of the standard form of a composition but a finishing theme added to the end to give the composition closure.

development: The second large part of a sonata form movement, during which the themes are developed in a generally unstable harmonic environment.

exposition: The first part of a sonata form, during which the principal themes are introduced.

flat: Accidental (sign/symbol) placed to the left of a note indicating that the pitch should be lowered by a semitone.

recapitulation: The third large part of a sonata form movement, during which the themes return in their original order.

Mozart—Piano Concerto No. 24 in C Minor
Lecture 6—Transcript

We return to *The 30 Greatest Orchestral Works*. This is Lecture 6, and it is entitled "Mozart—Piano Concerto No. 24 in C Minor."

We begin at the beginning. We're going to listen to the opening 35 seconds of the first movement of Mozart's Piano Concerto in C Minor of 1786. We will hear the first theme of the movement played twice: first quietly and ominously by the strings and bassoons and then loudly and most dramatically by the entire orchestra. Mozart, Piano Concerto in C Minor, movement 1, theme 1. [**Music selection**: Mozart Piano Concerto in C Minor, K. 491, movement 1.]

We're going to hear that again. This time, let's notice that the first, quiet iteration of the theme occurs in orchestral unison, without any accompaniment or harmonic support. This lack of accompaniment forces us—as we hear the theme for the first time—to focus entirely on the thematic melody itself, and a craggy, dissonant, and pause-laden melody it is! [**Music selection**: Mozart Piano Concerto in C Minor, K. 491, movement 1.] It is an article of faith that the classical style—of which we today consider Wolfgang Mozart to be a leading exponent—was about tunes: about lyric, engaging, in all ways "natural" (meaning accessible) thematic melody.

Back to Mozart's "theme." The theme begins with a slowly rising idea that suddenly leaps upwards, followed by a silence. [**Piano demonstration**.] That upwards leap spans an interval called a diminished seventh. [**Piano demonstration**.] That interval of a diminished seventh implies a harmony called a diminished seventh chord. [**Piano demonstration**.] A diminished seventh chord is a dissonance: It is, in fact, the single most dissonant harmony in Mozart's harmonic vocabulary. By definition, a "dissonance" is an unstable harmony that must resolve. So does Mozart's diminished seventh "resolve," for example, like this? [**Piano demonstration**.]

No. Mozart's diminished seventh does not resolve. Instead the theme continues with a lower version (or "sequence") of the opening phrase which also concludes with an upwards leap that outlines yet another diminished seventh that implies yet another diminished seventh harmony. [**Piano demonstration**.]

Does that diminished seventh resolve? No it does not! Instead, we hear a still lower version of the opening phrase, this one ending with an upwards leap that implies yet another diminished seventh chord. [**Piano demonstration**.] From here Mozart goes on to "liquidate" the phrase: Two more upwards leaps are followed by a serpent-like rising chromatic line that brings the first part of the theme to its conclusion. [**Piano demonstration**.] Once more, let's hear this opening part of theme 1. [**Piano demonstration**.] Once again, let's hear the entire theme as played by the orchestra, first unharmonized and then harmonized. [**Musical selection**: Mozart Piano Concerto in C Minor, K. 491, movement 1.]

Again and we are told that Wolfgang Mozart was a leading exponent of what today is known as the "classical style," a style of music that was principally characterized by lyric, engaging, in all ways natural (meaning accessible) thematic melody. However, there's nothing lyric, engaging, or natural about Mozart's theme. On the contrary, it is a dark, dissonant, jagged beastie of shocking modernity, an utterly unconventional thematic idea that conjures up an alien musical environment far beyond the "traditional" melodic and harmonic boundaries of classicism.

Mozart's opening theme is calculated to shock. It is a shock we must feel as well if we are to hear Mozart's music as his contemporaries heard it: as being dramatically intense, complicated, and in all ways modern.

So much for the tiresome, post-Beethoven opinion still held by some folks that Mozart was an expressive lightweight, a composer whose effortlessly lyric music betrays a lack of emotional depth and gravity. My friends, in truth, Mozart was a musical utopian: a composer of such lyric, dramatic, and technical gifts that his music transcends completely the stylistic rituals and clichés of classicism, someone who in his own time was considered outside the contemporary compositional mainstream. No one appreciated Mozart's uniqueness more than did his friend Joseph Haydn.

Wolfgang Mozart met Joseph Haydn in Vienna in December of 1783. Despite their 24-year age difference, Mozart and Haydn became real friends. It was a friendship founded on their mutual respect for each other as musicians. When Mozart died in December of 1791, Haydn was living in London. He was devastated when he heard the news. From London, Haydn wrote their mutual friend, Michael Puchberg:

> I was quite beside myself about his death. I could not believe that Providence should so quickly have called [this] irreplaceable man into the other world. Have the kindness, dear friend, to send me a list of Mozart's works not yet known here, and I will do my utmost to push them in the interest of the widow.

Haydn wrote the publisher Broderip, informing him that "[Mozart] was a truly great musician. Friends often flatter me that I have some genius, but [Mozart] stood far above me."

In 1807, 16 years after Mozart's death, when a friend mentioned Mozart's name in Haydn's presence, Haydn broke down and cried, saying later, "Forgive me, I must ever weep, ever weep when I hear the name of my Mozart."

Mozart and the Piano

Wolfgang Mozart was born in the Austro-Bavarian city of Salzburg on January 27, 1756. He was one of the most accomplished child prodigies of all time. The "keyboard" instrument Mozart learned to play as a child was the harpsichord. A harpsichord is a mechanical harp, the strings of which are plucked not by hand but rather, by picks activated from a keyboard. At the time of Mozart's birth, the piano was only beginning to make inroads against the harpsichord. Invented around 1700 by a Florence-based harpsichord builder named Bartolomeo Cristofori, the piano employs hammers to strike, rather than pluck, its strings.

On a piano, the intensity with which the hammers strike the strings is variable, depending upon how hard the keys are pushed, which gives the piano a degree of dynamic gradation and expressive nuance far beyond what is possible on a harpsichord. However, like any new and complex technology, it took time to get the bugs out and even more time for keyboard players to embrace what was a very different sort of instrument.

While piano technology developed tremendously during Mozart's lifetime, the piano was still, in Mozart's day, a relatively small, lightweight and light-sounding instrument, a far-cry from the modern grand pianos that came into being during the 1860s, some 70-plus years after Mozart's death.

By the mid-1770s Mozart had come to consider himself as being primarily a pianist and not a harpsichordist, although it was only in 1782, after he moved to Vienna, that Mozart began performing exclusively on pianos.

Mozart's Piano Concerti

Mozart is credited with having composed 27 piano concerti. This is technically correct but misleading. Mozart's first four "concerti" are actually arrangements of works by other composers. Also lumped into that total of 27 are Mozart's concerto for two pianos and his concerto for three pianos. In reality, Mozart composed 21 solo concerti for piano. The final 17 of them were composed between 1781 and 1791, when he lived in Vienna.

Mozart's 17 "Viennese" piano concerti are, like Johann Sebastian Bach's six Brandenburg concerti and Joseph Haydn's 12 "London" symphonies, a very, very special body of work: a concentration of masterworks in a single genre composed over a relatively brief period of time with few equals in the history of Western music. Mozart's Piano Concerto in C Minor, K. 491 is the 14 of his 17 Viennese piano concerti.

Opera, Drama, and the Self-Expressive Urge

Mozart completed his Piano Concerto in C Minor on March 24, 1786, just about a month after he put the finishing touches on his operatic masterwork *The Marriage of Figaro.*

My friends, Mozart was born to compose operas. He was, in my humble opinion, the greatest opera composer who has yet to live. Like the greatest dramatists—Shakespeare, Ibsen, Chekhov, Pirandello, Shaw—Mozart had a sixth, seventh, and eighth sense for character development and interaction, for dramatic line and the inner workings of the human psyche. Unlike the aforementioned writers, however, Mozart expressed himself through music, music that reveals the hidden souls of his characters and creates meaning and pathos far beyond what words can do themselves. OK. That was my opinion.

Of all Western instrumental genres, the concerto most closely approaches the dramatic condition of opera. The earliest concerti—with their confrontation between the soloist and orchestra, a metaphor for the individual versus the collective—grew out of baroque operatic practice. And although the concerto proceeded to evolve on a path of its own making, its relationship to the dramatic impulse and characterization of opera was never far away.

It should come as no surprise, then, that from a quantitative and qualitative point of view, Mozart was also the greatest composer of concerti who has yet to live. Aside from his piano concerti, Mozart also composed five violin concerti, four horn concerti, a bassoon concerto; a concerto for flute and harp; a clarinet concerto; an oboe concerto; two flute concerti (the second of which is an arrangement of the oboe concerto); and two *Sinfonie Concertante*, that is, symphonic works that feature solo instruments (concerti by any other name).

One of the things that make Mozart's Viennese piano concerti particularly special is their degree of self-expressive originality, a result of the fact that most of these concerti were created as performance vehicles for himself.

As in so much of the music Mozart composed after moving to Vienna in 1781, the Piano Concerto in C Minor walks a fine line between delivering to the ticket-buying public what it expected while satisfying Mozart's own creative muse, which was moving ever more beyond public taste. This is precisely the issue addressed by Hermann Abert in his monumental biography of Mozart, first published in 1924:

> In the rest of the [classical era] repertory, concertos in a minor key are very much the exception. One almost has the impression that in writing [this concerto], Mozart was conducting an experiment

in order to see how far it was possible to reconcile the spirit of "*Gesellschaftsmusik*" [meaning "social" or "popular" music] with his subjective emotions as an artist. After all, he was still attached, at least in part, to the old order with its *galant* zest for life and [melodic vivacity]. As a result, [this concerto] became an example of an art in which audience [expectations] and [artistic self-expression] both had a part to play, though it is clear [in the C minor concerto] that the focus of his activity shifted from the audience and increasingly towards the composer.

In other words, Mozart's self-expressive urge was beginning to trump the expressive standards of what we, today, consider the "classical style," a point painstakingly illustrated at the outset of this lecture!

Piano Concerto in C Minor, K. 491 (1786)

Further evidence of Mozart's increasingly "personalized" approach to the genre of concerto lies in the instrumentation of the C minor. We must remember that the pianos of Mozart's time were small and tinny-sounding instruments, easily drowned out by an orchestra. In his earlier concerti, Mozart did what he could to balance the piano with the orchestra by employing what was known as a "Neapolitan" scoring: a small orchestra consisting only of strings, oboes, and horns.

Well, not in the C minor concerto, in which the orchestra is a full, symphonic ensemble consisting of two flutes, two oboes, two clarinets, two bassoons, two horns, two trumpets, timpani, and a full string complement. Now obviously, Mozart was way too much of a pro to allow the orchestra to drown out the piano, so lighter orchestral textures are the rule while the piano plays. However, when the piano is not playing, orchestral passages in the C minor have a symphonic impact and expressive gravity far beyond what was, to its time, considered appropriate to a concerto. Simply put, from an expressive and orchestral point of view, Mozart's Concerto in C Minor of 1786 was a game changer, a work that had a profound influence on a young composer named Ludwig van Beethoven who began composing his first piano concerto just a few years later.

Movement 1: Double Exposition Form

Typical of Mozart's concerti, this first movement is cast in double exposition form. Double exposition form is an adaptation of sonata form to the particular dramatic requirements of the concerto. A typical sonata form movement has four main sections: an exposition, development, recapitulation, and a coda. It is in the exposition that the principal themes, usually two in number, are introduced. Sonata form expositions are typically repeated in their entirety, the better for us to get the contrasting themes and their key areas in our ears. The development section is the "action sequence," during which the themes are fragmented, or metamorphosed, or overlapped, or whatever, all of it occurring in a predominately unstable—meaning modulatory— harmonic environment. The recapitulation sees the themes return in their original order, though with the second theme now heard in the same key as the first. The coda is a closing section of music that brings the movement to its conclusion.

Mozart's double exposition form movements differ from sonata form in a number of ways, of which we will identify two. One: instead of repeating the exposition, there are two separately composed expositions. The first, called the "orchestral exposition" sees the orchestra play the themes. The second, called the "solo exposition," sees the soloist play the themes.

Difference number two: In a Mozart double exposition form movement, a third theme will typically be introduced and played only by the solo instrument, a theme generally referred to as the "solo theme."

Taken together, these compositional elements represent a structural template, a series of expectations. How Mozart manipulates (or even disregards) these expectations will contribute mightily to the expressive message and impact of a given movement.

Well, in the first movement of his Piano Concerto in C Minor, Mozart takes these expectations and throws them under the bus. For example, the orchestral exposition introduces one theme and one theme only, the craggy, dissonant, decidedly "non-classical melody" that we heard and discussed at the beginning of this lecture.

Now, during the course of the orchestral exposition there are moments when we think we "might" be hearing a second contrasting theme; most notably, the following passage based on a descending scale. [**Musical selection**: Mozart Piano Concerto in C Minor, K. 491, movement 1.]

In reality, that passage is a diversion, what Cuthbert Girdlestone calls "One of those engaging snares thanks to which Mozart avoids casting his concertos in the moulds of orthodoxy. It is not the second subject, [as] it will not reappear in the [solo exposition]." In truth, the entire orchestral exposition constitutes a statement and development of a single thematic idea: the ominous, dissonant, oh-so-ripe-for-development theme 1. Lacking thematic contrast, the orchestral exposition is not so much an "argument" as it is an introduction: an overture. And what operatically conceived character does it introduce? Why, the solo piano, of course.

We are going to spend the bulk of our examination of this first movement discussing the solo exposition for three reasons. One, it is in the solo exposition that contrasting themes are finally introduced; two, it is in the solo exposition that the solo piano is introduced and given a depth of "personality" analogous to a character in an opera; and three, the solo exposition beautifully demonstrates the sort of orchestrational and dramatic fluidity characteristic of the entire concerto, as the piano and elements of the orchestra enter and exit and the mood swings from the darkly dramatic to the most exquisite beauty with hardly a cadence to disturb the flow of the music!

The Solo Exposition: Enter the Piano

One hundred measures into the movement, the piano enters all by itself, with a sighing and reflective solo. With its entry, there is a palpable sense that the action is now "joined." [**Musical selection**: Mozart Piano Concerto in C Minor, K. 491, movement 1.] The piano's voice is that of a character who acknowledges—bravely but sadly—that it is about to enter a world of hurt, a world in which it will attempt to maintain its lyric equilibrium in the face of the dark and dissonant harmonic environment around it.

All of this is made inescapably clear the moment the piano concludes its "entrance solo" and the orchestra boldly and insistently re-enters with the opening of Theme 1. Rather than be drawn into an argument with the huge orchestra—an argument it physically cannot win—the piano instead quiets things down by reflecting on Theme 1. Like a 120-pound therapist calming down her 350-pound client, the piano acknowledges the expressive issues inherent to Theme 1 and then, having done so, launches into a brisk, scalar passage that enlivens the mood as it heads for the brighter harmonic world of E-flat major. Let's hear this passage, beginning with the orchestra's fateful reassertion of the opening of theme. [**Musical selection**: Mozart Piano Concerto in C Minor, K. 491, movement 1.]

Just like that, the piano has taken over the movement, having calmed the orchestra, engineered a key-shift to E-flat major, a mood-shift from dark angst to quiet good cheer, and is now prepared to introduce—finally—a contrasting theme. The theme is played first by the solo piano and then by the winds. [**Musical selection**: Mozart Piano Concerto in C Minor, K. 491, movement 1.]

That was an awkward cutoff because the piano, unexpectedly and joyfully breaks in. Buoyed by the lyric beauty of theme 2, the piano blazes through a dazzling episode, deftly accompanied by a flute, oboe, clarinet, bassoon, and very quiet strings. [**Musical selection**: Mozart Piano Concerto in C Minor, K. 491, movement 1.] Overlapping with the piano's conclusion, a solo oboe begins what is the third and final theme, a gentle, exquisite melody that descends with feather-lightness. The theme's first phrase is played by the winds and its second phrase is played and embellished by the piano. [**Musical selection**: Mozart Piano Concerto in C Minor, K. 491, movement 1.]

The craggy, C minor darkness that began the movement seems, for now, a distant memory. The "new," contrasting key of E-flat major will predominate for the remainder of this solo exposition. Let's hear the conclusion of the solo exposition: a lengthy and brilliant episode for the solo piano followed by a celebratory conclusion in E-flat major. [**Musical selection**: Mozart Piano Concerto in C Minor, K. 491, movement 1.]

E-flat major; ah, good times. Sadly, they're not going to last. The comparatively compact development section will swing the music back towards the dark harmonic side, after which the recapitulation will hammer away on the key—and dark mood—of C minor. We're going to rejoin the movement during the volcanic coda that brings it to its conclusion. The coda begins with one last tutti iteration of theme 1, after which things come to rest on a very special harmony, a harmony called a cadential six-four chord. [**Piano demonstration**: Mozart Piano Concerto in C Minor, K. 491, movement 1.]

While the term "cadential six-four chord" might not mean a whole lot to most listeners, the sound of that final harmony should be familiar to anyone who has ever heard a classical era concerto, because it is the stock-in-trade setup for the cadenza. A concerto "cadenza"—or "cadence solo"—is a passage in which the solo instrument has an opportunity to go out on its own and strut its stuff, unhindered by the orchestra.

During the classical era, soloists were usually expected to prepare their own cadenzas. Mozart himself wrote down very few cadenzas, primarily morning-after transcriptions of cadenzas he'd improvised in performance the evening before. Over the years, cadenzas for Mozart concerti have been written and published by many performers and composers, so performers today can create their own cadenza or choose one from the accumulated repertoire.

Our performer, the Hungarian pianist Jenö Jandó, has chosen to play a cadenza by his Hungarian compatriot, the composer and piano virtuoso Johann Nepomuk Hummel, who lived from 1778 to 1837. The choice is extremely appropriate, as Hummel was a student of Mozart's, who actually lived in Mozart's home for two years, when he was between the ages of 8 and 10. Let's hear the remainder of the movement, beginning with Hummel's most virtuosic cadenza through the concluding passage scored (quietly) for full orchestra and the solo piano. [**Musical selection**: Mozart Piano Concerto in C Minor, K. 491, Movement 1.]

Movement 2: Rondo Form

This exquisite second movement "Larghetto" (meaning slowly) is as structurally straightforward as the first movement is idiosyncratic. A gentle, singing theme in E-flat major acts as a refrain. We will hear it—whole or in part—three times across the span of the movement. This theme alternates with two contrasting episodes, the first of which is set in C minor and the second in A-flat major, after which a coda brings the movement to its conclusion. The rondo theme is introduced by the piano. Here's the opening of its first appearance. [**Musical selection**: Mozart Piano Concerto in C Minor, K. 491, movement 2.]

The two contrasting episodes both begin with wind instruments alone. Here's how the first contrasting episode begins. [**Musical selection**: Mozart Piano Concerto in C Minor, K. 491, movement 2.] And here's the beginning of the second contrasting episode. [**Musical selection**: Mozart Piano Concerto in C Minor, K. 491, movement 2.]

Mozart had a special affinity for the sound and combination of wind instruments; instruments which "breathe" in a manner very much like the human voice. By scoring this concerto for large orchestra, Mozart had a full wind choir at his disposal. His use of the winds imbues this second movement with a vocality that is, to my ear, very operatic in sound and feel.

Movement 3: Theme and Variations Form

Mozart's Theme is marked "Allegretto," meaning moderately fast. It is, according to the Mozart scholar Cuthbert Girdlestone, "measured but not slow, spare but not dry; it reminds us of both a march and a hymn." The orchestra introduces the theme, while the role of "varying it" will fall principally to the piano. Let's hear the theme. [**Musical selection**: Mozart Piano Concerto in C Minor, K. 491, movement 3.] Six variations and a coda now follow.

Variation 1: the solo piano gently embellishes the theme over a quiet string accompaniment. Variation 1, opening: [**Musical selection**: Mozart Piano Concerto in C Minor, K. 491, movement 3.] Variation 2 is a dialogue between the wind choir and the solo piano. Variation 2, opening: [**Musical selection**: Mozart Piano Concerto in C Minor, K. 491, movement 3.]

In variation 3, the theme becomes a ferocious march to war, initiated by the solo piano. [**Musical selection**: Mozart Piano Concerto in C Minor, K. 491, movement 3.] Variation 4 features a jaunty version of the theme set in A-flat major, played initially by the winds. [**Musical selection**: Mozart Piano Concerto in C Minor, K. 491, movement 3.] Variation 5 opens with a sinuous version of the theme in the solo piano, set back in C minor. [**Musical selection**: Mozart Piano Concerto in C Minor, K. 491, mmovement 3.] Variation 6 is absolutely adorable. We should enjoy it while we can, because it constitutes the last "light" expressive moment in the concerto, which is not destined to have a "happy ending." Set in C major, variation 6 is initiated by the winds. [**Musical selection**: Mozart Piano Concerto in C Minor, K. 491, movement 3.]

The lengthy coda, set back in C minor, begins with the theme played by the orchestral violins for the first time since the very beginning of the movement. Let's hear the coda in its entirety, with its brief cadenza (composed by Mozart himself) through the blazing conclusion of the movement and the concerto. [**Musical selection**: Mozart Piano Concerto in C Minor, K. 491, movement 3.]

Conclusion

In his seminal work, *Mozart and His Piano Concertos*, the English musicologist and Mozart scholar Cuthbert Morton Girdlestone writes, "[Mozart's C minor] concerto is in all respects one of his greatest; we would fain say, the greatest, were it not impossible to choose between four or five of them."

We cannot disagree. If Mozart is indeed (as I have asserted) the greatest composer of concerti yet to grace our planet, then his Piano Concerto in C Minor must be considered among a handful of the most extraordinary concerti ever composed.

Certainly, Ludwig van Beethoven believed this to be true. Having attended a performance of Mozart's Piano Concerto in C Minor with his friend, the pianist and composer Johann Baptist Cramer, Beethoven famously cried: "Cramer! Cramer! We shall never be able to do anything like that!"

Thank you.

Mozart—Symphony in C Major, "Jupiter"
Lecture 7

Mozart's Symphony in C Major is his longest and most expressively brilliant symphony. It is truly imperial in its scope and power, and so it deserves the nickname "Jupiter"—the king of the gods—that Johann Peter Salomon bestowed upon it soon after Mozart's death. Of course, had Mozart lived long enough to be inspired by Haydn's *London Symphonies* or Beethoven's "Eroica," who knows what kinds of masterpieces he might have composed.

As recently as the 1930s, there were thought to be 49 symphonies that Mozart composed. This total of 49 symphonies has, today, been reduced to 41, as works erroneously attributed to Mozart have been removed. Anyway, there are still more than enough to make him a major symphonist. But in truth, Mozart's symphonies occupy a secondary place in his compositional output. Only the last 10 symphonies were written after 1775, when he had achieved his full musical maturity. Only the final three—the E-flat major, the G minor, and the C major (also known as "Jupiter")—which were transcribed during the summer of 1788, were conceived as a cohesive and coherent symphonic unit.

Symphony in C Major, "Jupiter"

In truth, composing symphonies was never a high priority for Mozart. In his heart, he was an opera composer who wrote piano concerti for money and chamber music for his friends. With the exception of his final three, Mozart's symphonies were occasional works—works composed for particular occasions—or pieces written while he was on tour when he needed something new to perform. To this day, we know that only one of Mozart's symphonies was performed only once in his lifetime, and it was probably "Jupiter."

Movement 1

The first movement opens with a theme that immediately sets the tone for the remainder of the movement and that alternates a vigorous, martial, masculine phrase scored for the entire orchestra with a yearning, lyric, feminine phrase. The masculine aspect of the theme is a rhythmic idea represented by upward-sweeping motives. Conversely, the feminine aspect is pure melody that consists of a gentle, yearning **tune**. The second part of theme 1 is entirely masculine, as the martial, fanfare-like opening of the theme takes over. The regular rhythmic pattern and simple harmonic structure of this passage give it a drum-corps-like effect, which is entirely in keeping with the spirit of the masculine opening phrase.

According to the formal orthodoxy of classical-era sonata form, having stated theme 1, Mozart is next supposed to introduce a transitional passage called a modulating bridge that will transit

Wolfgang Amadeus Mozart (1756–1791) created entire works in his head and carried them around until deadlines forced him to write them down.

to the contrasting second theme. However, Mozart is so enamored of the masculine-feminine dichotomy his first theme represents that he begins to develop the theme immediately. Next, he superimposes a new, feminine-styled melodic idea in the flutes and oboes over the opening of theme 1.

Theme 2 is cast in three parts. Part 1 is a playful, bubbly tune of incredible grace and charm, feminine in its spirit and impact. The feminine spirit of theme 2 is made explicit in its second part, as the rising, feminine element of theme 1 is heard in dialogue with a new melodic phrase. Just as theme 1 represented a unity of masculine and feminine, so does theme 2. The third part of theme 2—set initially in C minor—is explosive and martial. It jump-starts the action and pitches the music headlong toward the cadence material—and, with it, the conclusion of the exposition.

The first part of the cadence material is familiar: It is a masculine development of the once-feminine phrase of theme 1. Because we expect this fire-breathing music to culminate with a powerful cadence, we are very surprised when it quietly descends and then just stops. Then, an entirely new theme appears, and it's more than just a cadence theme—it is a genuine third theme that is the most memorable melodic idea we have heard thus far in the movement. Using the melody of a concert aria that he had only just composed, Mozart plugged in this theme at the very last moment of the exposition, which is followed by the drum-corps-like music that brings it to its conclusion.

Movements 2 and 3
The second movement is a lyric **andante** cast in sonata form; it is a movement scored without trumpet and drums that is particularly notable for the way Mozart embellishes and varies the themes at each new iteration. The third movement is a broad and courtly minuet and trio.

Movement 4
The final movement contains four themes that are designed to be stacked and overlapped. We will refer to these four thematic elements as: thematic melody 1, thematic melody 2, the fanfare motive, and the bridge motive.

Movement 4, Theme 1
Theme 1 features two of the four thematic elements: thematic melody 1 and the fanfare motive. Thematic melody 1 is made up of a head and a tail. The head consists of a four-note motive that drives the bulk of the fourth movement. This thematic head is followed by a brilliant tail. We get a hint of the polyphonic games to come when Mozart brings theme 1 to its conclusion via a five-part **fugato**—a section of music that sounds like the opening of a fugue—based on the head motive of thematic melody 1.

Movement 4, The Fanfare Motive
The fanfare motive is the blaring, martial musical idea that follows thematic melody 1 and that begins overlapping with itself the moment it is first introduced. Mozart quietly concludes the exposition with a swirling, overlapping treatment of the fanfare motive.

Movement 4, Theme 2

Like theme 1, theme 2 consists of a thematic melody followed by the fanfare motive. Like thematic melody 1, thematic melody 2 consists of a head and tail. Like the head of thematic melody 1, the head of thematic melody two consists of sustained notes. Like the tail of thematic melody 1, the tail of thematic melody 2 consists of faster, descending notes. Like theme 1, the fanfare motive concludes theme 2.

Movement 4, The Bridge Motive

The final thematic entity of the movement is the bridge motive—a rising, trilling melodic idea introduced during the modulating bridge of the exposition. The bridge motive first appears in an overlapping dialogue between upper and lower strings.

As recently as the 1930s, there were thought to be 49 symphonies that Mozart composed.

The major "characters" of the movement, as aforementioned, are thematic melodies 1 and 2, the fanfare motive, and the bridge motive. It is their seemingly limitless combination and interaction that is the generative dramatic idea of the movement. As the movement approaches its conclusion, Mozart stages a curtain call for all his melodic characters, set as a canon in five parts. This episode is followed by the conclusion of the movement and the symphony.

There is hardly a measure of this fourth movement that is not witness to some kind of polyphonic interplay, from simple imitation to the five-part, canonic episode at the conclusion of the last movement. For all of its polyphonic arcana, the compositional techniques Mozart employs in this movement do not alone constitute the larger expressive point of the movement. Rather, the movement's polyphonic complexity serves a higher expressive message—a utopian message that reflects the contemporary spirit of the Enlightenment by joining together a multiplicity of independent and diverse elements to create a joyful, energized, and **consonant** finale. ■

andante: Moderately slow.

consonance: A musical entity or state that can be perceived as a point of rest.

fugato: A fugal exposition inserted into a movement that is not otherwise a fugue.

tune: Generally sing-able, memorable melody with a clear sense of beginning, middle, and end.

Mozart—Symphony in C Major, "Jupiter"
Lecture 7—Transcript

We return to *The 30 Greatest Orchestral Works*. This is Lecture 7, and it is entitled "Mozart—Symphony in C Major, " 'Jupiter.' "

Mozart's Facility

Mozart had a compositional facility that leaves the rest of us crinkle-browed and shaking our heads. It's not just that he composed with incredible speed. Oh no. The fact is that Mozart created entire works in his head and then carried them around the way the rest of us carry multi-gigabyte flash memory sticks. For Mozart, actually writing down a piece—"copying it out" as he called it—was but a last, tiresome task; hateful drudgery that he often put off for as long as he could until deadlines forced his hand. I offer up one anecdotal example—of the many that have come down to us—of Mozart's facility in "copying out" a piece on deadline: the story of the overture to *Don Giovanni* of 1787. I offer two different accounts of the story.

The first was written by Franz Xaver Niemetschek, a contemporary of Mozart and Mozart's first biographer. Here's Niemetschek's version of the story:

> Mozart wrote this opera in Prague in 1787; it was already finished and had been rehearsed and was due to be performed in two days' time, but the overture was still missing. The anxiety and worries on the part of his friends, which grew with each passing hour, seemed merely to be a source of amusement to him; the more concerned they became, the more nonchalant Mozart pretended to be. Finally, on the eve of the first performance, having joked to his heart's content, he went to his room at around midnight, started to write and completed this extraordinary masterpiece within a matter of hours.

Writing in the third person, Mozart's wife, Constanze, described the events of that night in a bit more detail.

> On the eve of the first performance of *Don Giovanni*, after the final dress rehearsal had already taken place, [Mozart] told his wife that he intended to write the overture that night and asked her to make some punch for him and to remain by his side in order to keep him awake. She did so, telling him tales of Aladdin's lamp, Cinderella and so on, while tears of laughter rolled down his cheeks. But the punch made him so sleepy that he nodded off whenever she stopped and [he] worked only when she told him these stories. But the effort involved, together with his frequent tendency to nod off and then suddenly start up again, made the work so difficult that his wife finally encouraged him to lie down on the couch and sleep, promising to wake him after an hour. But he slept so soundly that she did not have the heart to wake him and it was not until two hours later that she did so. It was now 5 o'clock. The copyist had been told to come at 7; by 7 the overture was finished.

In his magisterial, 1500 page biography of Mozart, Hermann Abert writes:

> [The] truth to the story is that [Mozart] had long since worked out the [overture] in his head and merely wanted to put off to the last minute the tiresome task of writing it down. Given Mozart's dislike of writing anything down, it is entirely [likely] that a large number of his works were simply never written down. Strange though it may sound, only a part of his oeuvre has survived: The rest he himself kept from us.

And when did Mozart "compose"—in his mind—his amazing, utopian masterworks? The answer: all the time. When he was eating, talking, mating, playing bocce, whatever; a significant portion of his mind was independent of ordinary interaction and was apparently never at rest.

Many people, today, ascribe Mozart's creative abilities to a medical condition or brain abnormality. It's an entirely understandable impulse, given the inexplicable mystery of his genius. It's just as possible that he was an alien installed here on earth by kindly extraterrestrials in an attempt to civilize our species. Whatever, Mozart has been making people shake their heads since he was about four years old.

Mozart's Symphonies

The numbering of Mozart's symphonies is problematic. As recently as the 1930s, there were thought to be 49 of them. (I own a score of Mozart's "Jupiter" Symphony published in 1929. In big, bold letters and numbers, the cover of the score lists this last of Mozart's symphonies as being No. 49.)

This total of 49 symphonies has, today, been reduced to 41, as works erroneously attributed to Mozart have been removed from the total. Even so, the number 41 is still misleading, because the symphony that we, today, still insist on calling "Mozart's Symphony No. 37 in G Major" was not composed by Mozart but rather by Michael Haydn, Joseph Haydn's baby brother. Michael Haydn, like Mozart's father Leopold, was a musician in the employ of the Archbishop of Salzburg and was a long-time friend of the Mozart family. Michael Haydn composed his G Major Symphony in 1783. A few months later, Wolfgang Mozart added a slow introduction to its first movement for a performance of the symphony in Linz, and there you have it, for the next 150 years everyone assumed that the entire symphony was by Mozart.

(My friends, it remains, then, one of the choicest traps available: that is, to ask a tiresome musical snob what he or she thinks of Mozart's 37th Symphony. He or she will likely wax eloquent on its sublime beauties. You will then have the option of either smiling or dropping the Michael Haydn bomb. Either way, the snob will have been owned.)

Anyway, if we take away the "ersatz" 37th, there are still some 40 Mozart symphonies, more than enough, it seems, to make him a major symphonist.

But in truth, Mozart's symphonies occupy a secondary place in his compositional output. The first 30 of them were written when he was just a tot; only the last 10 were written after 1775, when he had achieved his musical maturity. And of those 10 "mature" symphonies, composed in fits and starts between 1778 and 1788, only the final three, "copied out" during the summer of 1788, were conceived as a cohesive and coherent symphonic unit.

In truth, composing symphonies was never a high priority for Mozart. In his heart he was an opera composer who wrote piano concerti for money and chamber music for his friends. With the exception of his final three, Mozart's symphonies were "occasional works"—works composed for particular occasions—or pieces written while he was on tour when he needed to have something new to perform. Of course, had Mozart lived long enough to be inspired by Haydn's London Symphonies or Beethoven's Heroic Symphonies, who knows what he might have composed. But such a thing is best left unthought, such is the pain it can cause.

The Final Three

Mozart composed (or at least "copied out") his last three symphonies—the E-flat Major, the G Minor, and the C Major (also-known-as the "Jupiter")—during the summer of 1788.

His symphonies aside, it was a bleak time for Mozart. His finances were a wreck: unable to curb his spending, he had fallen deeply into debt, and his immediate financial prospects offered him little hope of climbing out of debt. The Habsburg Empire, having gone to war against the Ottoman Turks for the umpteenth time in 1787, was enforcing a policy of stringent austerity that closed the theaters and dried up cash in Vienna. One doesn't need a degree in economics to figure out that with the theaters closed, a freelance musician is going to have a hard time making a buck.

During the summer of 1788, Mozart's health—which had never been particularly good—was particularly awful. He was plagued by infections, kidney ailments, and viruses; you name it, he got it. On June 17, 1788, Mozart's finances forced him to take a flat in the 'burbs, outside the city walls of Vienna, the equivalent of a high-rolling Manhattanite being forced to move to New Jersey. Twelve days later—on June 29, 1788—his infant daughter Theresia—just six months old—died of some unspecified illness.

It was under these dismal circumstances that Mozart "copied out" his last three symphonies, one after the other. No. 39 in E-flat Major—"the locus classicus of Euphony," according to Sir Donald Francis Tovey—was completed on June 26. No. 40 in G Minor—anguished and tragic in tone—was completed a month later, on July 25. The Symphony No. 41 in C Major, the "Jupiter"—martial and celebratory in tone—was completed roughly two weeks later, on August 10. We still don't know exactly why Mozart composed these symphonies, though it seems likely that he intended to have them performed on a series of concerts he would personally produce, along the lines of the concerts for which he had composed so many of his piano concerti back in the early 1780s. If this was his intention the concerts never took place, and to this day, we know that only one of the symphonies was performed once in Mozart's lifetime, probably the "Jupiter."

Of these amazing symphonies, the French musicologist Georges de Saint-Foix rather lusciously writes:

> Never since he arrived at maturity had [Mozart] produced, at intervals of a few days only, a succession of compositions of the same caliber; the E-flat Symphony represents the immense portico through which the composer reveals to us all the warm and poetic beauty thronging his mind, before surrendering himself before our eyes to a struggle of exalted passion, to be manifest in the Symphony in G Minor; and finally he invites our presence at a sort of apotheosis of his musical genius, freed from all shackles, in what has come to be known as the "Jupiter" Symphony. This imposing [trinity is] his symphonic testament [which] sums up for us his inmost soul.

Gosh, I like that quote!

Symphony in C Major K. 551, The "Jupiter" of 1788

Mozart's "Jupiter" is his longest and most expressively brilliant symphony. According to Hermann Abert, "It breathes a spirit of proud strength found nowhere else in his output." It is truly imperial in its scope and power—and it well deserves the nickname "Jupiter"—the king of the gods—that Johann Peter Salomon bestowed upon it soon after Mozart's death.

Movement 1: Sonata Form

The first movement opens with a theme that immediately sets the tone for the remainder of the movement, a theme that alternates a vigorous, martial, masculine phrase scored for the entire orchestra with a yearning, lyric, feminine phrase. [**Musical selection**: Mozart, Symphony No. 41 in C Major, movement 1, theme 1.]

My identification of these opening phrases as being "masculine" and "feminine" is not an act of sexist stereotyping on my part. It was none other than the German poet and dramatist Johann Wolfgang von Goethe who is credited with coining the term "eternal feminine" in the late 18th century. Indeed, the back story of Goethe's epic version of *Faust* is a gender-transcending union of "masculine" and "feminine" "in a redemptive return to a primal unity."

Consequently, the issues of uniting the masculine and feminine into a "unified, redemptive whole" were common philosophical and artistic issues in 1788. The first movement of Mozart's "Jupiter" Symphony grows out of this very issue. Back to the first part of the first theme.

The "masculine" aspect of the theme is represented by upwards-sweeping motives. [**Piano demonstration**.] This "thematic idea" is based on a type of drum stroke called a "four-stroke ruff": three very fast strokes followed by an accented stroke. As such, the "masculine" element of theme 1 is essentially a "rhythmic" idea. Conversely, the "feminine" aspect is pure melody: It consists of a gentle, yeaning tune that step-ladders its way upwards. [**Piano demonstration**.] Let's hear this first part of theme 1 again. [**Musical selection**: Mozart, Symphony No. 41 in C Major, Movement 1, Theme 1.]

The second part of theme 1 is entirely masculine, as the martial, fanfare-ish opening of the theme takes over. The regular rhythmic pattern and simple harmonic structure of this passage give it a "drum and bugle corps-like" effect, which is entirely in keeping with the spirit of the "ruff-dominated" opening phrase. Let's hear the second part of theme 1. [**Musical selection**: Mozart, Symphony No. 41 in C Major, movement 1, theme 1.]

Now, according to the formal orthodoxy of classical era sonata form, having stated theme 1, Mozart is next "supposed" to introduce a transitional passage called a modulating bridge that will transit to the contrasting second theme. Well, so much for formal orthodoxy. Mozart is so enamored of the masculine-feminine dichotomy his first theme represents that he begins to develop the theme immediately. He next superimposes a new, "feminine-styled" melodic idea in the flutes and oboes over the opening of theme 1. Check it out: Once again, here's the opening of theme 1. [**Piano demonstration**.] Here's the flute and oboe tune that will be superimposed over the opening of theme 1. [**Piano demonstration**.] And now both together: [**Piano demonstration**.] Let's hear this gentle, quiet, and feminine development/extension of the opening of the theme. [**Musical selection**: Mozart, Symphony No. 41 in C Major, movement 1, theme 1.]

Its time, once again, for the masculine aspect of the theme to take front and center. A vigorous development of the "new" flute and oboe tune as well as the formerly feminine phrase of theme 1 ensues, followed by the "drum and bugle corps" music that concluded theme 1: all of this in lieu of a modulating bridge! [**Musical selection**: Mozart, Symphony No. 41 in C Major, movement 1, theme 1.]

Theme 2 now finally arrives. The theme is cast in three parts. Part one is a playful, bubbly tune of incredible grace and charm, feminine in its spirit and impact. [**Musical selection**: Mozart, Symphony No. 41 in C Major, movement 1.] The "feminine spirit" of theme 2 is made explicit in its second part, as the rising, "feminine" element of theme 1 is heard in dialogue with a new melodic phrase. [**Musical selection**: Mozart, Symphony No. 41 in C Major, movement 1. Ahhhh, Sugar 'n' spice and everything nice—but not for long!

Just as theme 1 represented a unity of masculine and feminine, so does theme 2. Thus the third part of theme 2—set initially in C minor—is explosive and martial. It jump-starts the action and pitches the music headlong towards the cadence material and with it, the conclusion of the exposition. Theme 2, part

3: [**Musical selection**: Mozart, Symphony no. 41 in C Major, movement 1.] The cadence material now begins and brings with it a surprise. The first part of the cadence material is familiar enough: It is a most masculine development of the once feminine phrase of theme 1. We expect this fire-breathing music to culminate with a powerful cadence, so we are very surprised—to say the very least—when it quietly descends and then just stops! Cadence material, part 1: [**Musical selection**: Mozart, Symphony No. 41 in C Major, movement 1.]

OK. You've got our attention Herr Mozart. And a good thing, too, because out of the blue, an entirely new theme now appears. More than just a cadence theme, that is, a melody associated with the endings of large sections, this is a genuine third theme, by far the most memorable melodic idea we have heard thus far in the movement. Here it is. [**Musical selection**: Mozart, Symphony No. 41 in C Major, movement 1.]

OK. We expected the exposition to end and instead we got an entirely new and most memorable theme. What's up? My friends, Mozart has plugged in a "loaner theme" at the very last possible moment of the exposition. He borrowed it from himself: It is the melody of a concert aria entitled *Un bacio di mano*—"A Kiss on the Hand"—that he had only just composed. Here's how the aria begins. [**Musical selection**: Mozart, *Un bacio di mano*.]

Once again, here's that melody as dropped into the first movement of the "Jupiter," followed by the "drum and bugle corps" music that finally brings the exposition to its conclusion. [**Musical selection**: Mozart, Symphony No. 41 in C Major, movement 1.]

All right: Let's recap the action of this utterly idiosyncratic sonata form exposition! Themes 1and 2 represent (and reconcile) the "feminine" and "masculine." Theme 1 is developed in lieu of a modulating bridge, and then a third theme is shoehorned in at the last possible moment for reasons still unexplained! The explanation for "theme 3" comes in the form of the development section, which is based almost entirely on theme 3, on *Un bacio di mano*! Why? Because over the course of the exposition, Mozart already "developed-and-extended" the great bulk of his thematic materials. Not only did Mozart require some new thematic grist for the development section, he also wanted to shift the dramatic focus away from the masculine/feminine dichotomy that dominates the exposition (and will dominate the recapitulation as well) towards something different and more musically abstract.

How do we know all of this? We know it by listening to the music. We're going to hear the development section in its entirety. And let us appreciate the comic irony here: that the masculine/feminine melding depicted by themes 1 and 2 is sealed in the development section with *Un bacio di mano*—with a kiss on the hand! [**Musical selection**: Mozart, Symphony no. 41 in C Major, movement 1.] As development sections go, this one feels to my ears almost like a respite, a break from the intensity of the action of the exposition. Usually, it's the other way around: Typically, the dramatic weight of a movement lies firmly in the development section. Then again, there's nothing "typical" about this remarkable first movement.

Movement 2

The second movement is a lyric andante cast in sonata form, a movement scored without trumpets and drums and particularly notable for the way Mozart embellishes and varies the themes at each new iteration. Let's hear the long-limbed theme 1 as it appears at the beginning of the movement. [**Musical selection**: Mozart, Symphony No. 41 in C Major, movement 2.]

Movement 3

The third movement is a broad and courtly minuet and trio. [**Musical selection**: Mozart, Symphony No. 41 in C Major, movement 3.]

Movement 4: Sonata Form

Mozart's father Leopold garnered international fame by writing a textbook on violin playing that was published in 1756, the same year Wolfgang was born. What many folks don't know is that Wolfgang himself also wrote a textbook, a textbook on polyphonic compositional technique. The difference: Wolfgang's textbook is in the form of a symphonic movement: the fourth movement of the "Jupiter" Symphony!

Our examination of this miraculous finale will focus on its four themes, themes specifically designed to be capable of all sorts of stacking and overlapping. these four thematic elements are thematic melody 1, thematic melody 2, the fanfare motive, and the bridge motive.

Theme 1

Theme 1 features two of the four thematic elements: "thematic melody 1" and the "fanfare motive." We will isolate and examine each of these thematic elements, but first let's hear theme 1 in its entirety. [**Musical selection**: Mozart, Symphony No. 41 in C Major, movement 4.] Thematic melody 1 is made up of a "head" and a "tail." The head consists of four sustained notes. [**Piano demonstration.**]

That four-note motive is the engine that drives the bulk of this fourth movement. Let's hear it again. [**Piano demonstration.**] This thematic "head" is followed by a brilliant "tail." [**Piano demonstration.**] Let's hear thematic melody 1 as played by the orchestra at the beginning of the movement. [**Musical selection**: Mozart, Symphony No. 41 in C Major, movement 4.] Back, for a moment, to the "head" of theme 1. [**Piano demonstration.**]

Had we examined the entire third movement minuet and trio, we would have heard the following outburst smack-dab in the middle of the movement. [**Musical selection**: Mozart, Symphony No. 41 in C Major, Movement 3.] Here's what we just heard. [**Piano demonstration.**] Once again, here's the head of the fourth movement's thematic melody one. [**Piano demonstration.**] One more time, the outburst from the third movement. [**Piano demonstration.**] Thus the seed from which the fourth movement grows was planted in the third movement. That's really very nice.

We get a hint of the polyphonic games to come when Mozart brings theme 1 to its conclusion with a five-part fugato, that is, a section of music that sounds like the opening of a fugue based on the "head motive" of thematic melody 1. Let's hear that fugato. [**Musical selection**: Mozart, Symphony No. 41 in C Major, movement 4.]

The Fanfare Motive

The fanfare motive is the blaring, martial musical idea that follows thematic melody no. 1, a musical idea that begins overlapping with itself the moment it is first introduced. [**Musical selection**: Mozart, Symphony No. 41 in C Major, movement 4.] Mozart concludes the exposition with a swirling, overlapping treatment of the previously heard fanfare motive. Let's hear this canonic episode followed by the quiet conclusion of the exposition. [**Musical selection**: Mozart, Symphony No. 41 in C Major, movement 4.]

Theme 2

Like theme 1, theme 2 consists of a thematic melody followed by the fanfare motive. Like thematic melody 1, thematic melody 2 consists of a head and a tail. Like the head of thematic melody 1, the head of thematic melody 2 consists of sustained notes. [**Piano demonstration**.] Like the tail of thematic melody 1, the tail of thematic melody 2 consists of faster, descending notes. [**Piano demonstration**.] Like theme 1, the fanfare motive concludes theme 2. Here, then, is theme 2 consisting of the head and tail followed by the fanfare motive. [**Piano demonstration**.] Let's hear theme 2 as it appears in the exposition. [**Musical selection**: Mozart, Symphony No. 41 in C Major, movement 4.]

Just a few measures later, Mozart takes the head of thematic melody 2 for a polyphonic test drive, creating from it a canon in *stretto*, meaning that as it overlaps with itself, the overlaps become closer and closer (or "tighter and tighter," which is what the Italian verb *stretto* means, to tighten). Let's hear this canonic episode as played by the orchestra. [**Musical selection**: Mozart, Symphony No. 41 in C Major, movement 4.]

The Bridge Motive

The final thematic entity of the movement is the bridge motive, a rising, trilling melodic idea introduced during the modulating bridge. It sounds like this. [**Piano demonstration**.] Let's hear the bridge motive as it first appears during the modulating bridge of the exposition in an overlapping dialogue between upper and lower strings. [**Musical selection**: Mozart, Symphony

No. 41 in C Major, movement 4.] These, then, are the major characters of the movement: thematic melodies 1 and 2, the fanfare motive, and the bridge motive. It is their seemingly limitless combination and interaction that is the generative dramatic idea of the movement.

Mozart saves the best for last. As the movement approaches its conclusion, he stages a curtain call for all of his melodic characters, set as a canon in five parts. Let's hear this episode, followed by the conclusion of the movement and the symphony. [**Musical selection**: Mozart, Symphony No. 41 in C Major, movement 4.]

There is hardly a measure of this fourth movement that is not witness to some kind of polyphonic interplay, from simple imitation to the five-part, everything-including-the-kitchen-sink canonic episode we just heard, to a passage in which Mozart puts the head motive of thematic melody 1 in double counterpoint at the tenth while simultaneously creating a canon in inversion at the octave! (This is something I did not demonstrate, because, as you might well imagine, it would have taken half a lecture to explain.)

For all of its polyphonic arcana, the compositional techniques Mozart employs in this fourth movement do not constitute, unto themselves, the larger expressive point of the movement. Rather, the movement's polyphonic complexity serves a higher expressive message. It is, my friends, a utopian message, one that reflects the contemporary spirit of the Enlightenment. Mozart, who was himself a free-thinker and a dedicated Mason, creates here a movement in which a multiplicity of independent and diverse elements join together to create a joyful, energized, and consonant whole far greater than the sum of its individual parts. It is an incredible finale, one that looks forward to the utopian, highly polyphonic, Enlightenment-inspired fourth movement finale of Beethoven's Symphony No. 9, a work 36 years in the future.

Thank you.

Beethoven—Symphony No. 3
Lecture 8

Beethoven's Symphony no. 3, otherwise known as the "Eroica," is an experimental artwork. In its fourth and final movement, Beethoven was attempting to do the impossible: to reconcile the classical tradition of playful, upbeat finales with the revolutionary, heroic expressive content of the other three movements. In the "Eroica," Beethoven made the epic leap toward conceiving his music as self-expression, a conception that changed the substance and spirit of Western music forever.

L udwig van Beethoven, who idolized Napoleon Bonaparte as the personification of the revolution that would sweep Europe clean of absolutism, took the news that Napoleon had crowned himself emperor poorly. Although Beethoven's Symphony no. 3 was originally subtitled "Bonaparte" as a sign of respect, upon hearing the news, Beethoven renamed it *Sinfonia Eroica*," or the "Heroic Symphony."

Symphony No. 3 in E-flat Major, "Eroica"
In reality, the hero Beethoven memorialized in this symphony was himself, whose aspirations for happiness were cut short by a progressive hearing loss that began in 1796 and who experienced a suicidal crisis over that loss in the fall of 1802. He virtually reinvented himself in the guise of a hero struggling with and overcoming fate in late 1802 and 1803. Beethoven expressed that struggle in his Symphony no. 3 of 1803 and 1804, which became more like a last will and testament, suicide note, and rant and rave against God, humankind, and intractable fate.

Movement 1
The symphony begins with two proud and powerful E-flat major chords, chords that anchor the harmony unambiguously in E-flat major and establish a martial and masculine mood. These opening chords are followed by a lengthy theme in four phrases. Although the theme concludes in a heroic blaze of glory, this theme—and consequently the male character it represents—carries within it the seeds of ruin and despair, which are musically depicted by melodic and harmonic dissonance and rhythmic ambiguity.

Just seven measures into the movement, the theme and its harmony take a completely unexpected and dissonant turn toward the dark side of G minor.

It is the 'cello—the voice of the hero—that pulls the music down toward the dark side by playing a shocking chromatic descent from an E-flat to a D to a C-sharp, which is a pitch that is not found in the key of E-flat major. This C-sharp in the 'cellos implies a sudden and shocking move toward the key of G minor. The C-sharp, and the dark key of G minor it implies, is a dissonant musical element—an element that implies harmonic chaos and disruption, a potentially fatal character flaw in the personality of the theme.

© iStockphoto/Thinkstock.

Ludwig van Beethoven (1770–1827) began conceiving his music as self-expression with the "Eroica."

During the third phrase of theme 1, the triple meter beat that has characterized the movement up to this point suddenly and unexpectedly begins to alternate with groupings of two beats. It is a passage of extraordinary rhythmic ambiguity. Like the C-sharp in phrase 1, the rhythmic ambiguity in phrase 3 is a character flaw, a seed of chaos and despair buried within an otherwise heroic personality. The fourth and final phrase of the theme is the least ambiguous and most outwardly heroic of the phrases.

The storyline of movement 1, then, is the flawed personality that theme 1 initially represents. Those flaws—as represented by dissonance and rhythmic ambiguity—combine at the very center of the movement to bring the hero to the very brink of destruction. It is here, at the center of the development section, that Beethoven depicts the abyss, a spiritual black hole from which no hope can emerge. It is a passage of extraordinary musical nihilism, during which the dissonance and rhythmic ambiguity present in theme 1 come together to create a terrifying climax.

During the course of the passage, isolated diminished seventh chords—the most dissonant harmony in Beethoven's tonal arsenal—are repeated in alternating patterns of two and three beats. These dissonant chords effectively destroy any sense of tonal gravity, and their alternating groups of two and three beats obliterate any sense of rhythmic regularity. Taken together, it is one of the most shocking, modern, and original passages in the orchestral repertoire.

In reality, the hero Beethoven memorialized in this symphony was himself.

Having survived the abyss, the development section slowly recovers and turns back, harmonically, toward the heroic key of E-flat major. That the struggle with harmonic dissonance and rhythmic ambiguity has been won is made clear by the version of theme 1 that begins the recapitulation. Theme 1 of the recapitulation begins as it did in the exposition but soon diverges, as the dissonant descent to C-sharp now continues downward to C-natural, a move that instantly dispels the darkness and harmonic tension that were implied in the exposition.

Theme 1 now consists of three (rather than four) phrases, because in the recapitulation, the phrase that contained the rhythmic ambiguity is no longer heard. The life and death struggle played out during the development section has been won by life itself. The hero—as represented by theme 1—has overcome the flaws that once threatened to destroy him. The movement ends as it began, with a series of detached E-flat major chords. The first movement of the "Eroica" is a stupendous achievement, a brilliant combination of narrative storytelling, abstract musical structure, and autobiographical confession—all couched in a musical language that stretches the contemporary musical elements of melody, harmony, and expressive content.

Movement 2
Beethoven conceived this second movement, also known as the funeral march, as an essential element in the large-scale dramatic progression of the symphony. Movement 1 is about heroic struggle, while movement 2

acknowledges the inevitability and finality of death. Movement 3 reanimates the symphony and sets the stage for movement 4, which is about apotheosis.

Movement 3
Beethoven's brilliant third movement scherzo reanimates the symphony through its pure, visceral, rhythmic power. It's hard to imagine a greater, more uplifting contrast than the one this movement provides after the funeral march. This third movement ends on an explosive, celebratory note, which sets up the genuinely burlesque opening of the fourth movement.

Movement 4
We know that Beethoven identified with the heroic image projected by Napoleon and that Beethoven appropriated that heroic image in his own rebirth and subsequent composition of this Third Symphony. However, even more important than Napoleon to the genesis of the "Eroica" was the image of the mythical hero Prometheus. In 1801, Beethoven, in collaboration with the choreographer Salvatore Vigano, composed a ballet score entitled *The Creatures of Prometheus*.

Beethoven makes the connection between his Prometheus music and his Third Symphony explicit by basing the fourth movement finale of the "Eroica" on a theme originally composed for the celebratory finale of the ballet. Beethoven's message is that Prometheus's rebirth is his own rebirth, and the apotheosis that marks the conclusion of the ballet is his own apotheosis at the conclusion of the Third Symphony. The dramatic and symbolic elements of the Prometheus story—struggle, death, reanimation, and apotheosis—constitute the large-scale dramatic progression of the Third Symphony, which parallel Beethoven's own despair, thoughts of suicide, and subsequent artistic rebirth.

The fourth and final movement of the "Eroica" is curious, as its comic opening behaves more like music-hall burlesque than the capstone of a great spiritual journey. The movement begins with dramatic, downward-rushing strings followed by an explosive and fanfare-like cadence. This grand, magnificent introductory music must anticipate an event of signal importance. Surprisingly, a silly little theme emerges—what we'll refer to as the bass theme—and when it emerges a second time, it is answered by out-of-step winds and is followed by a full measure of silence. The strings then resume their dainty bass theme along with the winds, brass, and percussion. This is an odd way to begin a movement that purports to be the apotheosis of a heroic struggle.

The bass theme then presents two variations of itself in which it accessorizes with various accompanimental elements. However, the bass theme still doesn't assume thematic responsibility. Then, with the appearance of the master theme, it is made clear that the bass theme is not a theme but the bass line—the support staff—for an infinitely more memorable master theme. This is the music that Beethoven borrowed from the finale of *The Creatures of Prometheus* ballet.

The remainder of the movement consists of a series of alternating variations of the bass theme and the master theme, which create an intricate and whimsical fugue together. The fugue concludes with the same sort of fanfare that concluded the movement's opening introduction—the same dramatic, downward-rushing strings. This time, however, the fanfare precedes a thrilling series of musical events: a version of the master theme heard in the horns, followed by what is among the longest and most exciting final cadences in the symphonic repertoire. ■

Beethoven—Symphony No. 3
Lecture 8—Transcript

We return to *The 30 Greatest Orchestral Works*. This is Lecture 8, and it is entitled. "Beethoven—Symphony No. 3."

It was Beethoven's student Ferdinand Ries who did it, who dashed to Beethoven's Viennese flat sometime in December of 1804 to report that Napoleon Bonaparte had crowned himself emperor.

Beethoven—who idolized Napoleon as the personification of the Revolution that would sweep Europe clean of absolutism—took the news poorly. Here is Ries's account of what happened.

> Not only I myself but several of Beethoven's friends had seen [his Third Symphony], in full score, lying on his table; at the head of the title page was the word BONAPARTE. [It was 1804.] I was the person who brought him the news that Napoleon had declared himself emperor. Thereupon he flew into a rage and cried out, 'He too is nothing but an ordinary man! Now he will trample underfoot all the rights of man and only indulge his ambition: He will now set himself on high and become a tyrant!' Beethoven went to the table, seized the title page from the top [of the symphony], tore it up completely, and threw it on the floor.

In truth, Beethoven—who was never one to discard a piece of paper—did not actually destroy but rather, altered the title page of the symphony. That title page had originally carried the inscription *Sinfonia grande, intitolata Bonaparte*: "Large Symphony entitled Bonaparte." Beethoven scratched out the words "entitled Bonaparte," leaving only "Large Symphony." Two years later, when the parts were printed, the symphony bore the title *Sinfonia Eroica*, the "Heroic Symphony," and sometime after that that Beethoven further extended the title with the inscription: "composed in celebration of the memory of a great man." Writes Beethoven biographer Walter Riezler: "This sounds as if the great man [of Beethoven's title] were dead; and, indeed, for Beethoven the greatness of Napoleon was a thing of the past once he had become emperor. So much is known fact."

OK. Here's another fact. The real "hero" was memorialized in the *Eroica* was Ludwig van Beethoven, a composer of Flemish descent who grew up in the Rhineland city of Bonn; who moved to Vienna a few weeks shy of his 22nd birthday; whose aspirations for happiness were cut short by a progressive hearing loss that began in 1796 and who experienced a suicidal crisis over that hearing loss in the fall of 1802; who virtually reinvented himself in the guise of a "hero" struggling with and overcoming fate in late 1802 and 1803; a composer who—thanks to his genius—found a way to express that struggle in his Symphony No. 3 of 1803 and 1804; and isn't this the longest run-on sentence we'll hear today!

My friends, let there be no doubt about it: Beethoven's "heroic symphony" is about Beethoven himself. The struggles, trials, and victories depicted in the *Eroica* are Beethoven's own and not those of Napoleon Bonaparte. Yes, the "idea" of Napoleon helped Beethoven to frame his own newly minted self-image of a "hero battling fate," but we should go no further than that. So, why did Beethoven initially entitle his Third Symphony "Bonaparte"? The answer: for marketing reasons, as Beethoven in 1804 was planning to move to Paris! We begin our story there.

The Move to Paris

The French Revolution "began" on July 14, 1789, with the sacking of the Paris city jail: a 14th-century fortress named the "Bastille." By 1795, the Revolution had bled itself out; among its victims were the king and queen of France— Louis XVI and Marie Antoinette—as well as the most radical revolutionaries themselves, including Georges Danton and Maximilien de Robespierre.

In October of 1795—with the new French government called the "Directory" at war with the Austrian Empire—a 26-year-old, Corsican-born artillery officer of Florentine descent named Napoleon Bonaparte began his meteoric rise to power. On December 24, 1799, the 30-year-old Napoleon was appointed "First Consul" and thus became the most powerful person in France.

By 1803, Napoleon appeared to be poised to bring the anti-monarchial, Enlightenment-inspired French Revolution to all of Europe. He was described by contemporary pundits as "Alexander reincarnate," "invincible," and "the righteous hand of God." "Bonapartism" became the central political and philosophical issue in post-French Revolution Europe. Émile Zola later wrote: "Napoleon's destiny acted like a hammer-blow on the heads of his contemporaries. ... All ambitions waxed large; all undertakings took on a gigantic air."

Napoleon's admirers included such German and Austrian patriots as Kant, Hegel, Goethe, and Schiller. Goethe kept a bust of Napoleon in his bedroom. And in 1806, Hegel called Napoleon: "A soul of worldwide significance ... an individual who encompasses the world and rules it."

Beethoven's identification with Napoleon was personal. Napoleon—who was a Florentine among Corsicans and a Corsican among the French—was an outsider who had mastered his world through his own genius and industry. For Beethoven—a Rhinelander among the Viennese, hearing impaired among the hearing healthy, a man of genius struggling to achieve the sublime—well, for Beethoven, he and Napoleon were like two peas in a pod.

In 1803 Beethoven informed his friends that he was going to move to Paris. He had lots of reasons to do so, all of them good ones. Paris in 1803 was the home of "the Revolution," of Napoleon, and the capital of the "new Europe." In 1803, Paris was the patronage capital of the world, with enough money floating around to make Vienna appear a backwater by comparison.

So it was that in 1803 Beethoven began the process of easing himself into the Parisian musical scene. He dedicated his new Sonata for Violin and Piano in A Major to Rodolphe Kreutzer and Louis Adam, who he called, "The first violinist and pianist of Paris." To this day the piece is known as the "Kreutzer Sonata."

Beethoven also decided to write an opera on the sort of escape-from-tyranny story so popular in post-Revolutionary France, choosing a text called "Leonore" (which eventually became the opera *Fidelio*). Finally, almost certainly after having completed the piece, Beethoven decided to "subtitle" his Third Symphony "Bonaparte." However, when Napoleon declared himself "emperor" in 1804, his name came off the symphony and Beethoven put his plan to move to Paris on permanent hold.

The Hearing Loss

It began around 1796, sometime before Beethoven 26th birthday. It began as a ringing in his ears followed by a slow and inconsistent loss of high frequency hearing in both ears. The image of the young Beethoven suddenly struck deaf is a myth; for years Beethoven had good hearing days and bad hearing days, and it wasn't until 1818—22 years after the symptoms first began—that Beethoven could be considered clinically deaf.

However, the emotional and spiritual toll Beethoven's progressive hearing loss took on him cannot be overestimated. Terrified that his disability would be discovered and that his career would crash and burn, Beethoven began to withdraw from public life. A few chosen friends knew what was going on, and they were distressed beyond measure. For example, two of Beethoven's friends who "knew" were Stephan von Breuning and Franz Wegeler. In 1804 von Breuning wrote Wegeler: "You cannot believe what an indescribable—I should say terrifying—impression the waning of his hearing has had upon him. ... He has become very withdrawn and often mistrustful of his best friends, and irresolute in many things!"

(Let's just get this out of the way now. Beethoven's hearing loss was not—I repeat, was not—caused by either syphilis or lead poisoning. He almost certainly contracted typhoid fever at the age of 16, which initiated a condition called "otosclerosis," the progressive calcification of the tiny bones in his ears.)

By the fall of 1802, Beethoven had come to realize that his hearing loss was unstoppable and incurable. He became deeply depressed, and in October of 1802—while in the throes of this depression and living in the Viennese suburb of Heilegenstadt—he wrote a letter to his brothers now known as the "Heilegenstadt Testament." It is an amazing document: part last will and testament, part suicide note, part rant and rave against God, humankind, and intractable fate. The Testament was written as an act of catharsis in which Beethoven cataloged his despair over his hearing and his intention to struggle against his fate. Once written, the letter was filed away and left unsent.

According to Walter Riezler, the Heilegenstadt Testament is: "The despairing cry of a man who sees no future but a life of isolation, who fears he may not have the strength to bear such a fate; the cry of a heart, overflowing with love for mankind and a longing for fellowship, but tormented by the fear of being misunderstood."

Beethoven's Symphony No. 3—which he began composing just a few months after having written the Heilegenstadt Testament—is nothing less than a musical version of the Testament itself. During the course of the Heilegenstadt Testament, Beethoven writes "So I must bid you farewell." According to Maynard Solomon:

> The Heilegenstadt Testament is a leave taking—which is to say, a fresh start. Beethoven metaphorically enacted his own death in order that he might live again. He re-created himself in a new guise, self-sufficient and heroic. The testament is the literary prototype of the *Eroica* Symphony, a portrait of the artist as hero, stricken by deafness, withdrawn from mankind, conquering his impulses to suicide, struggling against fate, hoping to find [in Beethoven's words] "but one day of pure joy." It is a daydream compounded of heroism, death, and rebirth, a reaffirmation of Beethoven's adherence to virtue and [Kant's] categorical imperative.

In the increasingly sealed-off padded-cell that was Beethoven's creative mind, it was time to put the "daydream" into musical action. In doing so, Beethoven created a symphony the likes of which no one had ever before imagined.

Symphony No. 3 in E-flat Major, Op. 55, "Eroica"

Movement 1, Sonata Form

The symphony begins with two proud and powerful E-flat major chords, chords that anchor the harmony unambiguously in E-flat major and establish a martial and masculine mood. [**Musical selection**: Beethoven, Symphony No. 3 in E-flat Major, op. 55, movement 1.]

These opening chords are followed by a lengthy theme in four phrases. Note particularly—during our first listening to the theme—that the thematic melody is heard initially in the orchestral 'cellos, the baritone voice of the orchestra, imbuing it with a masculine character and great expressive gravitas. Beethoven, Symphony no. 3, Movement 1: [**Musical selection**: Beethoven, Symphony No. 3 in E-flat Major, op. 55, movement 1.]

Although the theme concludes in a heroic a blaze of glory, this theme—and consequently the male character it represents—carries within it the seeds of ruin and despair. These seeds of ruin and despair are musically depicted by melodic and harmonic dissonance and rhythmic ambiguity.

First the dissonance. Just seven measures into the movement, the theme and its harmony take a completely unexpected and dissonant turn towards the dark side of G minor. It is the 'cello—the voice of the "hero"—that pulls the music down towards the "dark side," by playing a shocking chromatic descent from an E-flat to a D to a C-sharp, C-sharp being a pitch that is not to be found in the key of E-flat major! Let's hear that descent to "the dark side, starting at the beginning of the theme." [**Piano demonstration**.] That C-sharp implies a sudden and shocking move towards the key of G minor. Let me harmonize this theme and show you what I'm talking about. [**Piano demonstration**.]

This C-sharp in the 'cellos—and the dark key of G minor it implies—is a dissonant musical element, an element that implies harmonic chaos and disruption, a potentially fatal character flaw in the personality of the theme.

Back to theme 1. During its third phrase, the triple meter beat that has characterized the movement to this point, suddenly and most unexpectedly begins to alternate with groupings of two beats. It is a passage of extraordinary rhythmic ambiguity, and like a suddenly irregular heartbeat, it bodes poorly for the health of the hero the music represents.

Once again, let's hear the theme in its entirety. This time around I will count and conduct it so that we might be aware of the rhythmic ambiguity contained in phrase 3. [**Musical selection**: Beethoven, Symphony No. 3 in E-flat Major, op. 55, movement 1.]

Like the C-sharp in phrase 1, the rhythmic ambiguity in phrase three of the theme is a character flaw, a seed of chaos and despair buried within an otherwise heroic personality. (My friends, this theme is a perfect metaphor for Beethoven's newly created self-image as a "hero" struggling against his own flaws and the chaos and despair that are the possible consequences of those flaws. It's a fabulous theme.)

The fourth and final phrase of the theme is the least ambiguous and most outwardly heroic of the bunch. Having heard the theme, then, the burning question is which of its aspects will, in the end, triumph: its heroic aspirations as heard in phrase four or its potentially destructive pre-conditions, as heard in phrases 1 and 3? We'll find out. But first, let's hear the theme one more time, from the beginning of the movement. [**Musical selection**: Beethoven, Symphony No. 3 in E-flat Major, op. 55, movement 1.] That is not a standard sonata form theme 1 but something much more. This theme is nothing less than a character, a masculine person with some serious issues, a person who carries within himself the potential for both triumph and tragedy, a sort of musical Bill Clinton.

A number of other thematic entities make their appearance during the course of the exposition. They are all spin-offs from the first theme we've just discussed, as each of them isolates and highlights some aspect of the heroic personality that is theme 1. The storyline of this movement, then, is theme 1 and the flawed personality it initially represents. Those flaws—as represented by dissonance and rhythmic ambiguity—combine at the very center of the movement to bring the hero to the very brink of destruction. It is here, at the center of the development section, that Beethoven depicts the abyss, that spiritual black hole from which no hope can emerge. It is a passage of extraordinary musical nihilism, during which the dissonance and rhythmic ambiguity present in theme 1 come together to create a terrifying climax.

During the course of the passage, isolated diminished seventh chords—the most dissonant harmony in Beethoven's tonal arsenal—are repeated over and over again, in alternating patterns of two and three beats. These dissonant chords effectively destroy any sense of tonal gravity, and their alternating groups of two and three beats obliterate any sense of metric regularity. Taken together, it is one of the most shocking, modern, and original passages in the entire orchestral repertoire.

We'll listen to the fugue-like "run-up" to the abyss, the abyss itself, and then the resolution that mercifully brings the passage to its conclusion. I will count the alternating groups of two and three beats as they occur. [**Musical selection**: Beethoven, Symphony No. 3 in E-flat major, op. 55, movement 1.]

In his seminal book, *Beethoven and His Nine Symphonies* (first published back in 1896), George Grove wrote of this passage:

> [The hapless fugue] is crushed by an outburst of rage, which forms the kernel of the whole movement, and in which the most irreconcilable discords of the harmony and the most stubborn disarrangements of the rhythm unite to form a picture of obstinacy and fury, a tornado which would burst the breast of any but the gigantic hero whom Beethoven believes himself to be portraying, and who was certainly more himself than Bonaparte.

Having survived the abyss, the development section slowly "recovers" and turns back, harmonically, towards the heroic key of E-flat major. That the struggle with harmonic dissonance and rhythmic ambiguity has been won is made clear by the version of theme 1 that begins the recapitulation.

With the onset of the recapitulation, theme 1 begins more or less as it did in the exposition, but soon diverges, as the dissonant descent to C-sharp now continues downwards to C-natural, a move that instantly dispels the darkness and harmonic tension that were implied in the exposition. Listen! Here's theme 1 as it began in the exposition. [**Piano demonstration**.] And here's theme 1 as it begins in the recapitulation. [**Piano demonstration**.]

Here in the recapitulation, the dissonance is overcome. But there's more! Theme 1 now consists of three (rather than four) phrases, because now—in the recapitulation—the phrase that contained the rhythmic ambiguity is no longer heard! The life and death struggle played out during the development section has been won by life itself. The "hero"—as represented by theme 1—has overcome the flaws that once threatened to destroy him! Let's hear it. Recapitulation, theme 1: [**Musical selection**: Beethoven, Symphony No. 3 in E-flat Major, op. 55, movement 1.] The movement ends as it began, with a series of detached E-flat major chords. [**Musical selection**: Beethoven, Symphony No. 3 in E-flat Major, op. 55, movement 1.]

The first movement of the *Eroica* is a stupendous achievement, a brilliant combination of narrative story telling, abstract musical structure, and autobiographical confession, all couched in a musical language that pushes entirely the contemporary envelopes of melody, harmony, and expressive content.

Our essential goal in examining the second, third, and fourth movements of the *Eroica* will be to understand in what way they contribute to the large-scale dramatic progression of struggle and triumph that lies at the heart of this symphony.

Movement 2: "Funeral March"

Let's hear the opening of this *"Marche funebre"*—"Funeral March"—after which we'll discuss "for whom this bell tolls." [**Musical selection**: Beethoven, Symphony No. 3 in E-flat Major, op. 55, movement 2.])

For whom does this march toll? For Napoleon? (Is Beethoven saying, "I have come to bury Caesar, not to praise him"?)

No. The movement was composed long before Beethoven's "break" with Napoleon. Rather, Beethoven conceived this second movement as an essential element in the large-scale dramatic progression of this symphony. Movement 1 is about heroic struggle. Movement 2 acknowledges the inevitability and finality of death. Movement 3 reanimates the symphony and sets the stage for movement 4, which is about apotheosis.

Movement 3

Beethoven's brilliant third movement scherzo reanimates the symphony through its pure, visceral, rhythmic power. It's hard to imagine a greater, more uplifting contrast than the one this movement provides after the Funeral

March. [**Musical selection**: Beethoven, Symphony No. 3 in E-flat Major, op. 55, movement 3.] This third movement ends on an explosive and celebratory note, which sets up the genuinely burlesque opening of the fourth movement.

Movement 4

OK, we know that Beethoven identified with the heroic "image" projected by Napoleon, and that Beethoven appropriated that heroic image in his own rebirth and subsequent composition of the Third Symphony. However, even more important than Napoleon to the genesis of the "Eroica" was the image of the mythical hero Prometheus.

In 1801, Beethoven—in collaboration with the choreographer Salvatore Vigano—composed a ballet score entitled *The Creatures of Prometheus*. The ballet was Beethoven's first major work for the stage and one of his earliest public successes.

Prometheus stole fire from the Gods, fashioned it into knowledge and art, and then gave these as gifts to mankind, for which he was rather severely punished: chained to a rock, an eagle descends daily to devour his liver. (Painful, yes, though probably preferable to living in South Jersey.) Though physically chained, Prometheus is spiritually free. In the world of myth, there is no more powerful symbol of resistance to the arbitrary exercise of authority.

In the version of the story Beethoven and Vigano used—a version compatible with the spirit of the Enlightenment—Prometheus's agony on the rock is replaced by a procession of death and rebirth. In the ballet, Prometheus's gifts to humanity are not immediately appreciated, and as such, Prometheus's agony comes to parallel the plight of the misunderstood artist.

Beethoven makes the connection between his Prometheus music and his Third Symphony as explicit as he possibly could, by basing the fourth movement finale of the "Eroica" Symphony on a theme originally composed for the celebratory finale of the ballet! Back-to-back: First, here's the conclusion of the ballet during which Prometheus—the hero of the ballet— is reborn. [**Musical selection**: Beethoven, *Creatures of Prometheus*, op. 43

(1801), Act II finale.] And now, the principal theme of the fourth movement of the *Eroica*. [**Musical selection**: Beethoven, Symphony No. 3 in E-flat Major, op. 55, movement 4.]

Beethoven's message could not be more explicit: Prometheus's "rebirth" is his own rebirth, and the apotheosis that marks the conclusion of the ballet is his own apotheosis at the conclusion of the Third Symphony. The dramatic and symbolic elements of the Prometheus story—struggle, death, reanimation, and apotheosis—constitute the large-scale dramatic progression of the Third Symphony, and they parallel, as well, Beethoven's own despair, his thoughts of suicide, and subsequent artistic rebirth. The fourth and final movement of the *Eroica* is also something of a curiosity, as its comic opening behaves more like music-hall burlesque than the capstone of a great spiritual journey!

The movement begins with dramatic, downwards rushing strings followed by an explosive and fanfare-ish cadence. This grand, magnificent introductory music must surely anticipate an event of signal importance! [**Musical selection**: Beethoven, Symphony No. 3 in E-flat Major, op. 55, movement 4.] Ta-da! Well, after all that fuss, what follows comes as something of a surprise! A silly, mousy little theme emerges on tippy-toe. (We're going to call it the bass theme for reasons that will become clear in a moment.) We were prepared for a king, and instead we get a clown! [**Musical selection**: Beethoven, Symphony No. 3 in E-flat Major, op. 55, movement 4.]

This bass theme is heard again, this time answered by out-of-step winds and followed by a full measure of silence. [**Musical selection**: Beethoven, Symphony No. 3 in E-flat Major, op. 55, Movement 4.] OK. The winds, brass, and percussion wonder if anybody's home: Knock, knock, knock! Hmm? [**Musical selection**: Beethoven, Symphony No. 3 in E-flat Major, op. 55, movement 4.] Blithely unaware, the strings resume their tip-toeing bass theme. [**Musical selection**: Beethoven, Symphony No. 3 in E-flat Major, op. 55, movement 4.] Suddenly the strings wake up—"Did someone knock?"—to which the winds, brass, and percussion reply: Yes, we did! "Hmm?" says the strings. "Hmm!" answers the rest of the band, at which point the strings and winds complete their out-of-step version of the bass theme. [**Musical selection**: Beethoven, Symphony No. 3 in E-flat Major, op. 55, movement 4.]

This is an odd way to begin a movement that purports to be the apotheosis of a heroic struggle. Sir Donald Francis Tovey describes this passage as "Quite absurd." Frankly, what's most disconcerting about this passage is not its humor but its slap-stick humor, which is why many 19th century conductors simply left the movement out of performances entirely, and chose, instead, to conclude the symphony with the second movement Funeral March!

The bass theme next takes a crack at "thematic respectability" by presenting two variations of itself in which it "accessorizes" with various accompanimental elements. Let's hear the opening of the first of these two variations. [**Musical selection**: Beethoven, Symphony No. 3 in E-flat Major, op. 55, movement 4.] With or without accessories, the bass theme still doesn't cut it. It's too spare and too clownish to carry the movement!

So, what's Beethoven's game? The "game" becomes clear, finally, with the appearance of the master theme: The boss is home! The truth is revealed. The bass theme is not a theme at all but the bass line—the support staff—for an infinitely more memorable master theme! Here's the bass theme. [**Piano demonstration**.] And here's the master theme. [**Piano demonstration**.] And here they are together! [**Piano demonstration**.] This is the music that Beethoven "borrowed" from the finale of *The Creatures of Prometheus* ballet.

Now, the master theme may be home but the bass theme, having had the "run-of-the-house" for the first two minutes of the movement, will not give up its primacy easily. The remainder of the movement consists of a series of alternating variations as the bass theme and the master theme vie for control; back and forth they go until finally, they create an intricate and whimsical fugue together. The fugue concludes with the same sort of fanfare that concluded the introduction. [**Musical selection**: Beethoven, Symphony No. 3 in E-flat Major, op. 55, movement 4.]

Two more variations of the master theme follow, which is followed by a lengthy coda that we will join at its midpoint.

Our excerpt will start with the same dramatic, downward rushing strings that began the movement, though this time they precede a truly thrilling series of musical events: a version of the master theme heard in the horns, followed by what is among the longest and most exciting final cadences in the symphonic repertoire. Like ending a novel with three pages of exclamation marks, Beethoven concludes the *Eroica* at a pitch so fevered that if your pulse doesn't race you've got metabolic issues far beyond pharmaceutical intervention! [**Musical selection**: Beethoven, Symphony No. 3 in E-flat Major, op. 55, movement 4.]

The debate continues: Does this comic fourth movement "belong" in a symphony entitled "The Heroic"? I offer these observations in conclusion.

The "*Eroica*" is an experimental art work. In its fourth and final movement, Beethoven was attempting to do the impossible: to reconcile the classical tradition of playful, "upbeat" finales with the revolutionary, heroic expressive content of the other three movements. No, it doesn't quite work, and you know what, that's OK. Soon enough, Beethoven would come to conceive his finales not just as "closers" but as intensifications of everything that came before them, thus imbuing them with the same degree of dramatic thrust and import as his first movements.

But everything in time; Vienna was not built in a day. The key point is that in the "*Eroica*" Beethoven made the epic leap towards conceiving his music as self-expression, a conception that changed the substance and spirit of Western music—taken as widely as we please—forever.

Thank you.

Beethoven—Piano Concerto No. 4
Lecture 9

Between 1803 and 1812—that is, in the nine years after his reinvention—Beethoven composed six symphonies: nos. 3, 4, 5, 6, 7, and 8. During that same period, he composed three solo concerti: his piano concerti nos. 4 and 5 and the Violin Concerto in D Major. In his fourth and fifth piano concerti, Beethoven pushes the dramatic importance and virtuosic envelope of the solo piano to the point that it becomes, virtually, a second orchestra.

Beethoven was born in the German city of Bonn on December 16, 1770. He grew up hard and fast, a lonely and abused child for whom music was his solace. It was also his ticket out of Bonn and into the Habsburg capital of Vienna, where he settled in late November or early December of 1792, almost exactly a year after Mozart's death. Beethoven became a source of endless fascination for the local sophisticates, who encouraged his predisposition toward experimentation and novelty. That Beethoven did not have to spend time early in his career composing in a popular style gave him a degree of artistic freedom that few composers of his time ever enjoyed.

Piano Concerto No. 4 in G Major

Beethoven reinvented himself musically in the autumn of 1803 in response to his progressive hearing disability. Pressed to the edge of suicide, he had recast himself as a hero battling fate. The notion of such middle-class heroism was rife in Napoleonic Europe after the French Revolution, and Beethoven took advantage of this. He was a revolutionary man living during a revolutionary time, and he believed that his music was part of that revolution. Beethoven came to treat the compositional rituals, forms, and even genres of classicism contextually, using them only to serve his expressive needs—at which point he'd compose freely. A perfect example is the opening of Beethoven's Piano Concerto no. 4 of 1806.

Movement 1

The first movement is set in a musical form called double exposition form, which is sonata form adapted to the particular needs of a concerto. In performance, the sonata form expositions are typically repeated verbatim, so that listeners can absorb the contrasting themes and their key areas. In double exposition form, however, the exposition is not repeated; rather, there are two separately composed expositions. In the first exposition, called the orchestral exposition, the orchestra plays the themes. In the second, called the solo exposition, the soloist plays the themes.

Going against all convention, the piano begins the concerto by itself. It plays a hushed, chorale-like version of theme 1 that establishes the tonic key of G major and a mood both haunting and lyric. The orchestra responds with a similar phrase, but one that begins in the distant key of B major. The dramatic impact of this harmonic leap is subtle but very powerful. In this brief and gentle opening, Beethoven has reconciled the piano and the orchestra to each other not just as soloist and ensemble, but as equals.

Established as an equal partner to the orchestra, the solo piano steps back and lets the orchestra proceed with the orchestral exposition. Back in the home key of G major, the orchestra expands upon theme 1, building to a powerful climax. Theme 2 begins, without a transition, in the dark key of A minor but ends the theme back in the tonic key of G major. A royal and triumphant cadence theme follows, fading away with a series of rustling, downward **scales**.

In a traditional double exposition form movement, this is the point at which we'd anticipate the entrance of the soloist and the advent of the solo exposition. However, in this movement, the solo piano already appeared in the beginning of the orchestral exposition, so it makes sense that it will also conclude the exposition. Winds and violins echo between them the three repeated notes that initiated theme 1. The solo piano then enters with these same repeated notes and brings this orchestral exposition to its conclusion, seamlessly transitioning to the series of flourishes, scales, and trills that begin the solo exposition.

The solo exposition is double the length of the orchestral exposition, not just because of its extended and virtuosic piano episodes, but also because Beethoven introduces a third theme in the key of D major. In the solo exposition, themes 1, 2, and 3 are shared: Each theme is played first by the orchestra and embellished by the piano. Likewise, the cadence theme is shared: It is initially played by the orchestra and embellished by the piano, and then played by the orchestra alone. Together, these themes—and the various permutations Beethoven will derive from them—combine to create one of the most melodically varied movements Beethoven ever composed.

Beethoven reinvented himself musically in the autumn of 1803 in response to his progressive hearing disability.

The remaining formal landmarks of this first movement are the beginning of the development section and the beginning of the recapitulation. The development section begins with a lengthy and increasingly dramatic episode based on material the piano played at the conclusion of the orchestral exposition. The recapitulation begins with another shared version of theme 1. This time, the chorale-like opening of theme 1 is grandly played by the piano, after which the orchestra plays the theme supported by a brilliant, filigreed accompaniment in the piano.

Movement 2
The second movement is scored for solo piano and strings only. This movement is often referred to as "the lyre of Orpheus" because of the way the piano calms and eventually tames the wild beast that is the string section. In the opening of the movement, the growling and gnashing strings, playing in orchestral unison, are first confronted by the lyre of Orpheus as portrayed by the piano. As the movement unfolds, the dialogue between two completely different chunks of music—between the ferocious strings and the lyric piano—becomes increasingly intense, until the string ensemble is finally captivated and subdued. Thus, the ancient vision of music as having the power to enlighten—as personified by Orpheus—becomes a symbol of the power of the individual (Beethoven) to enlighten and tame the collective.

Movement 3

The third movement, the finale cast in rondo form, begins without a pause. For the first time in the concerto, we hear the entire orchestra as the trumpets and drums finally enter, giving this movement a glitz and festive edge new to the concerto. Nevertheless, thanks to its fabulous melodic substance and variety, its rhythmic energy and sharp-edged brilliance, and the collaboration between equals that marks the relationship between the solo piano and the orchestra, this third movement perfectly complements the first movement.

The rondo theme is set in four phrases: a, a^1, b, a^2. Phrase a is played quietly by the strings. In the spirit of sharing, the solo piano plays phrase a^1: a slightly embellished version of the opening phrase, intimately accompanied by a single 'cello. A slightly contrasting phrase b is evenly split between the strings and the piano. The fourth and final phrase of the rondo theme, a^2, is played by all instruments—the trumpets and drums make their first appearance in the concerto.

The first contrasting episode begins energetically, but soon transits to a radiant theme we will refer to as theme B. The coda that concludes the movement features a mix of everything: the rondo theme, theme B, transitional music, and so forth. The cadenza occurs about halfway through the coda. Soon after the cadenza concludes, the tempo picks up, and the rondo theme returns and careens forward to the conclusion of the concerto. Beethoven's Piano Concerto no. 4 is brilliant at every level: in its thematic content, in its pianistic virtuosity, and in particular, in the revolutionary manner by which Beethoven treats the piano and the orchestra as musical and expressive equals.

With the composer at the piano, Beethoven's Piano Concerto no. 4 received its premiere during the single most famous concert in the history of Western music: the "marathon concert" of December 22, 1808. The concerto has been a mainstay of the repertoire since that evening, although Beethoven himself never played it again. Nobody present that night—including Beethoven himself—could have guessed that because of his deteriorating hearing, this performance would mark his last as a soloist in a concerto. ∎

scale: All the pitches inside a given octave, arranged stepwise so that there is no duplication. The names of the chords built on the scale steps are: tonic, supertonic, mediant, subdominant, dominant, sub-mediant, and leading tone.

Beethoven—Piano Concerto No. 4
Lecture 9—Transcript

We return to *The 30 Greatest Orchestral Works*. This is Lecture 9, and it is entitled "Beethoven—Piano Concerto No. 4."

Beethoven the Pianist

From the moment he arrived in Vienna in late November or early December of 1792, the nearly 22-year-old Beethoven put the piano-crazed Viennese on their ears. Beethoven, whose first paying job back in his hometown of Bonn was as an organist, spent much of his life trying to wrest from the lightweight Viennese pianos of his time the same degree of power, sonority, and orchestral range of color that he got from a pipe organ. Well, the poor little Viennese pianos didn't stand a chance with Beethoven.

Beethoven's friend, Anton Reicha, related that one evening, when Beethoven was playing a Mozart concerto at court:

> He [Beethoven] asked me to turn pages for him. But I was mostly occupied in wrenching the strings of the pianoforte which snapped, while the hammers stuck among the broken strings. Beethoven insisted on finishing the concerto, and so back and forth I leaped, jerking out a string, disentangling a hammer, turning a page. I worked [much] harder than Beethoven.

Beethoven's tendency to destroy pianos might have been good theater, but it did not endear him to everyone, particularly, piano builders. In his essay "Brief Remarks on the Playing, Tuning, and Maintenance of the Fortepiano," the Viennese piano builder Andreas Streicher—undoubtedly referring to Beethoven—discussed a "nameless" pianist as being:

> Unworthy of imitation. A player, of whom it is said "he plays extraordinarily, like you have never heard before," sits down (or rather throws himself) at the fortepiano. Already the first chords will have been played with such violence that you wonder whether the player is deaf. … He … treats his instrument like a man who,

bent on revenge, has his archenemy in his hands and wants to torture him slowly to death ... He pounds so much that suddenly the maltreated strings go out of tune; several fly towards bystanders who hurriedly move back in order to protect their eyes. He makes only harsh sounds, and we hear only a disgusting mixture of tones. Is this description exaggerated? Certainly not!

Streicher wasn't the only one of Beethoven's contemporaries who criticized his playing. In 1805, the pianist and composer Camille Pleyel wrote: "[Beethoven] has ... flare, but no schooling and his execution is not polished ... He pounds a bit too much. He manages diabolical difficulties, but he does not play them precisely."

Muzio Clementi, himself one of the great pianists of his generation, commented that, "[Beethoven's] playing was not polished and was frequently impetuous, like [the man] himself."

Beethoven's pianistic critics were versed in what we might call the "Mozart" school of piano playing, a type of pianism defined by the physical limitations of contemporary pianos. For them, Beethoven's lack of what they considered "proper pianistic schooling," his body language at the piano, his occasional lack of precision, and his endemic disrespect for the instruments he played were fatal flaws in his musicianship.

However, some very influential Viennese aristocrats were fascinated by Beethoven the pianist and Beethoven the composer. Wealthy musical connoisseurs like Baron Gottfried von Swieten and Prince Karl Lichnowsky—who had a taste for difficult, serious music—actually encouraged Beethoven's predisposition towards experimentation and novelty. Lucky Beethoven: Thanks to his aristocratic patrons, he never had to curry the favor of musical "conservatives" or, for that matter, the general musical public.

That Beethoven did not have to spend time early in his career composing in a popular style gave him a degree of artistic freedom that few composers of his time ever enjoyed. Professor Timothy Jones of the University of Exeter explains further:

[Beethoven's] career as a pianist-composer was not typical. His financial security was guaranteed by a small but powerful group of Viennese aristocratic sponsors, and this protected him from the mass-market forces that weighed heavily upon his rivals. He was the only major keyboard player of his time never to set foot in Paris or London, [and he] rarely played in large, public spaces. His performances were largely confined to Vienna's most elite aristocratic salons where, since the death of Mozart in 1791, the select audiences had become increasingly receptive to high musical seriousness [that was at odds with most widespread popular tastes]. [Beethoven's patrons] encouraged him to pursue his already marked bent towards novel, difficult, and more densely argued-music. ... Free from the need to be a popular composer, he could afford to [reject] middlebrow ... values in his performances and compositions.

Beethoven quickly came to be considered a pianist and a composer for the connoisseur, an "acquired taste," a "musician's musician." His patrons gave him tremendous freedom to "be himself" and to therefore develop on a path of his own making. And this he did.

Beethoven's Attitude

Beethoven was born in the German city of Bonn on December 16, 1770. He grew up hard and fast, a lonely and abused child for whom music was his solace. It was also his ticket out of Bonn and into the Habsburg capitol of Vienna, where he settled in late November or early December of 1792, almost exactly a year after Mozart's death. Beethoven became a source of endless fascination for the local sophisticates. Writes Dieter Hildebrandt:

In Vienna, Beethoven ... established his fame and his notoriety with three strokes of genius: his impetuous virtuosity at the keyboard, his unprecedented talent for improvisation, and his rudeness, which must have reminded civilized Vienna of that archetypal character of the 18th century novel, the noble savage.

In 1811, when Beethoven was in his 41st year, his friend and fellow composer Franz Xaver Schnyder von Wartensee wrote to the publisher Hans Nageli that:

> [While] great thoughts drift through Beethoven's mind, he cannot express them in any form but music; he has no command over words. His whole education has been neglected and, apart from his art, he is coarse, but honest and unaffected; he says quite bluntly whatever he may be thinking.

The Beethoven von Wartensee described in 1811 was not just a "noble savage" but a very alienated man, a man who had been withdrawing from the world for a decade due to his increasingly bad hearing.

Beethoven reinvented himself musically in the autumn of 1803 in response to his progressive hearing disability. Pressed to the edge of suicide, he had recast himself as a "hero" battling "fate" itself. The notion of such middle-class heroism was rife in post-French Revolutionary, Napoleonic Europe and Beethoven ran with it for all he was worth.

Beethoven was a revolutionary man living at a revolutionary time. And he came to believe completely that his music was part of that revolution. It is this revolutionary spirit that the philosopher Theodor Adorno addressed when he wrote that:

> If [Beethoven the man] is already the musical prototype of the revolutionary bourgeoisie, he is also the prototype of a music that has thrown off its social obligations, a fully autonomous aesthetic, no longer in service of anyone [but the composer himself].

All of Beethoven's many compositional innovations can be boiled down to one, titanic, Enlightenment-inspired, hearing disability-triggered belief: that his music must be, first and always, a mode of self-expression, what Adorno refers to as "a fully autonomous aesthetic, no longer in service of anyone" but the composer himself.

What this means in real musical terms is that Beethoven came to treat the compositional rituals, forms, and even genres of classicism contextually, meaning that he used them only up to the point that they served his expressive needs. At which point he'd do whatever he pleased.

A perfect case in point is the opening of Beethoven's Piano Concerto No. 4 of 1806.

Piano Concerto No. 4 in G Major, Op. 58 (1806)

Movement 1: Double Exposition Form

A well-nigh invariable ritual of the concerto as Beethoven inherited it was its first movement musical form, a musical form called double exposition form. Double exposition form is sonata form adapted to the particular needs of a concerto.

A typical sonata form movement features four main sections of music: an exposition, a development section, a recapitulation, and a coda. It is in the sonata form exposition that the principal themes are introduced. In performance, sonata expositions are typically repeated verbatim, the better for us to get the contrasting themes and their key areas deeply in our ears. The biggest difference between sonata form and double exposition form is that in double exposition form, the exposition is not repeated, but rather, there are two separately composed expositions (thus, the name "double exposition form"). The first exposition, called the "orchestral exposition" sees the orchestra play the themes. The second, called the "solo exposition," sees the soloist play the themes.

This ritual has a distinctly operatic feel to it, which should come as no surprise given that the instrumental genre of concerto grew out of operatic practice. In the opera house, an instrumental overture almost always precedes and builds anticipation for the entrance of the soloists, the actual "characters": the individual singers themselves.

As Charles Rosen points out in his indispensable book, *The Classical Style*: "The most important fact about [double exposition form] is that the audience waits for the soloist to enter." Well, not in Beethoven's Piano Concerto no. 4! Going against all convention, the piano begins the concerto all by itself. It plays a hushed, chorale-like version of theme 1 that establishes the tonic key of G Major and a mood both haunting and lyric. [**Musical selection**: Beethoven, Piano Concerto No. 4 in G Major, op. 58, movement 1, orchestral exposition, theme 1.]

The orchestra responds with a like phrase, but one that begins in the distant key of B major. The dramatic impact of this harmonic leap is subtle but very powerful. The piano and orchestra are acknowledging right here, right at the very beginning of the concerto, that they will share as equals the thematic material. From the beginning: we hear the piano entry in G major followed by the orchestra's entry, initially in the key of B major. [**Musical selection**: Beethoven, Piano Concerto No. 4 in G Major, op. 58, movement one, orchestral exposition, theme 1.] In this brief and gentle opening, Beethoven has accomplished something earth shattering: He has reconciled the piano and the orchestra to each other not just as "soloist" and "ensemble" but as equals. And equals they will remain, through the remainder of the concerto!

The "Symphonic" Concerto

Between 1803 and 1812—that is, in the nine years after his "re-invention of self"—Beethoven composed six symphonies: nos. 3, 4, 5, 6, 7, and 8. During that same period he composed three solo concerti: his piano concerti Nos. 4 and 5 and the Violin Concerto in D Major. Beethoven scholar Walter Riezler observes: "With these three works Beethoven created a new [genre]: that of the symphonic concerto—a [genre] later employed by Schumann and Brahms." My friends, such a "symphonic concerto" is one in which a full symphony orchestra is used to full symphonic effect and not merely as an accompaniment to the soloist.

In his Fourth and Fifth Piano Concerti, Beethoven pushes the dramatic importance and virtuosic envelope of the piano to the point that it becomes, virtually, a second orchestra. A reminder: the pianos Beethoven played at the time he composed these concerti were only slightly bigger than those played by Mozart 20 years before, Mozart understood the pianos of his time for what they were: light, not particularly resonant instruments that could not compete on equal terms with a full orchestral complement. Conversely, Beethoven perceived the piano not as it was but rather, as he wanted it to be: a big, resonant instrument with the dynamic power and tonal range of an organ. Like the guy who drives his family's mini-van like the race car it is not, so Beethoven pushed his pianos to the breaking point and then beyond, as we have already observed.

Back to Beethoven's Piano Concerto No. 4, Movement 1

Having established itself as an equal partner to the orchestra and having informed us, the audience, that it will come and go as it pleases, the solo piano steps back and lets the orchestra proceed with the orchestral exposition. Back in the home key of G Major, the orchestra expands upon theme 1, building to a powerful climax. Theme 1: [**Musical selection**: Beethoven, Piano Concerto No. 4 in G Major, op. 58, movement 1.]

Theme 2 begins without a transition. It starts in the rather dark key of A minor, but by theme's end the key has moved back to where tradition says it ought to be: that is, in the tonic key, in the key of G major. Let's hear it, theme 2. [**Musical selection**: Beethoven, Piano Concerto No. 4 in G Major, op. 58, movement 1.] A royal and triumphant cadence theme follows, fading away with a series of rustling, downwards scales. [**Musical selection**: Beethoven, Piano Concerto No. 4 in G Major, op. 58, movement 1.]

The orchestral exposition is almost over. In a traditional double exposition form movement, this is the point at which we'd begin to anticipate the entrance of the soloist and the advent of the solo exposition. Except! Except that in this movement, the soloist has already appeared, having played theme 1 all by itself at the beginning of the orchestral exposition.

Thus it is most appropriate that the solo piano should also bring the orchestral exposition to its conclusion, and that is precisely what happens. Winds and violins echo between them the three repeated notes that initiate theme 1. The solo piano then enters with these same theme 1-derived repeated notes and brings this orchestral exposition to its conclusion, before seamlessly transitioning to the series of flourishes, scales, and trills that begin the solo exposition. [**Musical selection**: Beethoven, Piano Concerto No. 4 in G Major, op. 58, movement 1.]

The appearance of the solo piano at the beginning and conclusion of the orchestral exposition integrates piano and orchestra in a manner that changes, entirely, the roles and rituals usually observed between the soloist and the ensemble in a concerto.

Here in Beethoven's Piano Concerto No. 4, the solo piano is a free spirit that will be neither constrained nor controlled by the dictates of tradition. Given that Beethoven composed this concerto as a performance vehicle for himself, we would not be off base if we interpreted the freedoms exhibited by solo piano part as a metaphor for the artistic freedom Beethoven demanded for himself. When we talk about Beethoven's contextual use of form—about his willingness to adhere to traditional musical forms and rituals only to the point that they serve his expressive needs—this is exactly what we're talking about.

Just as Beethoven famously shrieked at the violinist Ignaz Schuppanzigh, "Do you really believe I think about your miserable fiddle when the muse strikes me?!" So he might just as easily shout at the so-called "classical style," "Do you really believe I think about your miserable rituals when the muse strikes me?!"

The Solo Exposition

The solo exposition is double the length of the orchestral exposition, not just because of its extended and virtuosic piano episodes, but also because Beethoven introduces a new theme, a third theme, in the key of D major. Let's hear the beginnings of all four themes in the order in which they appear in the solo exposition: theme 1, then theme 3, then theme 2, and finally, the cadence theme. While listening, let's be aware of the total integration of piano and orchestra, meaning the collaborative manner by which piano and orchestra share the themes. In the solo exposition, theme 1 is shared: It is played first by the orchestra and then embellished by the piano. [**Musical selection**: Beethoven, Piano Concerto No. 4 in G Major, op. 58, movement 1.] The "new" theme 3 is likewise shared; the orchestra plays it first and then the piano embellishes it. [**Musical selection**: Beethoven, Piano Concerto No. 4 in G Major, op. 58, movement 1.] In the solo exposition, theme 2 is also "shared," played first by the orchestra and then again embellished by the piano. [**Musical selection**: Beethoven, Piano Concerto No. 4 in G Major, op. 58, movement 1.]

Collaboration is the name of the game. In this solo exposition the cadence theme is also shared. It is initially played by the orchestra and embellished by the piano, and then played by the orchestra alone. [**Musical selection**: Beethoven, Piano Concerto No. 4 in G Major, op. 58, movement 1.] Taken together, these themes represent an incredibly rich thematic palette for Beethoven, who not infrequently will construct an entire movement using only one or two melodic ideas. Taken together, this multitude of themes—and the various permutations Beethoven will derive from them—combine to create one of the most melodically varied movements Beethoven ever composed.

Landmarks!

So that we might follow the large-scale structure of this first movement, let's hear the beginnings of the remaining formal landmarks: the beginning of the development section and the beginning of the recapitulation. The development section begins with a lengthy and increasingly dramatic episode based on material the piano played at the conclusion of the orchestral exposition: Here's the opening of the development section. [**Musical selection**: Beethoven, Piano Concerto No. 4 in G Major, op. 58, movement 1.]

The recapitulation begins with another shared version of theme 1. This time, the chorale-like opening of theme 1 is grandly played by the piano, after which the orchestra plays the theme supported by a brilliant, filigreed accompaniment in the piano. [**Musical selection**: Beethoven, Piano Concerto No. 4 in G Major, op. 58, movement 1.]

Beethoven composed two cadenzas for this first movement. A cadenza is a passage played exclusively by the solo instrument in a concerto. While cadenzas are traditionally supposed to sound like improvisations based on the thematic material at hand, they are, in reality, usually carefully prepared in order to put a performer's particular technical strengths on display. In the 200-plus years since its composition, any number of top-flight pianists and composers have written cadenzas for this concerto, including Johannes Brahms, Clara Schumann, Hans von Bülow, Leopold Godowsky, Ignaz Moscheles, Camille Saint-Saens, Nikolai Medtner, Anton Rubinstein, and Ferruccio Busoni.)

Beethoven himself composed cadenzas for the concerto, including two cadenzas for the first movement: a relatively easy one, prepared for the concerto's dedicatee, the Archduke Rudolf, and an obscenely difficult, piano-busting cadenza which he wrote for himself. My friends, in my opinion, when a composer composes his own cadenzas for his own concerti, performers should bloody well play them, particularly if the composer happens to be a control-freak named Ludwig van Beethoven. For our information, in our recording, the pianist Stefan Vladar uses the cadenza Beethoven composed for Archduke Rudolf. Let's hear the opening moments of this presumably easier cadenza. [**Musical selection**: Beethoven, Piano Concerto No. 4 in G Major, op. 58, movement 1.]

Movement 2

The second movement is scored for solo piano and strings only. This movement is often referred to as "the lyre of Orpheus" because of the way the piano calms and eventually tames the wild beast that is the string section. Let's hear the opening of the movement, during which the growling and gnashing strings—playing in orchestral unison—are first confronted by the exquisitely lyric "lyre of Orpheus" as portrayed by the piano. [**Musical selection**: Beethoven, Piano Concerto No. 4 in G Major, op. 58, movement 2.]

While the designation "lyre of Orpheus" was not of Beethoven's creation, it's hard to imagine a better description of what takes place over the course of the movement. As the movement unfolds, the dialogue between two completely different chunks of music—between the ferocious strings and the lyric piano—becomes increasingly intense, until at last the string ensemble is captivated and subdued. Thus the ancient vision of music as having the power to enlighten—as personified by Orpheus himself—becomes here a symbol of the power of the individual (an individual named van Beethoven) to enlighten and tame the collective! [**Musical selection**: Beethoven, Piano Concerto No. 4 in G Major, op. 58, movement 2.]

Movement 3: Rondo

The third movement rondo finale begins without a pause. For the first time in the concerto, we get to hear the entire orchestra, as the trumpets and drums—up to this point unheard—finally enter, giving this movement a glitz and festive edge new to the concerto. Nevertheless, thanks to its fabulous melodic substance and variety, its rhythmic energy and sharp-edged brilliance, and the collaboration between equals that marks the relationship between the solo piano and the orchestra, this third movement complements perfectly for the first movement.

Let's begin by hearing the rondo theme, which is set in four phrases that can schematicized as a, a^1, b, and a^2. Phrase a of the rondo theme is played quietly by the strings. [**Musical selection**: Beethoven, Piano Concerto No. 4 in G Major, op. 58, movement 3.] In the spirit of sharing, the solo piano plays phrase a^1: a slightly embellished version of the opening phrase, intimately accompanied by a single 'cello. [**Musical selection**: Beethoven, Piano Concerto No. 4 in G Major, op. 58, movement 3.]

A slightly contrasting phrase—b—is evenly split between the strings and the piano. [**Musical selection**: Beethoven, Piano Concerto No. 4 in G Major, op. 58, movement 3.] The fourth and final phrase of the rondo theme—a^2—is played by everybody as the trumpets and drums make their first appearance in the concerto. [**Musical selection**: Beethoven, Piano Concerto No. 4 in G Major, op. 58, movement 3.] From the beginning: Let's hear the rondo theme in its entirety. [**Musical selection**: Beethoven, Piano Concerto No. 4 in G Major, op. 58, movement 3.] A schematic layout of this entire movement would read: A (meaning the rondo theme)—B (first contrasting episode)—A (rondo theme returns)—C (basically a development section), B, A, and coda. The first contrasting episode begins energetically, but soon transits to a radiant theme we will refer to as theme B. Let's hear this theme B. [**Musical selection**: Beethoven, Piano Concerto No. 4 in G Major, op. 58, movement 3.]

167

The coda that concludes the movement features a bit of everything: the rondo theme, theme B, transitional music, and so forth. We're going to cut directly to the cadenza, which occurs about halfway through the coda. It is Beethoven's own cadenza, and I, for one, have never heard a performance of this third movement that didn't use it. Soon after the cadenza concludes, the tempo picks up, the rondo theme returns once more and like a runaway tractor-trailer on a 10 percent grade it careens forward to the conclusion of the concerto. We listen from the beginning of the cadenza to the end of the movement. [**Musical selection**: Beethoven, Piano Concerto No. 4 in G Major, op. 58, movement 3.] Beethoven's Piano Concerto No. 4 is brilliant at every level: in its thematic content, in its pianistic virtuosity and, in particular, in the revolutionary manner by which Beethoven treats the piano and the orchestra as musical and expressive equals.

The Premiere

With the composer at the piano, Beethoven's Piano Concerto No. 4 received its premiere during the single most famous concert in the history of Western music: the "marathon concert" of December 22, 1808. It was a concert that also saw the premiers of Beethoven's Fifth Symphony, Beethoven's Sixth Symphony, the Chorale Fantasy op. 80 for orchestra, chorus, and piano; the Vienna premiere of three movements from Beethoven's Mass in C Major, a concert aria entitled *Ah!, perfido,* and a lengthy improvisation by Beethoven. The concert went on for four hours in the freezing cold *Theater an der Wien*, where the heating system was on der fritz. Though the audience and the performers were half-paralyzed with cold, Beethoven insisted on going through with the entire concert.

The German composer and music journalist Joseph Friedrich Reichardt sat with Beethoven's patron Prince Franz Joseph von Lobkowitz in the prince's box. According to Reichardt: "[Our] patience was sorely tested by [the] many failures in performance." Yes, by all the mistakes they heard that frigid night. Nevertheless, the premiere of the Fourth Piano Concerto went quite well, a work Reichardt described as "a new forte-piano concerto of monstrous difficulty, which Beethoven played astonishingly well at the fastest possible tempos."

The concerto has been a mainstay of the repertoire since that evening, although Beethoven himself never played it again. We doubt that anyone present that night—including Beethoven himself—could have guessed that because of his deteriorating hearing, this performance would mark his last as a soloist in a concerto.

Thank you.

Beethoven—Symphony No. 9
Lecture 10

Beethoven's Symphony no. 9 was the most influential and important piece of music composed during the first half of the 19th century. By 1824, Beethoven had established his unassailable place in European music. His Ninth Symphony proved to the following generations of composers that something as basic as genre is contextual: The expressive needs of the artist must take precedence over any convention—no matter how sacred, time honored, or popular that convention may be.

Beethoven's Symphony no. 3 is generally acknowledged as his heroic breakaway piece, and each symphony that followed was unique, culminating in the still spine-tingling Symphony no. 9 of 1824. Somehow, Beethoven managed to once again reinvent himself compositionally after having reinvented himself through the composition of his Third Symphony. His experiences of 1815–1820—a custody battle over his nephew and the deterioration of his hearing to the point that he was deemed clinically deaf—forced Beethoven to acknowledge many of his deepest fears and desires, allowing his creativity and imagination to soar to unimagined places and to compose a series of works that redefined their genres.

Symphony No. 9 in D Minor

Beethoven's Ninth Symphony is an epic vision of struggle crowned by utopian triumph. Movements 1 and 2 deal with musical and expressive extremes, which we will interpret as the struggles of the present. These struggles are resolved in the song-like third movement. The fourth movement (which constitutes the second half of the symphony) describes a transcendent utopian vision of the future.

Movement 1

The first movement is about polar opposites and confrontations, a titanic struggle against the dark side of death and oblivion—as represented by the key of D minor. In this movement, the dark side is victorious; it ends with a funeral march in D minor. The monumental introduction of this symphony has no parallel in Beethoven's earlier symphonies. The Ninth Symphony emerges with a quietly throbbing open fifth A–E in the horns and strings.

There's no middle pitch—either a C-sharp or C-natural—that would tell us whether we're in major or minor, or even what key we're in. Falling As and Es in short-long rhythms appear increasingly quickly as more instruments enter. Finally, a sudden move to another open fifth (D–A) signals an impending change.

This principal theme of the movement is a ferocious thing of terrifying power, a compressed version of the falling notes and the short-long rhythms of the introduction. Most importantly, the theme outlines a complete triad, which finally signals that we are in the key of D minor. The first phrase of the theme represents a fearsome, expressive place. The next phrase is one of violent extremes; it alternates barking brass fanfares with pathetic, forlorn winds until—after a series of dissonant, off-beat chords—the theme collapses in on itself with a vicious downward swirl.

This opening version of theme 1—set in D minor—represents one expressive extreme: the dark side as represented by D minor. The primeval open fifth of the introduction resumes, now outlining a D–A. This reintroduction continues as did the original, but when theme 1 appears this time, it is not heard in minor but in major—in the key of B-flat major, in which the formerly tragic theme becomes heroic and magnificent. This is the other expressive polarity of the movement. The first movement is, therefore, about the struggle between the tragic and the heroic that is projected not so much via contrasting themes as by presenting the same themes in contrasting keys. This first movement ends in darkness, but the symphony's chief combatants—D major and D minor, metaphors for heroic triumph versus death and oblivion—will compete in the second movement.

Movement 2

The second movement begins in almost exactly the same manner in which the first movement ends. Movement 1 ends with one last loud playing of theme 1 that spells out a descending D minor harmony in short-long rhythms. Movement 2 begins in the same way but in long-short rhythms. This second movement is a scherzo, which was Beethoven's answer to traditional minuet and trio form. Like a classical-era minuet and trio form movement, a Beethoven scherzo is typically cast in three-part, A–B–A form. However, Beethoven's scherzi tend to be fast in tempo and do not adhere to the ritual phrase structure and repetitions.

It is in the second movement scherzo that the dramatic weight of the symphony shifts from the dark side toward the light, from D minor to D major. Beethoven achieves this shift two ways: by setting the middle B section and the coda of this second movement in D major, and by infusing the entire movement with a physical energy that blows away the deathly pall that concluded the first movement.

The scherzo section begins with a bouncing, fugue-like passage that, despite beginning in D minor, is filled with the life-affirming spirit of dance. This is music in expressive transition, animated by the physicality of dance. The B section that follows marks another step on the expressive journey. It is music unlike anything we have heard in the symphony: light, airy, rustic, charming, and set entirely in the key of D major. This second movement ends abruptly but joyfully and becomes the expressive fulcrum of the symphony: a movement that began on the dark side in D minor and concludes in the light of D major.

Movement 3
The third movement is gloriously beautiful. It shifts the expressive focus of the symphony from the visceral to the ethereal—from the personal to the universal—and paves the way for the statement of universal personhood that is the message of the fourth and final movement.

Movement 4
Beethoven's Ninth Symphony is truly universal music—music that inspires spiritual exaltation regardless of the nationality or religious affiliation of its listeners. In the fourth movement, that spiritual universality is explicitly evoked with its Enlightenment-inspired paean to collective personhood and democratic ideals. It is a paean that was premiered at a time (1824) when those ideals had largely been snuffed out by post-Napoleonic European governments. It is a paean that was premiered in a place where espousing such ideals could have been considered criminally subversive.

The final movement of Beethoven's Ninth Symphony is a vocal setting of Friedrich Schiller's poem "*Lied an die Freude*" ("Ode to Joy"). Beethoven spent a tremendous amount of creative energy trying to figure out how to incorporate human voices into the symphony, and his solution is brilliant. He begins the movement with what amounts to an overture for orchestra alone, during which the orchestra performs the same vocally conceived music the singers will sing when they make their entrance later in the movement. As a result, when the voices enter, it will sound as if they've been singing all along. A series of increasingly energized and joyful variations follow, as more instruments join in playing a new theme, a metaphor for an ever-growing number of people triumphantly embracing the enlightened message of the new theme.

Beethoven's Ninth Symphony is an epic vision of struggle crowned by utopian triumph.

Movement 4, Act I

In what we will refer to as act I of this fourth movement, the violent, dissonant, chaotic music of the movement's opening suddenly and brutally returns and, along with it, the key of D minor. The hero enters and rejects this orchestral chaos, just as he has rejected the efforts of the orchestra in all three previous movements. This time, however, the hero is a baritone singer who belts out in **recitative**.

A four-measure wind introduction punctuated with shouts of "Joy" from the chorus leads to verse 1 of Schiller's "Ode," with the hero in the lead. All at once, the implicit becomes explicit; "all men shall be brothers" is the meaning of the new theme—the "Ode to Joy" theme. By using voices to make his meaning explicit, Beethoven forever shattered the concept of the symphony as a purely instrumental genre. All at once, instrumental music and vocal music were fused in a manner entirely new, demonstrating unequivocally that a composer's expressive needs trump everything—including genre.

Movement 4, Act II

Act I of this fourth movement is about the promise of the Enlightenment. We discover that act II is about the victory of the Enlightenment and the triumph of the "Ode to Joy" because Beethoven turns the "Ode to Joy" theme into a triumphal march. From the distance we hear the "army of freedom" approach in a bass drum (the only appearance of a bass drum in any of Beethoven's symphonies) and bassoons. Having arrived before us, the army of freedom performs the "Ode to Joy" theme as a marching band tune (without strings)—a declaration of victory.

Movement 4, Acts III and IV

Act III is about thanksgiving and heavenly devotion. Finally, act IV is an extended celebration of light, life, and love that concludes the movement and the symphony. ■

Important Term

recitative: Operatic convention in which the lines are half sung, half spoken.

Beethoven—Symphony No. 9

Lecture 10—Transcript

We return to *The 30 Greatest Orchestral Works*. This is Lecture 10, and it is entitled "Beethoven—Symphony No. 9."

In early 1824, Beethoven received a letter signed by 30 of Vienna's leading musicians, publishers, and music connoisseurs. The word was out that Beethoven was about to complete a Ninth Symphony, and that it was going to receive its premiere in Berlin. The prospect of a Berlin premiere put the Viennese musical establishment into an absolute tizzy, and thus the letter to Beethoven was intended to convince him to stage the premiere in Vienna. It's a long letter; we read it in brief in part.

> Out of the wide circle of reverent admirers surrounding your genius in this, your second native city, there approach you today a small number of lovers of art to give expression to long-felt wishes, timidly to impart a long-withheld entreaty. …
>
> Do not withhold any longer from enjoyment, do not keep any longer from us that which is great and perfect: a performance of the latest masterwork of your hand. We know that a new flower grows in the garland of your glorious, unrivaled symphonies. For years, we have waited and hoped to see you distribute new gifts from the abundance of your wealth to the circle of your friends. Do not disappoint the general expectations any longer!

Beethoven was moved by the letter, reportedly saying, "It is very beautiful. It [pleases] me greatly!" The letter did the hoped-for trick: a date and Viennese location were set for the premiere of Beethoven's Symphony No. 9. The date: Friday, May 7, 1824. The time: 7 pm. The place: Vienna's Kärntnertor Theater, one of Vienna's two official court theaters. Built in 1741 and sadly demolished in 1868, it had an elegant, horseshoe shaped interior with five tiers of balconies. It was located on the *Kärntnerstraße* next to the old city wall and near the Carinthia Gate (which is what "Kärntner Tor" means), roughly on the spot occupied today by the Hotel Sacher, just behind the Opera House.

The performers: an orchestra of 82 players, of whom 44 were members of the Orchestra of the Kärntnertor Theater, and 38 amateurs and professional volunteers; and a chorus of between 80 and 90 singers, most of whom were members of the Kärntnertor Theater choir. There were also four vocal soloists: a soprano, contralto, tenor, and bass. The conductor was the 43-year-old violinist and composer Michael Umlauf, one of the six royal Kapellmeisters for the Imperial Court Theaters.

The all-Beethoven program featured *Consecration of the House* Overture; Kyrie, Credo, and Agnus Dei from the *Missa Solemnis*; and the premiere of Symphonie No. 9 in D Minor.

The buzz: The concert was the most anticipated "academy" (which is what public concerts were called at the time) in many years. The Viennese listening public was well aware that Beethoven's new symphony called for gargantuan performing forces; that at roughly 75 minutes in length, the symphony was three times as long as most other symphonies; that its final movement was a vocal setting of Friedrich Schiller's poem *Lied an die Freude* (which means song or ode to joy) and thus, heretically, the symphony called for voices as well as an orchestra! [**Musical selection**: Beethoven, Symphony No. 9, movement 4.]

Voices in a Symphony: Putting This in Context

We search, my friends, for like "heretical" musical parallels in our culture: the Mormon Tabernacle Choir singing a medley of greatest gangsta rap hits or Ozzy Ozbourne as Professor Harold Hill and Courtney Love as Marian the librarian in a remake of *The Music Man.* Voices in a symphony?! Hey, just why and where Beethoven got off doing such a thing is something we will discuss in due time. Some preliminaries first.

Biographical Background: Reinventions

Beethoven was born on December 16, 1770, in the German city of Bonn. Physically and emotionally abused by his alcoholic father, Beethoven grew up a lonely, angry survivor for whom music was a source of strength, solace, and even spiritual salvation.

Beethoven's mother died during the summer of 1787. By necessity, the 16 ½-year-old Beethoven became head of his household: its chief bread-earner and guardian of his two younger brothers and his increasingly narcotized father. His mother's death and his subsequent responsibilities were a crushing weight for a 16-year-old to bear, and bear it Beethoven did. But at a price: Beethoven—who had made great strides as a composer in his early teens—stopped composing entirely. Perhaps he had no time for it; perhaps he had no energy for it; certainly he had no spirit for it.

Reinvention No. 1

In 1789, the now 18-year-old Beethoven had had enough: He petitioned the elector to kick his father out of Bonn and to have half of his father's pension paid directly to himself and his brothers. It was, for young Ludwig, an emancipation proclamation, a demand to be freed from the burden of his father. His request was granted. Well, something clicked in Beethoven's brain, because after two years of compositional sterility, he suddenly began composing like a crazy person! Piano works, chamber works, cantatas; music flew from his pen, creating an artistic momentum that carried him to Vienna in late 1792.

In Vienna, Beethoven first rose to fame as a daring, keyboard-busting pianist whose playing captivated the piano-mad Viennese aristocracy. Soon enough, his reputation as a composer of new, really different, really modern music joined his rep as a piano player. By 1802, his compositional career was poised to go ballistic. Unfortunately, he was an emotional wreck, in despair, near suicidal.

Reinvention No. 2

Beethoven's slowly disabling hearing loss began in 1796. By the fall of 1802, Beethoven had come to realize that his progressive hearing loss was incurable. Beethoven fell into a suicidal depression. For the not-quite 32- year-old Ludwig van Beethoven, it was gut-check time, and he rallied. Somehow in the last months of 1802 and the first months of 1803, Beethoven reinvented himself once again and was spiritually and artistically reborn. Inspired by the revolutionary spirit of the time as well as the model of Napoleon Bonaparte—himself a middle class man whose success was product of his own genius—Beethoven sculpted for himself a new self-image as a hero battling and triumphing over fate itself!

Beethoven's heroic post-reinvention expressive impulse was based on a single, all-encompassing conviction: that the act of composing music was a consciously self-expressive act. Beethoven's Symphony No. 3 is generally acknowledged as his heroic break-away piece. Each of Beethoven's Symphonies that followed was unique, as Beethoven committed himself to saying something new and different in each successive work, culminating in the still spine-tingling Ninth Symphony of 1824.

Reinvention Number 3

Beethoven went through another crisis between 1815 and 1820. This one began with his fall from Viennese popularity in 1815 and continued with his ongoing attempt to literally steal his nephew Karl from Karl's mother, Beethoven's sister-in-law Johanna. The litigation over Karl went on until 1820, at which point Beethoven finally succeeded in gaining sole custody of the poor, messed-up kid. Along the way, Unkie Louis went just a little nuts: He became certifiably delusional; his nascent paranoia flowered like mold spores on six week-old cottage cheese; and his hearing deteriorated to the point that he was, finally, clinically deaf.

It remains, then, something of a miracle that Beethoven managed to once again reinvent himself compositionally in the years between 1818 and 1820. Somehow, the experiences of 1815–1820 forced Beethoven to acknowledge many of his deepest fears and desires, allowing his creativity and imagination to soar into unimagined places.

Between 1820 and late 1826, this angry, alienated, and sickly man composed a series of works that redefined their genres: his last three piano sonatas; the *Diabelli Variations* for piano; the *Missa Solemnis*; the Ninth Symphony; and his last five string quartets and the *Grosse Fugue.*

Beethoven's Symphony No. 9: The Big Story Line

Beethoven's Ninth is an epic vision of struggle crowned by utopian triumph. Movements 1 and 2 deal with musical and expressive extremes, which we will interpret as the "struggles of the present." These struggles are resolved in the song-like third movement. The fourth movement (which is, in reality, the second half of the symphony) describes a transcendent utopian vision of the future where, as the poet Schiller writes, "*Alle Menschen werden Bruder*," or "All men (all people) shall be brothers."

The principal goal of our examination of the symphony will be to observe its large-scale dramatic narrative: its story of struggle capped by triumph, expressed metaphorically in instrumental music in movements 1, 2, and 3, and then explicitly—with words and human voices—in movement 4.

Movement 1: Sonata Form

The first movement is about polar opposites and confrontations, a titanic struggle against the dark side of death and oblivion. Ultimately, here in the first movement, death and oblivion—as represented by the key of D minor—are victorious. How do we know that? We know it because the movement ends with a funeral march in D minor. [**Musical selection**: Beethoven, Symphony No. 9, movement1.]

Movement Introduction: "In the Beginning!"

Beethoven's primeval, monumental, even biblical introduction has no parallel in his earlier symphonies. The Ninth emerges from the ether—from silence—with a quietly throbbing open fifth *A*-E in the horns and strings. [**Piano demonstration**.] Are we in major or minor? We don't know, because there's no middle pitch here—either a C-sharp or C-natural—that would tell us whether we're in major or minor or even what key we're in! If we were in major it would have sounded like this. [**Piano demonstration**.] If we were in minor it would have sounded like this.[**Piano demonstration**.]

Only slowly does the cosmic machinery of the movement begin to turn. Falling *A*'s and *E*'s in short-long rhythms come more and more quickly as more and more instruments enter. [**Piano demonstration**.] Finally, a sudden move to another open fifth (*d* and *a*) signals an impending change. Let's hear this "from the void-styled" introduction. [**Musical selection**: Beethoven, Symphony no. 9, movement1.]

Theme 1 or Polarity No. 1!

This principal theme of the movement is a ferocious thing of terrifying power, a compressed version of the falling notes and the short-long rhythms of the introduction. Most importantly, the theme outlines a complete triad, and thus do we know—finally—that we are in the key of D minor. [**Musical selection**: Beethoven, Symphony No. 9, movement 1.]

That was the first phrase of the theme, and it represents a fearsome expressive place. The next phrase is one of violent extremes: It alternates barking brass fanfares with pathetic, forlorn winds until, after a series of dissonant, off-beat chords, the theme collapses in on itself with a vicious downward swirl. Let's hear the second phrase of theme 1. [**Musical selection**: Beethoven, Symphony No. 9, movement 1.] This opening version of theme 1—set in D minor—represents one expressive extreme, one polarity: the dark side as represented by the key of D minor.

What happens next is stunning and will define the struggle that characterizes the remainder of this first movement. The primeval, open fifth of the introduction resumes, now outlining a *D* and *A*. This "reintroduction" continues as did the original, although now, when theme 1 appears, it is not heard in minor but in major, in the key of B-flat major! [**Musical selection**: Beethoven, Symphony No. 9, movement 1.] Here in B-flat major, the formerly tragic theme becomes heroic and magnificent! This is the other expressive polarity of the movement, a polarity characterized here by the key of B-flat major.

This is what the first movement is all about: the struggle between the tragic and the heroic, a struggle projected not so much via contrasting themes as by presenting the same themes in contrasting keys. Another example, the massive development section concludes with a swirling, three-octave descent that drags the music downwards towards the recapitulation and presumably the tonic key of D minor. Let's hear the development section conclusion. [**Musical selection**: Beethoven, Symphony No. 9, movement 1.]

But wonder of wonders—to our everlasting shock—this descent alights and the recapitulation begins, not in D minor but in D major. [**Piano demonstration**.] The introduction now proceeds in D major!

Let's recall: When we first heard the introduction at the beginning of the movement, it outlined only an open fifth, and not a complete harmony in either major or minor. Thus, it has always been a possibility that the introductory material could be harmonized in major, although it's not something we had anticipated.

This recapitulatory version of the introduction is underlain by a teeth-rattling roll in the timpani. According to the musicologist Antony Hopkins, it is "Awe inspiring in the same way that a vision of the avenging angel would be: One's eyes would be dazzled by his radiance, even though one's heart would quake with terror."

Without a break in the drum roll, theme 1 then begins back in the key of D minor. and thus D major and D minor—which will turn out to be the great tonal protagonists of this symphony—are placed cheek by jowl. Let's hear it all: from the descent that concludes the development section, through the opening of the recapitulation, with the introduction set in D major and then theme 1 in D minor! [**Musical selection**: Beethoven, Symphony no. 9, movement 1.] As we know (because we've already heard its concluding funeral march), this first movement ends in darkness. But the symphony's chief combatants—D major and D minor, metaphors for heroic triumph versus death and oblivion—will now go toe-to-toe in the second movement.

Movement 2: Scherzo

The second movement begins in almost exactly the same way the first movement ends! Movement 1 ends with one last loud playing of theme 1, which spells out a descending D minor harmony in short-long rhythms. [**Piano demonstration**.] Movement 2 begins with a loud playing of a descending D minor harmony in long-short rhythms. [**Piano demonstration**.]

Its connection to the first movement thus established, this second movement scherzo proceeds. Scherzo was Beethoven's answer to traditional minuet and trio form. Like a traditional, classical-era minuet and trio form movement, a Beethoven scherzo is typically cast in three parts, A-B-A. However, Beethoven's scherzi tend to be fast to very fast in tempo, and bear no resemblance whatsoever to the courtly dance called the "minuet." Neither do Beethoven's scherzi follow the ritual phrase structure and repetitions that are fundamental to minuet and trio form. By calling his movements scherzi, Beethoven could do whatever he pleased without reference to the rituals of minuet and trio. As a result, Beethoven's scherzi serve the expressive context: Form follows expressive need, and not the other way around.

It is here, in the second movement scherzo, that the dramatic weight of the symphony shifts from the dark side towards the light, from D minor to D major. Beethoven achieves this shift two ways: by setting the middle B section and the coda of this second movement in D major, and by infusing the entire movement with a physical energy that blows away the deathly pall that concluded the first movement.

The scherzo section *A* begins with a bouncing, fugue-like passage that despite beginning in D minor is filled with the life-affirming spirit of dance. The disparate voices of this fugue-like passage coalesce into a raucous and most explicit dance! Taken all together, this is music in expressive transition, animated by the physicality of dance! [**Musical selection**: Beethoven, Symphony no. 9, movement 2.]

The B section, the middle section that follows, marks another step on the expressive journey. It is music the likes of which we haven't yet heard in the symphony: light, airy, rustic, charming, and set entirely in the key of D major. [**Musical selection**: Beethoven, Symphony no. 9, movement 2.]

(An awesome detail: This B section theme in D major will evolve into the fourth movement "Ode to Joy" theme, which is likewise set in D major! Here's a back-to-back. First the B section theme from movement 2: [**Piano demonstration**.] And the "Ode to Joy" theme from the fourth movement: [**Piano demonstration**.] This second movement ends—abruptly though joyfully—with a brief return to the music of the *B* section in D major. And thus this second movement becomes the expressive fulcrum of the symphony: a movement that began on the dark side in D minor concludes in the light side of D major. Here's that conclusion. [**Musical selection**: Beethoven, Symphony no. 9, movement 2.]

Movement 3

The third movement *Adagio molto e cantabile* ("slowly and very singing") is gloriously beautiful. It shifts the expressive focus of the symphony from the visceral to the ethereal; from the personal to the universal; and thus paves the way for the statement of "universal personhood" that is the message of the fourth and final movement.

Movement 4

Beethoven's Ninth is truly universal music, music that continues to inspire spiritual exaltation no matter what the nationality or religious affiliation of its listeners. It is here, in the fourth movement, that that spiritual universality is explicitly evoked, with its Enlightenment-inspired paean to collective personhood and democratic ideals. It is a paean that was premiered at a time (1824) when those ideals had largely been snuffed out by post-Napoleonic European governments. It is a paean that was premiered in a place (Metternich's Austria) where espousing such ideals could have been considered criminally subversive! It is a paean sung to words written by Friedrich von Schiller in 1803, in his poem *An die freude,* which translates song or "Ode to Joy."

"How to Do It?"

Yes, Beethoven spent a tremendous amount of creative energy trying to figure out how to incorporate human voices into the symphony, and his solution is brilliant. He begins the movement with what amounts to an overture for orchestra alone, during which the orchestra performs the same vocally-conceived music the singers will sing when they make their entrance roughly 6½ minutes into the movement. As a result, when the voices do enter it will sound as if they've been singing all along!

Let me show you what I mean. The movement begins suddenly and brutally with an incredibly dissonant harmony. [**Piano demonstration**.] Followed by a jaggedly outlined D minor harmony. We're back on the dark side, and it ain't pretty. [**Musical selection**: Beethoven, Symphony no. 9, movement 4.] This is Beethoven's evocation of the social chaos before the Enlightenment—trust me on this. The hero now enters, as portrayed by the 'cellos and basses, and attempts to calm the raging orchestra. Beethoven indicates in the score that the low string melody be played "in the character of an [operatic] recitative." [**Musical selection**: Beethoven, Symphony no. 9, movement 4.] Sadly, the hero's plea for peace falls on deaf orchestral ears. An even more furious outburst erupts from the orchestra, after which the hero again tries to calm things down. [**Musical selection**: Beethoven, Symphony no. 9, movement 4.]

"OK" says the orchestra. "We'll ixnay the chaos. Would you prefer this?" At which point the orchestra plays the introduction of movement 1, evoking— as it does—memories of struggle and death. [**Musical selection**: Beethoven, Symphony no. 9, movement 4.] The hero vehemently rejects the music of the first movement and the memory of despair associated with it. [**Musical selection**: Beethoven, Symphony no. 9, movement 4.] "OK then," says the orchestra. "How about this?" And the orchestra plays a brief bit of the second movement scherzo. Rather more gently, the hero rejects that music as well. [**Musical selection**: Beethoven, Symphony No. 9, movement 4.]

The orchestra is nothing if not game. It next offers up a brief a bit of the third movement, only to have the hero gently but firmly reject that music as well. With growing frustration, the hero—"Mr. Enlightened Everyman"—appears to ask, "Is this all you can offer me?" [**Musical selection**: Beethoven, Symphony no. 9, movement 4.] A choir of winds offers up a new melody, a melody in D major, and before they can play more than four measures the hero breaks in, "That's what I'm talking about!" And together, the hero and the orchestra together articulate a closed cadence in D major, bringing this first part of the overture to its close. [**Musical selection**: Beethoven, Symphony No. 9, movement 4.] Without accompaniment, the low string hero sings the "new theme" in D major just handed to him by the orchestra. [**Musical selection**: Beethoven, Symphony No. 9, movement 4.]

A series of increasingly energized, increasingly joyful variations follow, as more and more instruments join in playing the "new theme," a metaphor for an ever growing number of people embracing, ever more triumphantly, the Enlightened message of the "new theme."

How do we know that this "new theme" is, for Beethoven, a musical personification of the Enlightenment? Because of what happens next, in what I call "Act I" of the movement. The violent, dissonant, chaotic music of the movement's opening suddenly and brutally returns and, along with it, the key of D minor. [**Musical selection**: Beethoven, Symphony no. 9, movement 4.] Once again, the hero enters and rejects this orchestral chaos. Only now, the hero is a baritone singer who belts out in recitative. "*O Freunde, nicht diese Töne!*" "Oh friends, not this tone! Rather let us sing more pleasantly and more joyfully."[**Musical selection**: Beethoven, Symphony No. 9, movement 4.]

A four measure wind introduction punctuated with shouts of *Freude*— "Joy"—from the chorus leads to verse 1 of Schiller's "Ode," with the hero in the lead:

> Oh joy, thou lovely spark of God,
> Daughter of Elysium
> we enter, drunk with fire,
> immortal goddess, thy holy shrine.
> Thy magic does again unite
> what custom has torn apart;
> all men shall be brothers,
> where thy gentle wing is spread.

[**Musical selection**: Beethoven, Symphony no. 9, movement 4.] All at once, the implicit becomes explicit; *"alle Menschen werden Brüder,"* "all men shall be brothers." That is the meaning of the "new theme," of the "Ode to Joy" theme!

By using voices singing words to make his meaning explicit, Beethoven forever shattered the concept of the symphony as a purely instrumental genre. All at once, instrumental music and vocal music were fused in a manner entirely new. The lines between symphony, oratorio, and even opera were not just redrawn but largely erased, as Beethoven, by his example, demonstrated unequivocally that a composer's expressive needs trump everything, including genre.

Act II

Act I of this fourth movement is about the promise of the Enlightenment. Act II is about the victory of the Enlightenment and the "Triumph of the 'Ode to Joy.'" How do we know that? We know it because Beethoven turns the "Ode to Joy" theme into a triumphal march.

From the distance, we hear the "army of freedom" approach in a bass drum (the only appearance of a bass drum in any of Beethoven's symphonies), and bassoons. Having arrived before us, the "army of freedom" performs the "Ode to Joy" theme as a marching band tune (that is without strings). Let's hear them back to back: the "Ode to Joy" as originally heard and then as a march tune. Here's the original. [**Piano demonstration**.] And now as a march tune. [**Piano demonstration**.]

Verse four of Schiller's "Ode" follows:

> It is a declaration of victory.
> Happily, like the heavenly bodies
> through the glorious plain of heaven,
> brothers, run your course,
> joyful as hero to victory.

Note—while we listen—the cymbals and a triangle meant to portray the clanking of swords and the jingle of spurs. [**Musical selection**: Beethoven, Symphony o. 9, movement 4.] [**Male Tenor.**]

> Brothers, run your course,
> joyful as hero to victory.
> Like a hero to victory.
> joyful as hero to victory.

Acts III and IV

Act III is about thanksgiving and heavenly devotion. Finally, Act IV is party time, an extended celebration of light, life, and love. We hear the last 1½ minutes of the movement and the symphony. [**Musical selection**: Beethoven, Symphony No. 9, Movement 4.]

Opening Night

A description of the premiere of the Ninth comes to us from the violinist Joseph Böhm, who as a member of the orchestra had a front row seat for the deaf Beethoven's ludicrous behavior during the performance.

> Beethoven himself conducted, that is, he stood in front of a conductor's stand and threw himself back and forth like a madman. At one moment he stretched to his full height, at the next he crouched down to the floor, he flailed about with his hands and feet as though he wanted to play all the instruments and sing all the chorus parts. The actual direction was in [Michael Umlauf's] hands; we musicians followed his baton only. Beethoven was so excited that he saw nothing that was going on about him. He paid no heed whatever to the bursts of applause, which his deafness prevented him from hearing in any case.

Yes, the conductor—Michael Umlauf—had warned the players and singers not to even think about looking at Beethoven during the performance. It was one of the singers—the contralto soloist Karoline Unger—who famously turned the deaf Beethoven around so that he might be aware of the extraordinary ovation the symphony received.

Conclusion

Beethoven's Symphony No. 9 was the most influential and important piece of music composed during the first half of the 19th century. By its example—and Beethoven's unassailable place in European music by 1824—Beethoven's Ninth said to the next generations of composers (and that includes us here today!) that something as basic as genre is contextual: The expressive needs of the artist must always take precedence over any convention, no matter how sacred, time honored, or popular that convention may be.

Thank you.

Schubert—Symphony No. 9
Lecture 11

Franz Schubert put the finishing touches on his Symphony no. 9 in C Major in March 1828—almost one year after Beethoven died and just seven months before his own death at the young age of 31. In his Ninth Symphony, Schubert managed to reconcile classical lyricism with an expressive energy inspired by, but in no way an imitation of, Beethoven. When this work was discovered and performed in 1838, it provided an alternative to Beethoven's stylistic reign of the realm of symphonies.

At the time he composed the Symphony no. 9 in C Major, between 1825 and 1828, Franz Peter Schubert was grappling with an artistic problem that would plague the next two generations of composers: Maestro Ludwig van Beethoven, who completed and premiered his Ninth Symphony just one year before Schubert began his own Symphony no. 9. The legacy of Beethoven—his compositional innovations, his expansion of the expressive language of Western music—had to be dealt with to the degree that his legacy informed but did not overpower the music of those who followed him. Of the composers who can be considered Beethoven's contemporaries, only a very few—Carl Maria von Weber, Felix Mendelssohn, and Schubert—incorporated elements of Beethoven's mature style into their own music in Beethoven's lifetime.

Franz Schubert was born in Vienna on January 31, 1797. Of all the great masters of Viennese classicism—including Haydn, Mozart, and Beethoven—Schubert was the only native-born Viennese. For Schubert, these composers were not names in a textbook but real people, and their music was part of the contemporary scene in which he grew up. Although we do not know unequivocally that Schubert and Beethoven met at some point in their lives, we do know that Beethoven's music had a decisive influence on Schubert's late music, of which the crowning glory is his Symphony in C Major. And even beyond the technical influences of Beethoven on Schubert's late music, there seemed to be a spiritual influence that was even more profound.

Unfortunately, Schubert contracted syphilis sometime during the summer of 1822 at the age of 25. Periods of remission were followed by periods of relapse, which were accompanied by depression and despair. Schubert's illness certainly affected the nature and expressive substance of his music. With his diagnosis, an expressive depth entered his compositional vocabulary that was simply not there before. At the same time, Schubert's identification with Beethoven became personal, as his own disease gave him an insight into Beethoven—the man and composer that he might never have gained had he remained healthy. Schubert died on November 19, 1828, at the age of 31. Schubert was buried in Währing Cemetery—just three graves away from Beethoven.

Schubert called the symphony "The Great," here meaning a grand or large symphony.

Symphony No. 9 in C Major, "The Great"

Schubert began his last symphony, in C major, during the summer of 1825. It was substantially completed by early 1826, though Schubert didn't date the piece as being finished until March of 1828. Schubert called the symphony "The Great," here meaning a grand or large symphony. Inspired by Beethoven's Ninth, Schubert's Ninth Symphony typically runs a full hour in performance and is scored for a full orchestra. As the symphony makes clear, Schubert had, by the age of 29, been won over entirely by Beethoven's music.

Movement 1

The first movement is in sonata form and begins with an introduction that features a theme of great majesty and lyric beauty that is played first in unison by two unaccompanied horns and then by a choir of winds. This introductory tune is so sylvan and beautiful that we might not notice its incredibly complex and original phrase structure. The tune is eight measures long. Typically, a tune eight measures in length will break down into two (rather predictable) four-measure phrases, the first called an antecedent and the second called the consequent. However, this does not occur.

The first phrase of the tune is two measures long. Schubert follows this first phrase with a one-measure echo. The first three measures, then, consist of two phrases: a two-measure phrase followed by the one-measure echo. The next three measures are the same: we hear another two-measure phrase followed by another one-measure echo. The opening melody appears to be complete at the end of measure six, but it's not. Next, Schubert takes the echo that was measure six and repeats it, stretching out its note values so that it takes up two measures instead of one, creating what amounts to an echo of the echo.

Schubert then attaches this elongated version of the echo to the end of the tune, creating an eight-measure melody with a phrase structure of two measures

Franz Schubert (1797–1828) finished his Symphony no. 9 in March of 1828, which was just seven months before his untimely death.

plus one measure, two measures plus one measure again, plus two additional measures. Even as the horns conclude the melody, though, the strings enter at the very last moment as a tagline that smoothes the way for the next iteration of the melody, which is in the winds. This fabulous opening melody has a fluidity, flexibility, and sense of growth that is a product of its unpredictable phrase structure.

A sense of triumphant arrival greets the beginning of the fast-paced sonata form that follows the introduction. In this massive exposition, there are four component parts: theme 1, the modulating bridge, theme 2, and the cadence material. Theme 1 alternates a vigorous, dotted-note (meaning a long-short rhythm) melody in the strings and brass with chirping winds. The modulating bridge that follows grows directly out of this melody.

Theme 2 begins as a vaguely Slavic-sounding tune set initially in E minor and played initially by the winds. The second part of theme 2 is set in G major with alternating wind instruments and loud strings. The strings play a rustic, foot-stomping melody derived from the opening of the theme. Finally, rising trombone lines, based on rhythms drawn from the introduction, lead to a series of huge orchestral swells and the conclusion of this massive second theme. This huge exposition ends as the foot-stomping melodic idea of theme 2 leads to a brief but energized version of the opening of theme 1.

Movement 2

The second movement has been variously described as a march depicting a theme—described by critics as either a march of tragedy or a dance of seduction—that has a Slavic melodic feel characteristic of Viennese music, of which Schubert was very fond.

Movement 3

The third movement is a huge scherzo—a three-part, A–B–A form structure. The opening of the first A section is a rollicking peasant dance that initially alternates between heavy, masculine-sounding strings and light, delicate, feminine-sounding winds. The middle section of the movement, the B section, begins a full six minutes into the movement. At roughly 13½ minutes long in performance, Schubert's third movement scherzo even outlasts the scherzo in Beethoven's Ninth Symphony.

Movement 4

The fourth movement is a sprawling movement that runs over 1,150 measures in length; there are entire Haydn symphonies that are shorter. As is true throughout the symphony, Schubert's orchestration—the way he distributes thematic and accompanimental materials among the instruments of the orchestra—is wonderful. In this fourth movement, the independence with which Schubert treats the woodwind and brass instruments is particularly striking.

After the Leipzig premiere of the symphony, Felix Mendelssohn brought it with him to London and wasn't even able to get through the first rehearsal of the symphony before the performance was called off. It seems that the violinists could not handle the multitudinous consecutive measures of eighth-note triplets that accompany the fourth movement's second theme—the scale of Schubert's Symphony in C Major was completely new to them. ■

Schubert—Symphony No. 9
Lecture 11—Transcript

We return to *The 30 Greatest Orchestral Works*. This is Lecture 11, and it is entitled "Schubert—Symphony No. 9."

The Gorilla in the Living Room

Franz Schubert put the finishing touches on his C Major Symphony in March 1828, almost one year to the day after Beethoven died and just seven months before his own death at the absurdly young age of 31. At the time he composed the Symphony, between 1825 and 1828, Schubert was grappling with an artistic problem that would plague the next two generations of composers. The problem? What to do about the gorilla in the living room.

I present to you the gorilla: Maestro Ludwig van Beethoven, represented here by his Ninth Symphony, completed and premiered just one year before Schubert began his own "Symphony No. 9." [**Music selection**: Beethoven, Symphony No. 9, Movement 4.] Let's make this personal! For reasons beyond your control, you've got a 450-pound silverback (meaning adult male) gorilla in your living room. His presence has complicated your life; frankly, you'd rather he wasn't there. But there he is, and somehow, you've got to deal with him.

Now, one way to deal with him is to pretend he isn't there; quietly creep around and hope that he doesn't notice you. Just so, some 19th century composers did their level best to pretend that Beethoven didn't and had never existed, by composing music that harkened back to a classical style that, in retrospect, Beethoven had rendered largely irrelevant by 1810. We're referring here to the instrumental music of such composers as Johann Hummel and Ludwig Spohr, music that was much more popular than Beethoven's own in the years immediately following the great man's death in 1827.

Other 19th-century composers swung to the other extreme: They bought themselves gorilla outfits, brought in cartloads of bananas, redecorated their houses in faux-Angola, and did everything to be like Beethoven, forgetting that they couldn't really be like Beethoven because they weren't Beethoven. We're talking about you, Misters Berlioz and Liszt, composers whose music fascinates, but often gets lost in a sea of overstuffed schlock, schmeer, und kitsch.

Then there's the middle ground. "Hey, yo, Mr. Gorilla, let's lay down some ground rules so we can co-exist. There's the bathroom; use it. The towels are in the closet. Don't even think of messing with the remote. You wanna banana daiquiri?"

Now that's the ticket! The legacy of Beethoven—his compositional innovations; his expansion of the expressive language of Western music—had to be dealt with to the degree that his legacy informed but did not overpower the music of those who followed him.

Beethoven's Contemporaries

We need to make an important point: This "Gorilla in the living room" stuff must be understood not through our historical view—one that recognizes Beethoven's music as the game-changer it was—but through the eyes and ears of his contemporaries, whose view of Beethoven was rather more nuanced than ours. Those contemporaries who chose to ignore Beethoven's example did not do so out of innate conservatism. Oh no; they were still discovering and processing the music of Haydn and Mozart. According to musicologist Nicholas Temperley, for these composers, "Beethoven's mature art seemed an intrusive irrelevance."

Of the composers who can be considered Beethoven's contemporaries, only a very few incorporated elements of Beethoven's mature style into their own music in Beethoven's lifetime. That small, extremely talented, and most select group consists of Carl Maria von Weber, Felix Mendelssohn, and Franz Peter Schubert.

Franz Schubert

Schubert was born in Vienna on January 31, 1797. Of all the great masters of Viennese classicism—including Haydn, Mozart, and Beethoven—Schubert was the only native-born Viennese. At the time of Schubert's birth, Mozart had been dead for five years, Haydn was working on his epic oratorio, *The Creation,* and Beethoven, 26 years old, had been living and working in Vienna for just over four years. By the time Joseph Haydn died in May of 1809, Schubert was 12 years old and studying composition with none-other-than Antonio Salieri.

Mozart. Haydn. Beethoven. Salieri. For Schubert, these composers were not names in a textbook but real people, and their music was part of the contemporary scene in which he grew up. By the age of 14, his favorite orchestral works were Mozart's stormy G Minor Symphony of 1788 and Beethoven's Symphony No. 2 in D Major of 1802.

It is worth noting that Beethoven's Second is the last of his decidedly classical symphonies, and for Schubert himself, "classical clarity and discipline" marked his own instrumental music through the age of 20, by which time he had already composed his first five symphonies.

Schubert got his "Beethoven religion"—what the musicologist Christopher Gibbs goes so far as to call his "Beethoven complex"—around 1820, when he was 23 years old. If not before, Beethoven would have become aware of Schubert a couple of years later, in 1822, when Schubert dedicated his first major instrumental publication—his *Eight Variations on a French Song* for piano duet—to Beethoven. Schubert's dedicatory inscription reads, "To Herr Ludwig van Beethoven, by his Worshipper and Admirer Franz Schubert."

Which leads to one of the most frequently asked and still unanswerable questions in the Schubert literature: Did Schubert and Beethoven ever actually meet and, if so, when, where, and how many times? Sadly, no one really knows because the contemporaries of Schubert who were in the best position to know have left us with completely contradictory answers. For example, Schubert's brother Ferdinand claimed that Franz "met Beethoven frequently." However, Josef von Spaun, Schubert's oldest and greatest friend claimed that "Schubert often lamented, especially at the time of Beethoven's death, how much he regretted that [Beethoven] had been so inaccessible, and that he had never spoken to Beethoven."

At very least, they must have "run into each other" in Vienna. The population of Vienna in 1810 was roughly 275,000, about the size of Plano, Texas. Beethoven and Schubert lived and worked in a small, tightly-knit musical community. They had numerous friends, supporters, performers, and publishers in common. They strolled on the same streets and in the same parks and, before Beethoven's hearing-loss permanently precluded him from doing so, they attended the same theaters.

For several years during the early 1820s, Beethoven "held court" at the offices of the publisher Steiner and Co. a few mornings a week. Schubert almost certainly attended at least some of these sessions, though given his shyness it is unlikely that he would ever have said a word.

Some of the most tantalizing reports of contact between Schubert and Beethoven date to Beethoven's final days. Anselm Hüttenbrenner, who was a friend of both Beethoven's and Schubert's, stated for the record, "I know for an absolute fact that Professor Schindler, Schubert, and I visited Beethoven at his sickbed about a week before he died."

The "Professor Schindler" Hüttenbrenner refers to is Anton Schindler, Beethoven's on-again, off-again personal secretary. For his part, Schindler reported no such meeting. However, Schindler did claim that he brought to Beethoven's attention some 60 of Schubert's songs in February of 1827, roughly a month before Beethoven's death. According to Schindler, Beethoven was floored by the songs and exclaimed, "Truly, in Schubert there dwells a divine spark!" According to Schindler, "[Beethoven] simply could not believe at that time that Schubert had already written over 500 [songs]!"

Schubert biographer Brian Newbould claims that despite Schindler's notorious tendency to exaggerate and fabricate, there's no reason to doubt him in this case. Writes Newbould:

> The respect which Beethoven acquired for Schubert's talent was so great that he also wanted to see his operas and pianoforte works; but his illness had already developed to such an extent that he could no longer satisfy this wish. Nevertheless he often spoke of Schubert and prophesied "that he will make a great stir in the world" and,

at the same time, expressed regret at not having gotten to know him earlier.

Beethoven died on March 26 of 1827. His funeral was held three days later, on March 29. We know that Schubert attended the service, which was held at the Holy Trinity Church in the Alsergrund parish, and that afterwards he participated as a torch-bearer in the processional to the Währing district cemetery. Such an honor would likely not have been granted Schubert had he not known Beethoven personally, and there you go, we're back to square one, because we've no unequivocal evidence that they ever met.

To Matters Musical

What we do know is that Beethoven's music had a decisive influence on Schubert's late music, of which the crowning glory is his Symphony in C Major. And even beyond the technical influences of Beethoven on Schubert's late music, I would suggest that there is a spiritual influence that is even more profound. You see, Beethoven's mature music gave Schubert (who was, after all, still a young man in the 1820s) the expressive license to "be himself."

Franz Schubert: Necessary Biographical Background

This description of the adult Schubert was written by his friend Anselm Hüttenbrenner:

> Schubert's outward appearance was anything but striking. ... He was short of stature, with a full, round face, and was rather stout. ... Because of his short sight, he always wore spectacles, which he did not take off, even during sleep. Dress was a thing in which he took no interest whatever. ... He disliked bowing and scraping, and listening to flattering talk about himself he found downright nauseating.

Schubert had an adequate singing voice and was, according to his contemporaries, a barely passable pianist. Put simply, Franz Schubert was a composer. In his own words, "I work every morning. When I have finished one piece, I begin another."

To call Schubert a compulsive composer is something of as understatement. In the last 16 years of his life, between the ages of 15 and 31, Schubert produced, among other works: nine finished and unfinished symphonies; 10 orchestral overtures; 22 piano sonatas; six masses; 17 operas; over 1,000 works for solo piano and piano four-hands; around 145 choral works; 45 chamber works, including 15 string quartets and one string quintet; and 637 songs.

It was by composing songs for voice and piano that Schubert developed his amazing melodic and harmonic craft, and learned as well to convey laser-like literary and expressive meaning with great brevity.

Disaster

Schubert contracted syphilis sometime during the summer of 1822, at the age of 25. The first symptoms began to appear in the late fall of 1822 and became pronounced by January of 1823. My friends, in those days, the question wasn't will the disease kill, but simply when.

Schubert was terrified. Periods of remission were followed by painful periods of lymphatic swelling, pustules, rashes, hair loss, lesions in the mouth and throat, debilitating muscle aches, and so forth. Depression and despair accompanied the periods of relapse.

In March of 1825 a despondent Schubert wrote his friend Leopold Kupelwieser:

> I feel myself to be the most unhappy and wretched creature in the world. Imagine a man whose health will never be right again. Imagine a man whose most brilliant hopes have perished, to whom love and friendship have nothing to offer but pain, and I ask you, is he not a miserable, unhappy being? Each night, on retiring to bed, I hope I may not wake again, and each morning but recalls yesterday's grief.

We are compelled to ask the question, the same terrible question that is asked regarding Beethoven's progressive hearing loss. Did Schubert's illness affect the nature and expressive substance of his music?

The answer, as in Beethoven's case, is yes. Franz Schubert, who in his mid-20s should have had his entire life in front of him, was instead staring death in the face. With his diagnosis, an expressive depth entered his compositional vocabulary that was simply not there before. No longer would he compose works meant simply to please and amuse; there was no time for that. At the same time, Schubert's identification with Beethoven became personal, as his own disease gave him an insight into Beethoven the man and composer that he might never have gained had he remained healthy.

Symphony No. 9 in C Major, "The Great"

Schubert began his last symphony, in C Major, during the summer of 1825, a few months after having written the broken-hearted letter quoted just moments ago. It was substantially completed by early 1826, though Schubert didn't date the piece as being finished until March of 1828. Schubert called the symphony "the Great" not because he was some sort ego-freak bent on hyping the piece. Rather, Schubert called it a "*Grosse*" Symphony—meaning a "grand" or "large" symphony. And large it is! Inspired by Beethoven's Ninth, Schubert's Ninth typically runs a full hour in performance and is scored for fullest of full orchestras, with enough brass and drums to take down the walls of Jericho without raising a sweat. As the symphony makes clear, Schubert had—by the age of 29—been won over entirely by Beethoven's music. "The Great" is Schubert's "Beethoven" symphony, and we can only cry the bitterest tears that he didn't live long enough to build on this piece. The history of the symphony would likely have been very different had he the opportunity to do so.

Movement 1: Sonata Form

The first movement sonata form begins with an introduction that features a Theme of great majesty and lyric beauty, played first in unison by two unaccompanied horns and then by a choir of winds. [**Music selection**: Schubert, Symphony No. 9 in C Major, movement 1.])

This introductory tune is so sylvan, so beautiful that we might not notice its incredibly complex and original phrase structure. Well, let's notice it. The tune is eight measures long. Typically, a tune eight measures in length will break down into two (rather predictable) four-measure phrases, the first called an "antecedent" and the second called the "consequent." But that's not what happens here. The first phrase of the tune is two measures long. [**Piano demonstration**.] Schubert follows this first phrase with a sort of one measure "echo." [**Piano demonstration**.] The first three measures, then, consist of two phrases, a two-measure phrase followed by the one measure echo. [**Piano demonstration**.] The next three measures do the same thing. We hear another two-measure phrase. [**Piano demonstration**.] Followed by another one measure echo: [**Piano demonstration**.] And there you have it: For all intents and purposes, the opening melody is complete at the end of measure six. [**Piano demonstration**.]

But it's not complete, and here Schubert indulges in a bit of compositional magic. He takes the "echo" that was measure six. [**Piano demonstration**.] And repeats it, stretching out its note values so that it takes up two measures instead of one, creating what amounts to an "echo of the echo." [**Piano demonstration**.] Schubert attaches this elongated version of the echo to the tail-end of the tune, creating an eight-measure melody with a phrase structure of two measures plus one measure, two measures plus one measure, plus two measures.

But he's not quite done yet! Even as the horns have concluded the melody, the strings enter at the very last moment, with a sort of amen-like tag line that smoothes the way for the next iteration of the melody, which will be in the winds. Let's listen from the top! Horns, strings, and then winds: [**Musical selection**: Schubert, Symphony No. 9 in C Major, movement 1.]

This fabulous opening melody has a fluidity, a flexibility, a sense of growth and unfolding that, taken together, is a product of its utterly unpredictable phrase structure. There's a lot of art in that horn melody, and that's just the first 30 seconds of the symphony.

A sense of triumphant arrival greets the beginning of the fast-paced sonata form that follows the introduction! To get an idea of the massive,

Beethoven's Ninth-inspired proportions of this movement and, by extension, the entire symphony, let's examine, one by one, the four component parts of just the exposition of the sonata form: theme 1, the modulating bridge, theme 2, and the cadence material.

Marked "*Allegro ma non troppo*" (meaning "fast, but not too fast"), theme 1 alternates a vigorous, dotted note (meaning long-short rhythmed) melody in the strings and brass with chirping winds. [**Musical selection**: Schubert, Symphony No. 9 in C Major, movement 1.] The modulating bridge that follows grows directly out of the dotted-note string and brass melody and chirping winds that characterized theme 1. We hear the modulating bridge. [**Musical selection**: Schubert, Symphony No. 9 in C Major, movement 1.]

Theme 2 is massive. In performance it runs nearly two minutes in length, so let's break it up into three segments. The theme begins as a vaguely Slavic sounding tune set initially in E minor and played initially by the winds. [**Musical selection**: Schubert, Symphony No. 9 in C Major, movement 1.]

The next big chunk o' theme 2 is set in G major. This second part of the theme alternates wind instruments and loud strings. The strings play a rustic, foot-stomping melodic idea derived from the opening of the theme. I demonstrate. Here's the opening of the theme as heard in the winds. [**Piano demonstration**.] And here's the rustic, foot stomping melodic idea that is actually just the first three notes of the theme. Let's hear it: theme 2, part 2. [**Musical selection**: Schubert, Symphony No. 9 in C Major, movement 1.]

Finally, rising trombone lines, based on rhythms drawn from the introduction, lead to a series of huge orchestral swells and the conclusion of this massive second theme. [**Musical selection**: Schubert, Symphony No. 9 in C Major, movement 1.] This huge exposition finally ends as the foot-stomping melodic idea of theme 2 leads to a brief but energized version of the opening of theme 1. Let's hear it: the conclusion of the exposition. [**Musical selection**: Schubert, Symphony No. 9 in C Major, movement 1.]

My friends, in performance, we are roughly 6½ minutes into the movement, and we're only one third of the way through the movement. There's a scope and magnificence here, an expressive exuberance, and a range of expression that clearly mark this as a post-Beethoven symphony. Yet its wonderful melodic and harmonic content and its details of orchestration mark it as 100 percent Franz Schubert.

Movement 2

The second movement has been variously described as a march depicting a "heartbreaking show of spirit in adversity" (that according to Sir Donald Francis Tovey) and the "subtly seductive dance of a young gypsy woman" (that according to Michael Steinberg). Whatever Schubert's inspiration, the theme, presented initially by a solo oboe, has a Slavic melodic feel characteristic of Viennese music, a Slavic feel with which Schubert was quite enamored. Let's hear the opening of the movement, and let's try to determine—based on our performance—whether the theme is a march of tragedy or a dance of seduction. [**Musical selection**: Schubert, Symphony No. 9 in C Major, movement 2.]

Given the relatively brisk pace of our performance, this sounds—to my ear—much more like a slinky dance of seduction than a march of tragedy, though I am, admittedly, predisposed towards slink!

Movement 3

The third movement is a huge scherzo, a three-part, A-B-A form structure. Let's hear the opening of the first A section, a rollicking peasant dance that initially alternates between heavy, masculine-sounding strings and light, delicate, most feminine-sounding winds. [**Musical selection**: Schubert, Symphony No. 9 in C Major, movement 3.]

The middle section of the movement, the B section or trio, begins a full six minutes into the movement. For our reference, the third movement scherzo of Beethoven's Symphony no. 2 runs about 4½ minutes in its entirety; the third movement scherzi of Beethoven's Symphonies nos. 3 and 4 run about 5½ minutes in their entirety; and the scherzo of Beethoven's fifth runs about seven minutes in its entirety. At roughly 13½ minutes in performance, Schubert's scherzo even outlasts the scherzo in Beethoven's Ninth. Big! Everything about Schubert's C Major is "great," meaning, here, big.

Interlude: An Extraordinary Story

In 1838, 10 years after Schubert died, the composer, pianist, and music journalist Robert Schumann made a pilgrimage to Vienna. He visited Schubert's grave and then made a call on Schubert's brother Ferdinand. Schumann had heard that Ferdinand had a stack of Schubert manuscripts—pieces that no one wanted to play or publish—and he wanted to have himself a look-see.

Well, Schumann was flabbergasted by the music he saw. Among the masterworks he leafed through was this very C Major Symphony, which to that point had been rejected for performance because it was "*Schwierig und schwülstig*" ("too difficult and bombastic"). Schumann, bless him, immediately arranged for the piece to be sent to Leipzig's Gewandhaus orchestra, where Felix Mendelssohn conducted its premiere a few months later. It has been a mainstay of the repertoire since that performance.

Movement 4: Sonata Form

The fourth movement "*Allegro vivace*" ("fast, with life") is just sensational. According to musicologist A. Peter Brown, it is "a conflation of the heroic and the frantic."

An admirably succinct description of an otherwise sprawling movement, a movement that runs over 1,150 measures in length! There are entire Haydn symphonies that are shorter! As is true throughout the symphony, Schubert's orchestration, the way he distributes thematic and accompanimental materials among the instruments of the orchestra, is wonderful here in the fourth movement. In this fourth movement, the independence with which Schubert treats the woodwind and brass instruments is particularly striking. Let's hear theme 1 and the modulating bridge. [**Musical selection**: Schubert, Symphony No. 9 in C Major, movement 4.]

Great stuff, yes? Well, they didn't think so in London, at least not at first. After the brilliant Leipzig premiere of the symphony, Felix Mendelssohn brought it with him to London, where he was held in reverence by everyone, from Queen Victoria and her boy-toy Prince Albert on down. Well,

Mendelssohn didn't even get through the first rehearsal of the symphony before the performance was called off. It seems that the violinists first got the giggles and then collapsed in laughter when they came to the 88 consecutive measures of eighth-note triplets that accompany the fourth movement's second theme. Let's hear that second theme. [**Musical selection**: Schubert, Symphony No. 9 in C Major, movement 4.]

In all fairness to those naughty, naughty English violinists, the scale of Schubert's "Great" C Major Symphony was completely new to them. Out of context, the 88 consecutive measures of eighth-note triplets, if rehearsed without the theme-bearing-winds above, must have seemed crazy. Having said that, in a country where the national cuisine includes a desert called Spotted Dick, I'm not sure I would be casting aspersions at anything composed by Franz Schubert!

One last anecdote regarding this fourth movement. In his manuscripts, Schubert tended to write his accent marks, little wedge-shaped things, so big that they were sometimes mistaken for decrescendi—indications that the music should actually get quieter, rather than be accented. Such a thing occurred at the very end of this C Major Symphony: An accent was misread as a decrescendo, and for years, the last three measures of the symphony were played as dying away instead of as loud and punchy. My Dover edition score, edited by none other than Johannes Brahms and first published in 1885, has a decrescendo under the last three measures. My Eulenberg score, edited by Roger Fiske and published in 1984, has an accent and no decrescendo!

So here's the story, told by Michael Steinberg:

> Some years ago I heard one of the best conductors of our time rehearse this symphony, and when he got to the final note he sank into a deep knee-bend to produce the diminuendo in his score. Afterwards, I suggested that this ought really to be an accent, and he said, "Oh no, that is Schubert's gesture of humility before Beethoven."

Let's hear those closing moments as played with a final accent in our NAXOS performance. [**Musical selection**: Schubert, Symphony No. 9 in C Major, movement 4.] The Schubert scholar Brian Newbould breathlessly sums things up when he writes:

> Schubert's "Great" C Major is a glorious last re-affirmation of the classical principles of symphonic design, imbued with a [Beethovenian] spirit and impelled by an unflagging rhythmic verve. ... In its life-enhancing combination of richness and élan, it stands as a symbol of renewal. ... The last classical symphony it may be, but its message is newly-minted, its scope visionary, its momentum tireless.

A Concluding Story

Schubert died on November 19, 1828, aged 31 years, 9 months, and 20 days. Two days later, on November 21, Schubert's brother Ferdinand wrote their father. Schubert had been delirious and hallucinating near the end, and in his letter, Ferdinand described one of his brother's hallucinations:

> On the evening before his death, though only half conscious, he said to me: "I implore you to take me to my room, not to leave me here, in this corner under the ground." I answered him: "Dear Franz, believe your brother who loves you so much: you are in [your] room, lying on your bed!" And Franz said: "No, that's not true: Beethoven is not lying here." Could this be anything but an indication of his inmost wish to repose by the side of Beethoven, whom he so greatly revered?

Writes Schubert biographer Elizabeth McKay:

> Knowing Ferdinand's tendency to fabricate information when ... expedient, it is surely conceivable that [he] invented this scene ... in order to persuade their father to [bury Schubert at the Währing Cemetery], as close as possible to Beethoven.

Schubert's wish—real or fabricated—was granted, and he was buried in Währing Cemetery just three graves away from Beethoven. In 1888, Beethoven's and Schubert's remains were transferred to Vienna's main cemetery—the "Zentralfriedhof"—where they remain today, buried next to each other in what is called the "Garden of Honor."

Conclusions

In his Ninth Symphony, Schubert managed to reconcile classical lyricism with an expressive oomph inspired by, but in no way an imitation of, Beethoven. In doing so, Schubert tamed the gorilla, and when this work was discovered and performed in 1838, it provided "a viable [stylistic] alternative to Beethoven's domination of the symphonic landscape."

Thank you.

Mendelssohn—"Italian" Symphony
Lecture 12

> Mendelssohn's critics have claimed that the "Italian" Symphony is nothing but an unconnected series of *tableaux vivants*—that is, program music that would describe pictures of daily life—and a rather unsophisticated soundtrack to the travelogue of Mendelssohn's Italian tour that inspired the work. Of course, Mendelssohn's "Italian" Symphony is, like so much of his mature music, unclassifiable. It features the beauty of line and clarity of expression associated with classicism along with the personalized, programmatic content that is very much the territory of early-19th-century romanticism.

Felix Jacob Ludwig Mendelssohn was born in Hamburg on February 3, 1809. In 1812, when Felix was three years old, his family moved to Berlin. Mendelssohn was an absurd prodigy. There was nothing he couldn't master: the piano, composing, painting, languages. Between the ages of 12 and 14, he composed, among many other works, 13 symphonies for string orchestra.

Mendelssohn's teacher was Carl Friedrich Zelter, the director of the Berlin Singakademie. Zelter put Mendelssohn through a rigorous, J. S. Bach-dominated program of study, with some C. P. E. Bach and Mozart mixed in for the sake of modernity. Mendelssohn's Symphony no. 1 in C Minor—completed on March 31, 1824, just a month after he turned 15 years old—capped his education at Zelter's hands. From that point on, he moved on a compositional path of his own making. At 16, he composed his Octet in E-flat Major for strings, his first great masterwork. Mendelssohn went on to compose four more symphonies, the most famous of which is his Symphony no. 4 in A Major—the "Italian."

Symphony No. 4 in A Major, "Italian"
Felix Mendelssohn began work on his Symphony no. 4 in A Major during an extended trip through Italy in 1830 and 1831. At its core, the symphony is an impressionistic work based on the sights, smells, and emotions inspired by his Italian adventure. The music is among the most brilliant

Mendelssohn ever wrote, but he did not allow it to be published in his lifetime. He completely revised the second, third, and fourth movements, but never got around to rewriting the first movement—an unfortunate fact given his premature death at the age of 38. The symphony was published posthumously in 1851, four years after Mendelssohn's death. It was instantly embraced by symphonic audiences and has been a mainstay of the orchestral repertoire since.

Felix Mendelssohn (1809–1847) composed one of the most enduring orchestral works in the repertoire at the age of 17.

Movement 1

Mendelssohn spent a large portion of his stay in Italy in Rome. He was particularly enthralled by the pre-Lent season of Carnival, which runs for roughly a month. Many have compared Mendelssohn's leaping, throbbing, vivacious theme 1 to the Carnival season. A fanfare-like modulating bridge follows. Theme 2, graceful and lilting, is initially heard in the clarinets and bassoons. Theme 1 then briefly returns and brings the exposition to its conclusion.

A third theme makes an appearance about halfway through the development section, but supposedly this third theme had originally appeared in the exposition. According to the rules and regulations of classical-era sonata form, introducing a new theme in a development section is absolutely wrong, but Mendelssohn was living and working in the post-Beethoven expressive environment of 19th-century romanticism. The third theme returns in the recapitulation, and along with theme 1, it drives the movement to its glittering conclusion in A major.

Despite its programmatic content and idiosyncratic approach to sonata form, the overwhelming impressions the first movement of Mendelssohn's "Italian" leaves us with are its melodic brilliance and structural clarity; its expressive directness; its dancing, rhythmic character, and its complete lack of post-Beethoven angst. These descriptors apply to most of Mendelssohn's mature music. They apply, as well, to the music of the classical era—to the music of Haydn and Mozart. Thus, Mendelssohn is often classified in a manner that inadvertently denigrates his work even as it misleads, implying that the mature Mendelssohn was a conservative composer. This perception is intensified when we consider that Mendelssohn's first, youthful masterworks were anything but conservative.

Movement 2

At the heart of Mendelssohn's mature compositional style is lyricism: songlike melodic expression that explicitly invokes the human voice. The second movement is a quiet and melancholy processional, inspired perhaps by the religious processionals Mendelssohn witnessed during his stay in Italy. The opening of the movement is occupied by a single, direct, song-like melody accompanied by steady, marching, plucked low strings.

Typical of his mature music, Mendelssohn presents the principal theme of this second movement over a simple, straightforward accompaniment, without the more active, counter-melody-dominated accompaniments characteristic of his earlier music. This sort of direct thematic presentation is not an indication of encroaching conservatism; rather, it's a reflection of Mendelssohn's developing desire to cultivate voice-like lyricism and thematic clarity in his music.

Movement 3

The opening of the third movement strikes many listeners as being conservative and conventional when compared to such early Mendelssohn masterworks as the Octet in E-flat Major and the "Overture to a Midsummer Night's Dream." This perception of encroaching conservatism in Mendelssohn's later music has led many intelligent auditors to incorrectly categorize his work and development as a composer.

What most of us hear when we listen to this movement is a gentle, gliding, exquisitely lyric dance movement featuring a song-like phrase structure and muted contrasts—something that the mature Beethoven would probably not have composed. Thus, such a movement is considered by some to be conservative, as representing a pre-Beethoven aesthetic environment. The fact is that Mendelssohn developed on an artistic path of his own making, and as he got older, his compositional muse led him to an ever greater intensification of musical means—a less-is-more aesthetic attitude that is not unusual for a maturing artist.

Movement 4

This fourth movement finale is the most explicitly Italian music in the symphony. Mendelssohn labels the movement as being *saltarello*, a high-energy folk dance popular in southern Italy characterized by a hop on the last beat of every measure. This *saltarello* finale behaves like most classical-era symphonic finales, which were intended not as summations but, rather, to engage the listener by inspiring dance. However, at the same time, this last movement is a rarity: a minor-mode finale (set in A minor) for what is otherwise a major-mode symphony.

Once again, Herr Mendelssohn makes himself impossible to classify: something traditional, something different, all in the service of an entirely personal, an entirely "Mendelssohnian" movement. This finale also has that personalized, Mendelssohnian sound that is created by the light-as-a-feather opening thematic statement in the flutes, the steady-state triplets that characterize the theme and its accompaniment, and the dance-like beat that underlies it all.

The conclusion of the movement—and thus the symphony—is fabulous. A sinuous melody in the strings (which is theme 2, thus far unsampled) builds up to a last, climactic statement of theme 1, and then the music simply seems to fade away into the distance. Only at the very last second does the volume pick back up again in order to give some punch to the closing moments of the symphony. ■

Mendelssohn—"Italian" Symphony
Lecture 12—Transcript

We return to *The 30 Greatest Orchestral Works*. It is entitled "Mendelssohn—'Italian' Symphony."

Child Prodigies

Is there anything more tiresome, more downright irksome than so-called "child prodigies"? You know what I'm talking about: some singing six-year-old grinding her pelvis like a Vegas show girl on "American Idol" (or worse, lip-synching to another, less "attractive" prodigy during the opening ceremony of the Beijing Olympics).

Or the "cute kid" prodigies who would seem to embody all the wisdom of adulthood in their otherwise innocent, pre-pubescent punim: from Shirley Temple's pouty smarminess to Gary Coleman's off-color wise-cracks.

The real prodigies—the ones with genius—are the most offensive of all. The five-year-old "trained monkey" (as he was called) Wolfgang Mozart, sight-reading perfectly at the harpsichord while doing the Sunday Times acrostic with his left foot. The 11-year-old, 65-pound Midori Goto soloing with the New York Phil while discussing Proust with the concertmaster.

Prodigies: They stand as a mocking reminder of our own mediocrity, and if we could, we'd squash 'em all like the bugs they are. Honestly, is there a story that gives us a greater secret thrill than that of the "prodigy" who crashes and burns when the realities of life begin to kick in sometime around late adolescence? Hah hah hah!

Now, having told you more about myself than I probably intended to, we'd observe that the rarest prodigy of all is the creative prodigy. My friends, it's one thing to mimic adults, to repeat words that have been put into your mouth or to play music written by others; it's another thing entirely to actually write those words and compose that music yourself. To be able to do that, you need real life experience and half a lifetime of accumulated technical skills. We are still, thankfully, waiting for the first "great" 15-year-old novelist.

And while it is entirely true that Wolfgang Mozart, Frederic Chopin, and Alexander Scriabin all composed some first-rate music before they were 16, the fact remains that their early music was derivative, that is, based on pre-existing compositional models.

Now, in no way is that statement meant to demean these miraculously talented composers. In reality, no artistic pursuit is more difficult or demanding than writing instrumental music, and the mere fact that a 15-year-old can produce a polished piece of instrumental music is a miracle all by itself. But not even Mozart started composing genuine masterworks until he was 18, and as we all know, Mozart was a freak.

Which brings us to the extraordinary case of Felix Mendelssohn. Simply put, when it came to child prodigies, Felix Mendelssohn left 'em all in the dust, including the original "boy-wonder," Wolfgang Mozart.

Felix Mendelssohn and the "Jewish Thing"

Felix Mendelssohn came from some pretty solid intellectual stock: His grandfather was the Jewish philosopher Moses Mendelssohn, who has been referred to as the "father of Reform Judaism." Writes Mendelssohn biographer R. Larry Todd:

> [Moses Mendelssohn's] struggle to mediate between two German worlds—the dominant Christian society, tied to the monarchy of Frederick the Great, and the disenfranchised Jewish society and subculture—was not lost on Felix Mendelssohn ..., who, after his boyhood baptism as a Protestant, remained mindful of his Judaic roots.

In 1795, Moses Mendelssohn's eldest son, Joseph, founded a private bank. In 1804, four years before Felix was born, his father, Abraham, (Joseph Mendelssohn's younger brother), joined the business. Headquartered in Berlin, the firm of *Gebrüder Mendelssohn* (Mendelssohn Brothers & Co.) became one of the most important banking houses in all of Europe, and remained so until 1938, when it was "Aryanized" by the Nazis, who forced the family to sell its assets to Deutsche Bank.

Mendelssohn's mother Lea (born Lea Salomon) was a native Berliner. Her grandfather was a banker named Daniel Itzig, who in 1761 became only the third Berlin Jew to receive the status of "general privilege."

I explain: Jews in Berlin were classified into six categories. Those families in the top category—"general privilege"—were allowed to own property, found businesses, and to pass these privileges down to their children. Therefore, Felix's mother, Lea Salomon, came with what amounted to a hereditary title—"general privilege"—which made her one heck-of-a catch. She was smart and talented as well; we are told that she was:

> acquainted with every branch of fashionable information; [that she] played [piano] and sang with expression and grace; ... she drew exquisitely; she spoke and read French, English, Italian and ... Homer in the original [Greek]; [and that] she had made the acquaintance of [Johann] Sebastian Bach's music and [played Bach's] *Well-Tempered Clavier.*

Putting it all together: Felix Mendelssohn's parents lived, worked, and played in the highest of social circles, in which a premium was placed on education, culture, and assimilation. The perception among Abraham Mendelssohn and Lea Salomon's high-end Jewish contemporaries was that Judaism was no longer relevant, and that remaining Jewish could only lead to socio-economic martyrdom. The answer was conversion to Christianity and assimilation into German society.

Lea's brother, Jacob Levy Salomon, was among the first of their generation to convert, which he did in 1805 (and for which—incidentally—he was disowned by his mother, Bella). Jacob owned some property in Berlin, and he took as his surname the name of its former owner, "Bartholdy."

Lea's brother Jacob played a major role in convincing Abraham and Lea to baptize their four children—Fanny, Felix, Rebecca, and Jacob—which was done at Berlin's Jerusalemkirche, near the Gendarmenmarkt, on March 21, 1816. The name "Bartholdy" was attached to their names, as it was to Abraham and Lea when they themselves converted, six years later, in 1822.

According to Mendelssohn's contemporary, the poet Heinrich Heine—who was a German Jew who also converted to Lutheranism—conversion was: "The ticket of admission into European culture, although one not regarded as valid by everyone."

Ain't that the truth. These smart, talented, upwardly-mobile, cosmopolitan Jews thought that by converting they could re-invent themselves and in doing so, deflect the rampant anti-Semitism of the time. In truth, the conversions didn't fool anybody. Mendelssohn's conversion certainly didn't deflect Richard Wagner's hatred for "the Jew Mendelssohn"; we read that:

> [Typical of Wagner's] overt disdain of the Jewish race [was] his habit of conducting the music of Mendelssohn only while wearing gloves. At the end of the performance he would remove the garments and throw them to the floor, to be removed by the cleaners.

Conversion didn't keep the Mendelssohn banking business from being Aryanized and stolen from the family. Mendelssohn's conversion didn't keep his music from being banned as "degenerate" by the Third Reich or save any of the memorials to him in his native Germany. Eric Werner writes:

> Just before the 90th anniversary of Mendelssohn's death (in 1937), the city fathers of Leipzig removed the master's monument from the *Gewandhaus*, which [as a conductor] he had made world-famous, and sold it for scrap iron.

Far more than just a cautionary tale, these issues of conversion and assimilation have a tremendous impact on our perception of Mendelssohn's music as it developed during his all-too-brief career. We will discuss this at length in a few minutes. But first, some biographical background.

Felix Jacob Ludwig Mendelssohn (1809–1847)

Mendelssohn was born in "The Free and Hanseatic City of Hamburg" on February 3, 1809. In 1812, when Felix was three years old, his family moved to Berlin.

It was there that, according to Harold Schonberg:

> [Mendelssohn] grew up in an atmosphere of almost grim culture, grim because both parents were determined to see that their children had every advantage money and position could provide. ... [Abraham] and Leah not only directly supervised their children's education, but were also determined that the children be serious about it. That meant a great deal of work. ... Felix would be up at 5 am, ready to work at his music, his history, his Greek and Latin, his natural science, his contemporary literature, and his drawing [and painting]. (He was to retain that early rising hour all his life.) He thrived on the regimen.

Felix Mendelssohn was an absurd prodigy. There was nothing he couldn't master: the piano, composing, painting, languages; he was omnivorous. Between the ages of 12 and 14, he composed, among many other works, 13 symphonies for string orchestra, all of which were performed at the Mendelssohn's Berlin home. Yes, they are generally conservative works, but it would be a mistake to call them student works because Mendelssohn was no ordinary student.

Mendelssohn's teacher was Carl Friedrich Zelter, the director of the Berlin *Singakademie*. Zelter put Mendelssohn through a rigorous J. S. Bach-dominated program of study, with some C. P. E. Bach and Wolfgang Mozart thrown in for the sake of modernity. According to R. Larry Todd, "By the third of February 1824—[Felix's] 15th birthday—Zelter could proclaim him a member of the brotherhood of Mozart, Haydn, and Bach."

Mendelssohn's Symphony No. 1 in C Minor—completed on March 31, 1824, just a month after he turned 15 years old—capped his education at Zelter's hands. From that point on, he moved on a compositional path of his own making, a fact that became crystal clear the following year when, at 16, he composed his Octet in E-flat Major for Strings, his first great masterwork.

A year later, at 17, Mendelssohn composed one of the most enduring orchestral works in the repertoire, the *Overture to a Midsummer Night's Dream* for orchestra. At 17, Mozart had not accomplished anything even approaching it at a like age. Mendelssohn went on to compose four more symphonies. The most famous of them is his Symphony No. 4 in A Major, op. 90, the "Italian."

Mendelssohn, Symphony No. 4 in A Major, Op. 90, "Italian" (1833)

Felix Mendelssohn took his "grand European tour" from 1829 to 1832, between the ages of 20 and 23. Such a grand tour was:

> A common practice for well-to-do young men as a means of developing cultural literacy and taste. Such a grand tour generally included the major European capitals, especially Paris and Vienna, and Italy as the garden bed of culture for both classical antiquity and the Renaissance.

> There were various ways to capture the experience of one's Grand Tour. One obvious means was by writing a journal or a series of letters to one's family at home. Another was through drawing in pen or pencil, or paintings in watercolor, at which Mendelssohn was highly skilled. For Mendelssohn, not only letters and pictures filled this function, but also music.

Yes, two major works emerged from Mendelssohn's pen in direct response to his grand tour: the *Hebrides Overture*, inspired by the west coast of Scotland, and his Symphony in A Major, known as the "Italian."

Mendelssohn began work on the symphony during an extended stay in Italy in 1830 and 1831. At its core, the symphony is an impressionistic work based on the sights, smells, and emotions inspired by his Italian adventure. It must have been a great trip, because the music is among the most brilliant Mendelssohn ever wrote; even he remarked that the symphony "was the most cheerful piece [I] had yet composed."

Cheerful it is, although Mendelssohn did not allow it to be published in his lifetime. He completely revised the second, third, and fourth movements, but never got around to rewriting the first movement, an unfortunate if understandable fact given his premature death at the age of 38. The symphony was published posthumously in 1851, four years after his death. It was instantly embraced by symphonic audiences and has been a mainstay of the orchestral repertoire since. The usually tough-as-nails Viennese critic Eduard Hanslick was enthralled by it, writing that the symphony is "full of sweet enchantment; an intoxicating floral fragrance."

Movement 1, Sonata Form

Mendelssohn spent a large portion of his stay in Italy in Rome. Based on his letters back home, he was particularly enthralled by the carnival season, which officially begins on January 6—the Twelfth Night after Christmas, also-known-as the "Feast of the Epiphany"—and runs for roughly a month, until the beginning of Lent: the 40 days before Easter. Mendelssohn's leaping, throbbing, vivacious theme 1 has been compared to "Arlecchino" (or "Harlequin"), the nimble, acrobatic character archetype of the Italian *Commedia dell'arte* and Carnival season. Let's hear the theme and the fanfare-ish modulating bridge that follows. [**Musical selection**: Mendelssohn, Symphony No. 4 in A Major, op. 90, "Italian," movement 1.]

Theme 2—graceful and lilting—is initially heard in the clarinets and bassoons. Theme 1 then briefly returns and brings the exposition to its conclusion. Let's hear the remainder of the exposition, beginning with theme 2. [**Musical selection**: Mendelssohn, Symphony No. 4 in A Major, op. 90, "Italian," movement 1.] A third theme makes an appearance in the development section, a theme that sounds like this. [**Piano demonstration**.]

According to modern scholarship, this third theme had originally appeared in the exposition. But Mendelssohn removed the passage and transferred the theme to the development section. Now according to the rules and regulations of classical era sonata form, introducing a new theme in a development section is an absolute no-no, sort of like introducing a major character two-thirds of the way through a movie. But then, Mendelssohn was not living and working in the 18th century but rather, in the post-Beethoven, "do-what-you-want" expressive environment of 19th century romanticism.

Here's the third theme, heard in all its glory about halfway through the development section (and notice how the opening leap of theme

1 is appended to this third theme as it winds down). [**Musical selection**: Mendelssohn, Symphony No. 4 in A Major, op. 90, "Italian," movement 1.] This third theme returns in the recapitulation and along with theme 1, it drives the movement to its glittering conclusion in A major. [**Musical selection**: Mendelssohn, Symphony No. 4 in A Major, op. 90, "Italian," movement 1.]

The "Mendelssohn Problem"

Despite its programmatic content and idiosyncratic approach to sonata form, the overwhelming impressions the first movement of Mendelssohn's "Italian" leaves us with are its melodic brilliance and structural clarity; its expressive directness; its dancing, rhythmic character, and its complete lack of post-Beethoven schmerz and angst.

Melodic brilliance, structural clarity, expressive directness, dancing rhythms, and a lack of schmerz and angst. These descriptors apply to most of Mendelssohn's mature music. They apply, as well, to the music of the classical era, to the music of Haydn and Mozart.

Thus, given our compulsive need to pigeonhole, Mendelssohn the composer is often classified in a manner that inadvertently denigrates his work even as it misleads. Because of his identifiably classical leanings, Mendelssohn has been categorized as "conservative romantic," a "romantic classicist," and a "classical romantic." What these classifications imply is that the mature Mendelssohn was a conservative composer, a perception that is intensified when we consider that Mendelssohn's first, youthful masterworks were anything but conservative. For example, let's listen to the opening of the third movement of Mendelssohn's "Italian" Symphony. [**Musical selection**: Mendelssohn, Symphony No. 4 in A Major, op. 90, "Italian," Movement 3.] This music—which I personally find enthralling in its lyricism and rhythmic grace—strikes many listeners as being conservative and conventional, especially when compared to such early Mendelssohn masterworks as the Octet in E-flat Major and the *Overture to a Midsummer Night's Dream*. This perception of encroaching conservatism in Mendelssohn's later music has led all sorts of intelligent auditors to say all sorts of dumb things. Regarding this third movement, Mendelssohn biographer Eric Werner writes: "This minuet-like *Con Moto Moderato* is a 'Biedermeier Minuet': merry, lovable, but without the power of a Haydn, without the winged, noble grace of a Mozart—a real bourgeois minuet!"

Huh! "A real bourgeois minuet!" OK, let's hear the opening of the third movement again, and let's listen for the "bourgeois minuet-ness"—the "antiquated, middle class conventionality"—of which Professor Werner speaks. [**Musical selection**: Mendelssohn, Symphony No. 4 in A Major, op. 90, "Italian," movement 3.]

Speaking for myself, I do not hear in this music an "antiquated, middle class conventionality." What I do hear—and what we all hear when we listen to this movement—is a gentle, gliding, exquisitely lyric dance movement featuring a song-like phrase structure and muted contrasts. So a song-like dance movement in which contrasts are muted: The mature Beethoven, for one, would probably not have composed such a thing. Thus, such a movement is considered—by some—to be conservative, as representing a pre-Beethoven aesthetic environment. But why would Eric Werner call this movement "a real bourgeois [middle class] minuet?" What is that supposed to mean?

Here's what: Mendelssohn was married on March 28, 1837, to a woman named Cecile Jeanrenaud, who came from a wealthy Huguenot family. She was regarded as one of the great beauties of her time, and every extant image of her confirms that she was drop-dead gorgeous, a Biedermeier Michelle Pfeiffer with dark hair and crystal-fine features. We are told that:

> She was not well-read; this was quite to the taste of Felix, who could not stand blue-stockings [meaning highly educated and opinionated women, like Mendelssohn's own mother and his sister Fanny!]. In social matters, she seems to have been quite experienced, and an especially gracious hostess. She became a splendid housewife and mother, and a beloved companion for Felix, to whom she brought joy, beauty, and goodness. Felix remained totally dependent upon her [for the rest of his life].

According to Eric Werner, marriage and family (Felix and Cecile had five children) are to be blamed for the "bourgeois conservatism"—the "perceived conventionality"—that purportedly "crept" into Mendelssohn's music starting in the early 1830s.

Harold Schonberg, for many years the chief music critic of the New York Times, blames this "encroaching conservatism" on Mendelssohn's Jewish background and his desire to assimilate. According to Schonberg:

> Mendelssohn never lived up to his initial creative promise. A certain conservatism, an emotional inhibition, kept him from reaching the heights. His music, always skillful, became more and more a series of correct, polite gestures as he grew older. For this we can blame his background. Coming as he did from a distinguished, wealthy, conservative Jewish family, he was taught from childhood to be correct, to observe good form, to avoid offence. conservatism [was] ingrained within him. The combination of wealth and Jewish-ness in a strongly anti-Semitic Berlin kept Mendelssohn unconsciously over-careful, hesitant to obtrude, anxious to be accepted.

Harold Schonberg statement and Eric Werner's before it are both based on the perception that Felix Mendelssohn—a pillar of the German musical establishment who had fame, wealth, a beautiful wife and adorable children—chose not to rock the musical boat out of fear: that he rooted himself in the status quo because he had no desire to "mess with his success."

Mendelssohn's perceived "bourgeois conservatism" is put into even higher relief when he is compared to Mr. Angry himself—Ludwig van Beethoven—the quintessential outsider: a man alienated from his family, terrified of marriage; a provincial Rhinelander among the courtly sophisticates of Vienna, a natural-born loner made doubly so by his hearing disability. When it came to his later music, Beethoven had nothing to lose by letting his amazing imagination run free. By comparison—so say some pundits—Mendelssohn had everything to lose if he had let his muse run free, so consequently he did not.

So what does all of this mean apropos of Mendelssohn's mature music in general and the "Italian" Symphony in particular? It means absolutely nothing. The fact is, Mendelssohn developed on an artistic path of his own making, and "developed" is the right word. He did not "stand still," and as he got older his compositional muse led him to an ever greater intensification of musical means, a sort of less-is-more aesthetic attitude that is not at all unusual for a maturing artist. This so-called "Mendelssohn problem" is, in reality, a canard, a red herring, a groundless issue based on false assumptions.

Mendelssohn's early masterworks have led some observers to believe that he was, at 18 years of age, the second coming of Beethoven: that he was going to pick up where Beethoven left off by composing music characterized by intense contrast and high dramatic content, and that his seemingly "less dramatic" later music was thus an epic artistic copout!

Wrong. Mendelssohn was Jacob Ludwig Felix Mendelssohn, not Ludwig van Mendelssohn, and his early, Beethoven-inspired masterworks represented but his first great compositional flowering: early masterworks that were a step on the road to finding his own compositional voice.

My friends, it's a case of Mendelssohn's prodigious talent working against him. Because he composed such amazing music before he was 20, many observers have assumed that those youthful works represented his mature compositional voice. In reality, these early works represented steps in Mendelssohn's ongoing development as a composer.

Fanny Mendelssohn, who understood her baby brother personally and musically better than anyone, wrote in a letter to him in 1835: "We were young precisely in the time of Beethoven's last years, and it was only to be expected that we assimilated his manner, as it is so moving and impressive. But you have lived through it and written yourself through it."

And in this, Fanny is absolutely correct.

Mendelssohn's music did not become "less Beethoven-like" and thus less "modern" because he was a bourgeois, converted-and-assimilated Jew fearful of rocking the cultural boat. His music became more lyric, more dominated by vocally-conceived melody, because that's where his compositional muse took him.

Musicologist Michael P. Steinberg writes in the *Cambridge Companion to Mendelssohn*:

> There is no "Mendelssohn problem," just as there is no "Jewish problem." Both of these are phantoms of history. The "Mendelssohn" and "Jewish" problems emerge from the anxiety of classification. Classification is an act of authority, of control. Mendelssohn [is resistant] to classification.

Well! Amen brother!

"Italian" Symphony, Movement 2

Once again, at the heart of Mendelssohn's mature compositional style is lyricism: song-like melodic expression that explicitly invokes the human voice. The second movement andante is a quiet and melancholy processional, inspired, perhaps, by the religious processionals Mendelssohn witnessed during his stay in Italy. We're going to hear the opening two minutes and 12 seconds of the movement, which is occupied by a single, direct, song-like melody accompanied by steady, marching, plucked low strings. [**Musical selection**: Mendelssohn, Symphony No. 4 in A Major, op. 90, "Italian," movement 2.]

Typical of his mature music, Mendelssohn presents the principal theme of this second movement over a simple, straightforward accompaniment, without the more active, counter melody-dominated accompaniments characteristic of his earlier music. [**Musical selection**: Mendelssohn, Symphony No. 4 in A Major, op. 90, "Italian," movement 2.]

This sort of direct thematic presentation is not an indication of encroaching conservatism. Rather, it's a reflection of Mendelssohn's developing desire to cultivate voice-like lyricism and thematic clarity in his music. In a letter to Wilhelm von Boguslawski written in 1834—the year after he initially completed the "Italian" Symphony—Mendelssohn stated that a composer must be able "to clearly present his ideas and what he wants to express. I want [my thematic] ideas to be expressed more simply and more naturally."

According to the musicologist Thomas Schmidt-Beste:

> Mendelssohn's concept of the "[thematic] idea" can be traced back to Hegel's idealism—that "the idea" is the carrier of all meaning, and for that meaning to be "clear" and communicable, it has to become "concrete" in an adequate fashion. Mendelssohn, like many of his contemporaries, sought in music an "ideal" art. After having become disenchanted with the potential of [program music, Mendelssohn's frequent use] of self-contained, song-like "[thematic] ideas" as well as their clear presentation were steps in that direction.

"Hegelian idealism": Who says Mendelssohn wasn't up to date?

Movement 4: Sonata Form

This fourth movement finale is the most explicitly "Italian" music in the symphony. Mendelssohn labels the movement as being "*saltarello.*" As Mendelssohn understood it, a *saltarello* was a folk dance popular in south and south-central Italy; a high-energy dance characterized by a hop on the last beat of every measure. (And thus the name of the dance: the word "saltarello" is derived from the Italian verb *saltare,* which means "to jump.") Let's hear the *saltarello* dance-theme that dominates the movement. [**Musical selection**: Mendelssohn, Symphony No. 4 in A Major, op. 90, "Italian," movement 4.]

We would observe that this *saltarello* finale behaves—expressively—like most classical era symphonic finales, which were intended not as summations *a la* Beethoven but rather, to engage the listener by putting a bounce in her step and a smile on her face. However, at the same time, this last movement is a rarity: a minor mode finale (set in A minor) for what is otherwise a major mode symphony. Once again, Herr Mendelssohn makes himself impossible to classify: something traditional, something different, all in the service of an entirely personal, an entirely "Mendelssohnian" movement.

That adjective "Mendelssohnian" came into being to describe the sprightly and elfin scherzi Mendelssohn was so famous for composing. This finale also has that personalized, Mendelssohn sound: a sound created here by the light-as-a-feather opening thematic statement in the flutes, the steady state triplets that characterize the theme and its accompaniment, and the rock-steady, dance-like beat that underlies it all. Let's hear the *saltarello* theme one more time, and now let us be especially aware of the piping flutes and bristling rhythms that help give this music its trademark, "Mendelssohnian-sound." [**Musical selection**: Mendelssohn, Symphony No. 4 in A Major, op. 90, "Italian," movement 4.]

The conclusion of the movement (and thus the symphony) is fabulous. A sinuous melody in the strings (which happens to be theme 2, thus far unsampled) builds up to a last, climactic statement of theme 1. And then, well, and then, the music simply seems to fade away into the distance, like a receding memory. Only at the very last second does the volume pick back up again in order to give some punch to the closing moments of the symphony. We hear the conclusion. [**Musical selection**: Mendelssohn, Symphony No. 4 in A Major, op. 90, "Italian," movement 4.]

Oh, Those Critics

Mendelssohn's critics have claimed that the "Italian" symphony is nothing but an unconnected series of *tableaux vivants*—that is, program music that would describe "pictures of daily life": a rather unsophisticated soundtrack to the travelogue of Mendelssohn's Italian tour.

Of course, it is nothing of the sort. Mendelssohn's "Italian" Symphony is, like so very much of Mendelssohn's mature music, unclassifiable. Yes, it features the beauty of line and clarity of expression we associate with classicism, but the sort of personalized, programmatic content that is very much the territory of early 19th-century romanticism. It is music that sounds and acts like that of Felix Mendelssohn and no one else.

Thank you.

Schumann—Symphony No. 3
Lecture 13

From a purely compositional point of view, Schumann's "Rhenish" is the best of the post-Beethoven program symphonies, combining his impressions of the Rhineland—its scenery, atmosphere, legends, and history—with a Beethovenian concision and rhythmic drive. Specifically, the exhilarating music of the first movement is a reflection of the exhilaration Schumann felt during his first months in Düsseldorf. Schumann composed his Third Symphony, in a typical creative intensity, between November 2 and December 9 of 1850.

The early 19th century saw the first great flowering of an artistic mentality that saw composers, writers, and visual artists bent on expressing their own feelings and worldviews in their work. By the 1830s, the romantic era had arrived, in which personal self-expression and originality had become artistic ends unto themselves. It was a time when cutting-edge, post-Beethoven composers celebrated themes of the glorification of emotion, nostalgia for a deep and mysterious past, and an extraordinary enthusiasm for nature—wild, pure, and untamed.

Many of these composers believed that the future of music was tied to merging music with literature and, thus, creating a composite art form. In the case of instrumental music, this meant composing works that could evoke specific emotions, paint pictures, and even tell stories. No one believed more completely in the artistic necessity of synthesizing music, literature, and self-expression than did the pianist, composer, and wannabe poet Robert Schumann.

Just as romanticism initially grew from literature, so did Robert Schumann. His father, August Schumann, was an author, translator, and bookseller who passed on his passion for literature to his son. Schumann began writing poems around the age of ten and continued to fancy himself a poet through his teens. His musical talents developed alongside his literary ones. He began piano lessons at the age of seven, and by the age of eight he had composed his first music—a set of dances for the piano. Between 1830 and 1840, he composed a large number of extraordinary avant-garde works for solo piano.

Typical of his manic creative jags, Schumann sketched his First Symphony in four days: from January 23–26, 1841. He completed orchestrating it a few weeks later. Nicknamed "Spring," it received its premier under the baton of Felix Mendelssohn at the Gewandhaus on March 31, 1841. The premiere was a triumph, and Schumann churned out a series of symphonic masterworks over the next nine years, capped by his Symphony no. 3, the "Rhine" or "Rhenish" of 1850.

The musical talents of Robert Schumann (1810–1856) developed alongside his literary talents.

Symphony No. 3 in E-flat Major, "Rhenish"
On March 31, 1850, the almost 40-year-old Schumann accepted an offer to become the municipal music director for the city of Düsseldorf, situated on the Rhine River in Germany. Schumann, who had never spent any appreciable amount of time in the Rhineland before moving to Düsseldorf in 1850, was enthralled with its landscape and history. Schumann's Symphony no. 3 in E-flat Major—his "Rhenish" Symphony— is about his fascination with the Rhenish landscape and its history, as well as the surge of optimism he felt during those first, exhilarating months in Düsseldorf.

Schumann's "Rhenish" Symphony is what we now call a program symphony, which is a multi-movement orchestral work that tells a story and/or paints musical pictures across its span. The most famous precedent is Beethoven's five-movement Symphony no. 6 of 1808, the "Pastoral" Symphony, which is about impressions and emotions inspired by a day in the country. Like Beethoven's Sixth Symphony, Schumann's Third is cast in five movements.

Movement 1

This first movement begins with one of Schumann's greatest themes. It rolls forward inexorably, riding on a rhythmic wave created by its rocking triple meter and long-short rhythms. This theme is meant to evoke the breadth and grandeur of the Rhine River itself. However, for all its grandeur, this theme does not employ the sorts of stereotypical, explicitly programmatic, opera house–derived musical gestures that would evoke water. This first theme is in sonata form and creates an impression rather than a programmatic theme that uses familiar devices to paint an explicit picture.

Schumann's Symphony no. 3 in E-flat Major—his "Rhenish" Symphony—is about his fascination with the Rhenish landscape and its history.

The theme's rolling sensibility is created by its triple meter, and its grandeur is created by its royal, fanfare-like long-short rhythms. The theme's grandeur is also a product of its orchestration: Along with the strings and winds, four horns, two trumpets, and a busy timpani part create a royal and festive atmosphere. This music makes an impression that is as broad and magnificent as the Rhine itself as it passes through Germany.

More than anything else, the movement is a beautifully wrought sonata form, replete with a second, contrasting theme, a lengthy development section, and a bold and brilliant conclusion. Theme 2 does not evoke the magnificence of the Rhine—or water, for that matter: It is a lyric, delicate, contrasting theme initially introduced by the winds that travels from G minor to E-flat major. While Schumann will dutifully return to theme 2 during the development section and the recapitulation, the star of this movement is theme 1 and the river it implicitly evokes. The conclusion of the development section features the horns, which play an elongated version of theme 1, and then theme 1 begins the recapitulation.

Movement 2

Schumann originally entitled this second movement "Morning on the Rhine." He removed the title, and in its place substituted the generic designation "scherzo." Structurally, a scherzo it is: a three-part, A–B–A form movement. A movement labeled a scherzo is usually a brisk, up-tempo affair, but this one is a moderately paced dance—a rustic German three step called a *Ländler*. Once again, the gently rising-and-falling melody line that characterizes the outer A sections evokes an impression of the Rhine.

Movement 3

Schumann indicates that this third movement be played *nicht schnell*— meaning "not fast." However, everything about this charming, elegantly scored movement is "in the middle." The overwhelmingly easygoing nature of this third movement gives it the character of an **intermezzo**, which means "interlude," an ingratiating transition from the first half of the symphony to this five-movement second half.

Movement 4

This fourth movement—the only true slow movement in the symphony— is the most program-specific movement in the "Rhenish" as well as the expressive cornerstone of the entire work. It is quite evident that Schumann composed this fourth movement in praise of the Cathedral of Cologne and the mystery and majesty of Catholic ritual. In addition, it is only in the fourth movement that the three trombones—which have been mute since the beginning of the symphony—begin to play. The gravity and majesty they evoke is physically palpable.

The opening of the movement exhibits the distinctive sound of the trombones, the processional sense created by the slow but steady rhythms, and the use of a dated polyphony that gives this passage a vaguely archaic quality. As the movement approaches its conclusion, the forward motion of the processional stops. The brass, wind, and string choirs alternate long, sustained notes, just as choirs of voices would at the climax of a sacred ceremony. This closing passage is sublime, as is the manner by which Schumann manages to create a sense of lofty, echoing space on what is otherwise a concert-hall stage.

Movement 5

In this fifth movement, we transit from the explicit programmatic references of the fourth movement back to the more implicit, impressionistic character of movements 1 and 2. An exuberant, energized rondo theme begins the movement that evokes a certain popular dance-type element. It is a brilliant movement, made more so by a brass choir that now includes not just four horns and two trumpets but the three trombones that made their first appearance during the fourth movement.

Typical of Schumann, he takes the opportunity in this final movement of the work to subtly bring together musical elements from previous movements—most notably from the fourth and the first movement. For example, as this fifth movement approaches its conclusion, the brass and string instruments make a direct reference to the fourth movement processional. The reference is subtle, but clear enough to evoke the memory of the first movement and, thus, create the sense of a journey complete. ■

Important Term

intermezzo: An instrumental interlude between the acts of a performance.

Schumann—Symphony No. 3
Lecture 13—Transcript

Welcome back to *The 30 Greatest Orchestral Works*. This is Lecture 13, and it is entitled "Schumann—Symphony No. 3."

The Romantic Expressive Paradigm

The early 19th century saw the first great flowering of what we today might call "me-centrism": an artistic mentality that saw composers, writers, and visual artists bent on expressing their own feelings, their own issues, and their own world views in their work.

Nothing happens in a vacuum, and certainly, this "triumph of me" was a result of a complex series of events going back over 100 years. The growing middle class placed an entirely new set of pressures on 18th-century Western society, pressures that slowly altered the economic, political, and cultural landscapes of the Western world. These pressures manifested themselves in a philosophical movement called the Enlightenment, a movement that gave intellectual currency and a vocabulary to the social evolution already in progress.

In reality, what we call the "Enlightenment" was not a single movement but rather a generalized drift of thought, one that advanced reason in government and recognized the individual—a sort of idealized every person—as being the principal "unit" in Western society. Enlightened thinking posited that the central task of the individual was to revel in his individuality through a pursuit of happiness here on earth, meaning self-fulfillment through political self-determination, education, and cultivation of the arts.

The French and American revolutions were direct political outgrowths of Enlightenment thought. The American Declaration of Independence, the United States Bill of Rights, and the French Declaration of the Rights of Man and of the Citizen are documents rooted in Enlightenment principles.

During the Enlightenment, the arts were judged based on the degree to which they embodied naturalness: that is, reason. The music of the Enlightenment—

which today goes under the heading of "the classical style"—was music that celebrated—above all—direct and beautiful melody, clarity of phrase and formal structure, and expressive restraint and good taste. More than any other single composer, it was Joseph Haydn whose music came to epitomize the classical style.

The French Revolution and subsequent Napoleonic Age—which encompassed the 26 years from 1789–1815—shook the European world to its core and changed the nature and substance of European society forever. In the world of Euro-music, it was the "Bad Boy from Bonn"—Ludwig van Beethoven—whose music best embodied the radicalism, danger, and disruptive change characteristic of this time. Beethoven's revolutionary artistic belief, that music composition was at its essence a form of self-expression, was itself a reflection of the Enlightenment's emphasis on the rights of the individual; the anything goes radicalism engendered by the French Revolution; and the disruption of the European status quo wrought by Napoleon.

Yes, Beethoven had—as well—profound personal issues that pushed him to radicalize his music as he did, but in fact, he could not possibly have framed his mature music as he did without the environmental and intellectual pre-sets provided by the Enlightenment, the French Revolution, and Napoleon Bonaparte.

Despite the reassertion of monarchial power in the years after Napoleon's final defeat and exile, there could be no going back to the absolutism of the early 18th century or to the "period style" of the classical era, during which composers were willing to work within a common musical style.

Beethoven died in 1827. By the 1830s, the "age of the individual" had arrived, in which personal self-expression and originality had become artistic ends unto themselves. The period designation most commonly applied to this 19th-century "age of the individual" is the romantic era.

"Romanticism": Definition

The adjective "romantic" comes from the noun "Romance." A "Romance" was a medieval tale or poem about heroic persons or events, written in one of the Romance languages: one of the languages descended from the Roman language, meaning Latin. Thus, when the adjective romantic first came into use around the mid-1600s, it implied a distant, fantastic, and imaginary world beyond the reality of the everyday.

"romantic art," then, is art that plumbs the "fantastic" by exploring emotional extremes and levels of experience beyond the everyday. In terms of 19th-century art, the word "romantic" was first used to describe the me-centric literature of such early 19th-English writers and poets as William Wordsworth, Samuel Taylor Coleridge, Percy Bysshe Shelley, John Keats, and Lord George Gordon Byron. These writers and poets celebrated a number of particular themes: the glorification of emotion, in particular, love; nostalgia for a deep, mystic, legendary and mysterious past; and an extraordinary enthusiasm for nature—wild, pure, and untamed.

Cutting-edge, post-Beethoven, "me-centric" composers were enamored of these same themes. To that end, many of these composers believed that the future of music was tied to merging music with literature, and thus creating a composite art form. In the case of instrumental music, this meant composing instrumental works that could evoke specific emotions, paint pictures, and even tell stories.

For cutting-edge, "me-centric" 19th-century poets, writers, visual artists, and composers, spontaneous personal expression was the passkey to the sublime. No one believed more completely in the artistic necessity of synthesizing music, literature and intimate, spontaneous self-expression than did the pianist, composer, and "wannabe" poet Robert Schumann.

Robert Schumann (1810–1856)

Just as romanticism initially grew from literature, so did Robert Schumann. His father, August Schumann, was an author, translator, and bookseller who passed on his passion for literature to his son. Robert Schumann began writing poems around the age of 10 and continued to fancy himself a poet through his teens. Schumann's musical talents developed side-by-side with his literary ones. He began piano lessons at the age of seven, and by the age of eight he had composed his first music, a set of dances for the piano. According to Schumann's friend Emil Flechsig, "Schumann was absolutely convinced that he would eventually become a famous man."

What remained undecided for the teenaged Robert Schumann was whether his fame would come as a poet or a musician. Poet or musician? Well, as far as Schumann's mother Johanna Christiana Schumann was concerned, it would be neither. Schumann's father had died in 1826, when he was 16. There was a family business to run, and Schumann's mother had decided that it was time for her dreamy, artsy-fartsy son Robert to step up to the plate and to do his part. At her insistence, the 18-year-old Schumann was packed off to the University at Leipzig to study law.

Away in Leipzig, and consequently out of his mother's sight, Schumann did what 18-year-old boys have always done: exactly what he wanted to. According to Schumann's friend Emil Flechsig, "[Robert] never entered a lecture hall."

Instead, he took piano lessons with a teacher named Friedrich Wieck, who told Robert that he—Friedrich Wieck, the greatest piano teacher in the world!—would make Schumann one of the greatest pianists in all of Europe in just three years!

That's not what happened. Within a matter of months Schumann was experiencing numbness in what was likely the ring finger of his right hand. The cause: repetitive stress brought on by Wieck's tortuous regimen, which required that Schumann practice exercises for upwards of eight hours at a stretch. Within a couple of years, Schumann's injured finger was de facto useless for anything more complicated than stirring coffee. Schumann was devastated. But he had been composing all the while, and he was able to shift his core musical activity to composition pretty much without missing a beat. Between 1830 and 1840 he composed a large number of really extraordinary, avant-garde works for solo piano, including such repertoire staples as *Scenes from Childhood*, *Carnaval*, and *Kreisleriana*.

At the same time, Schumann fell hopelessly in love with his former piano teacher's daughter, the young and beautiful piano wunderkind Clara Wieck. The 25 year-old Robert and 16 year-old Clara shared their first kiss in November of 1835, and within a month they had pledged themselves to each other. Friedrich Wieck, Clara's father, was apoplectic when he found out, and for the next five years he did everything in his power to keep the two apart. In this he failed, and Robert and Clara were married on September 12, 1840.

Up to the time of his marriage, Schumann's compositional output consisted almost entirely of solo piano works and songs for voice and piano. Clara wanted to see him move on to bigger things. Early in their marriage she wrote: "Dear Robert, don't take it amiss if I tell you that I've been seized by the desire to encourage you to write for orchestra. Your imagination and your spirit are too great for the weak piano."

It was Clara's confidence in her new hubby that gave Schumann the electrified prod he needed to write his first mature symphony. It didn't hurt that he was also, at the time, living and working in Leipzig, where the director and conductor of the local orchestra, the Gewandhaus, was a man Schumann declared to be the second coming of Mozart: Felix Mendelssohn.

Mendelssohn had been appointed conductor of the Gewandhaus in 1835, at the age of 26. To a degree quite new for his time, Mendelssohn was fascinated by the music of the recent and relatively distant past. Under his leadership, the Gewandhaus concerts became repertoire events, at which listeners—including Robert and Clara Schumann—gathered to hear masterworks by such dead composers as J. S. Bach, Haydn, Mozart, Beethoven, and Schubert. Along with Clara's insistence that he, "think big and write a symphony," it was the inspiration provided by Felix Mendelssohn and the Gewandhaus orchestra that gave Schumann the nerve to compose his first symphony in 1841.

Typical of his manic creative jags, Schumann sketched the symphony in four days: from the 23rd to 26th of January, 1841. He completed orchestrating it a few weeks later, on February 20. Nicknamed "Spring," it received its premiere under the baton of Felix Mendelssohn at the Gewandhaus on March

31, 1841. The premiere was a triumph, and Schumann, bit by the "orchestra bug," churned out a series of symphonic masterworks over the next nine years, capped by his Symphony No. 3, the "Rhine" or "Rhenish" of 1850.

Düsseldorf

On March 31, 1850, the not quite 40-year-old Schumann accepted an offer to become the municipal music director for the city of Düsseldorf, situated on the Rhine River in west-central Germany. Robert, Clara, and their brood of children arrived in Düsseldorf on September 2 of 1850, where they were greeted with a love-fest that went on for a week: serenades, balls, banquets, and performances of Robert's music.

We can only hope the Robert and Clara felt the love, because the first six months in Düsseldorf turned out to be the last good time in Schumann's life, a good time capped by the composition of his Symphony No. 3 and its premiere on February 6, 1851. Soon enough, Schumann's epic inadequacies as a conductor ("Could someone remind me why did we hired this guy?") became apparent, and not long after that, madness carried him off to an insane asylum in Endenich, roughly 35 miles south of Düsseldorf. But we get ahead of ourselves. First the good times.

Symphony No. 3 in E-flat Major, Op. 97, "Rhenish" (1850)

Despite the fact that the Rhine River begins in the Swiss Alps and flows through the Netherlands before emptying into the North Sea, it is Germany's River. The Rhine is to German geography and culture what the Mississippi is to American geography and culture: not just Germany's longest river but a landmark, a treasure trove of folklore and legend, a personification of the nation itself.

Since ancient times, the Rhine has been a vital and navigable waterway, carrying people and goods to and from the interior of Germany. Over the centuries the river has marked both regional and international borders, and has historically been a major defensive line. It marked the northern-most border of the Roman Empire, and 2,000 years later, it was Nazi Germany's presumably "impregnable" western barrier. (So much for impregnable:

It was crossed in March 1945 when the Ludendorff Bridge at Remagen, just south of Bonn, was captured by soldiers of the American Army's 27th Armored Infantry Battalion.)

In 2002, a 40-mile stretch of the Rhine south of Düsseldorf was declared a UNESCO World Heritage Site. Framed by steep cliffs and dotted with over 40 castles—many in ruins—this part of the Rhine long ago became a basic component in Germany's national mythology. It is here that the Rhine maidens guarded their patrimony: the Rhine gold. It was here that Wotan, king of the gods, built his castle Valhalla. And it was here, on the banks of the Rhine, that the castle of the Gibichungs fell to ruins at the end of Wagner's music drama *The Twilight of the Gods* to conclude his epic *Ring Cycle*.

Schumann, who had never spent any appreciable amount of time in the Rhineland before moving to Düsseldorf in 1850, was enthralled with its landscape and its history. Schumann's Third Symphony—his "Rhine Symphony"—is about his fascination with the Rhenish landscape and its history, as well as the surge of optimism he felt during those first, heady months in Düsseldorf.

Program Symphony

Schumann's "Rhenish" Symphony is a critter we now call a program symphony. A "program symphony" is a multi-movement orchestral work that tells a story and/or paints musical pictures across its span. The most famous precedent is Beethoven's five movement Symphony No. 6 of 1808, the "Pastoral Symphony," which, according to Beethoven himself, is about impressions and emotions inspired by a day in the country.

Hector Berlioz's *Symphonie Fantastique* of 1830 is just such a program symphony, as is Franz Liszt's *Faust Symphony* of 1854. From a purely compositional point of view, Schumann's "Rhenish" is the best of the post-Beethoven bunch, combining his impressions of the Rhineland—its scenery, atmosphere, legends, and history—with a Beethovenian concision and rhythmic drive. Schumann composed the symphony in a typical "white creative heat" between November 2 and December 9, 1850. Like Beethoven's Sixth Symphony, Schumann's Third is cast in five movements.

Movement 1: Sonata Form

This first movement begins with one of Schumann's greatest themes. It rolls forward inexorably, riding on a rhythmic wave created by its rocking triple meter and long-short rhythms, something we'll discuss after we've first heard the theme. [**Musical selection**: Schumann, Symphony No. 3 in E-flat Major, op. 97, movement 1.]

This theme is meant to evoke the breadth and grandeur of the Rhine River itself. However, for all its ebb and flow and grandeur, this theme does not employ the sorts of stereotypical, explicitly programmatic, opera house-derived musical gestures that would immediately tell us water: for example, swirling, eddying, continuous triplets: [**Piano demonstration**.] Or watery little sparkles played by plucked strings or bells: [**Piano demonstration**.] No. This is a sonata form first theme that creates an impression, rather than a programmatic theme that uses familiar devices to paint an explicit picture. The theme's "rolling sensibility" is created by its triple meter. [1-2-3, 1-2-3, 1-2-3.] Its "grandeur" is created by its royal, fanfare-ish long-short rhythms. [Sing rhythms.]

The theme's grandeur is also a product of its orchestration: along with the strings and winds, four horns, two trumpets, and a very busy timpani part create a royal and festive atmosphere. [**Musical selection**: Schumann, Symphony No. 3 in E-flat Major, op. 97, movement 1.] This is no trickling tributary in the Swiss Alps—oh no; this music makes an impression that is as broad and magnificent as the Rhine itself as it passes through Germany!

But an impression it is. Because more than anything else, the movement is a beautifully wrought sonata form, replete with a second, contrasting theme, a lengthy development section, and a bold and brilliant conclusion.

Theme 2 does not evoke the magnificence of Rhine or water, for that matter: It is a lyric, delicate, contrasting theme initially introduced by the winds that shuttles from G minor to E-flat major. Let's hear it. [**Musical selection**:

Schumann, Symphony No. 3 in E-flat Major, op. 97, movement 1.] Yes; that was short. Let's hear it again. [**Musical selection**: Schumann, Symphony No. 3 in E-flat Major, op. 97, movement 1.] Yes, it's still short.

And while Schumann will dutifully return to this theme 2 during the development section and the recapitulation, the star of this movement is theme 1 and the river it implicitly evokes. Let's hear the conclusion of the development section, during which Schumann cuts the horns loose to play an elongated version of theme 1, and then theme 1 as it begins the recapitulation. [**Musical selection**: Schumann, Symphony No. 3 in E-flat Major, op. 97, movement 1.] This is exhilarating music, and its exhilaration level does not flag for a moment. It's a reflection of the exhilaration Schumann himself felt during his first months in Düsseldorf.

Movement 2: Scherzo

Schumann originally entitled this second movement "Morning on the Rhine." He removed the title, and in its place substituted the generic designation "scherzo." Structurally, a scherzo it is: a three part, A-B-A form movement. However, to my mind, he should have kept the title "Morning on the Rhine." A movement labeled a "scherzo" is usually a brisk, up-tempo affair, and this one is a moderately paced dance, a rustic German dance, a three-step called a "Ländler." But more than that, the gently rising-and-falling melody line that characterizes the outer A sections once again evokes an impression of the Rhine. [**Musical selection**: Schumann, Symphony No. 3 in E-flat Major, op. 97, movement 2.]

Movement 3

Schumann indicates that this third movement be played *nicht schnell*: "not fast." He might just as well have indicated that it be played "*nicht* too hot," "*nicht* too cold," but just right, because everything about this charming, elegantly scored movement is "in the middle." Yes, Goldilocks would love it. Let's hear its opening minute. [**Musical selection**: Schumann, Symphony No. 3 in E-flat Major, op. 97, movement 3.] The overwhelmingly "easygoing dude-ness" of this third movement give it the character of an intermezzo—

an interlude—an ingratiating transition from the first half of the symphony to this five-movement second half.

Movement 4

This fourth movement—the only true slow movement in the symphony—is the most program-specific movement in the "Rhenish" as well as the expressive cornerstone of the entire work.

Here's the scoop. On September 30, 1850, four weeks after they had arrived in Düsseldorf, Robert and Clara took the 30-mile trip on the brand-new railway line to Cologne, where they visited the Cathedral of Cologne. The cathedral, which was begun in 1248 but not completed until 1880 (and you thought your kitchen remodel took too long!) is the largest Gothic church in northern Europe. In Schumann's day, the Cathedral of Cologne was considered the most famous building in all of Germany. (An irresistible factoid, my friends: For four years, from 1880 to 1884, the north tower of the cathedral, at 515 feet, was the tallest manmade structure in the world. It was topped in 1884 when the Washington Monument was finally completed; it stands 555 feet, 5 inches tall. The Washington Monument held the record for five years, until 1889, when the Eiffel Tower—at a whopping 1,063 feet—became the world's tallest structure. The Eiffel Tower remained the world's tallest man-made structure for 40 years, until 1929, when it was eclipsed by the Chrysler Building in New York City, which was beaten out 11 months later by the Empire State Building and that's where we will stop!)

The point: Robert Schumann was awed by the Cathedral of Cologne. According to Schumann's early biographer Wilhelm Joseph von Wasielewski, it was this visit to Cologne that inspired Schumann to compose a symphony about the Rhine in the first place. Anyway, five weeks later, in early November, Schumann returned to Cologne and toured the cathedral. On returning home to Düsseldorf, he learned of the impending celebrations to be held at the cathedral in honor of the elevation of Archbishop Geissel of Cologne to the College of Cardinals.

Well, that did it. His creative engine now thoroughly lubed, the Lutheran Robert Schumann sat down and composed his fourth movement in praise of the cathedral and the mystery and majesty of Catholic ritual. No doubt imagining the installation ceremony for Archbishop Geissel, Schumann originally indicated that the movement be played, "In the character of an accompaniment to a solemn ceremony."

However, when the symphony was published in 1851, he removed the inscription, stating that: "There is no need to reveal one's heart to the world. It is better for people to be given a general impression of the work; then they won't make any false comparisons."

While we might admire Schumann's altruism, it didn't do him any good, because we know what he wrote in the first place! Besides, everything about this extraordinary movement screams "a solemn processional down a vaulted, echoing nave"!

One last point before we begin our listening. It is only here and now, in the fourth movement, that the three trombones—which have been sitting on stage, cooling their slides since the start of the symphony—begin to play. The gravity and majesty they evoke is physically palpable. The expressive impact of the trombones would have been even greater in Schumann's day, when their sound was more closely associated with the church and the opera theater than with the symphony hall.

Let's hear the opening two minutes of the movement. Let us listen, one, for the distinctive sound of the trombones at the beginning; two, the sense of processional created by the slow but steady rhythms; and three, Schumann's use of a sort of "ye olde time polyphony" that gives this passage a vaguely archaic quality. [**Musical selection**: Schumann, Symphony No. 3 in E-flat Major, op. 97, movement 4.]

As the movement approaches its conclusion the forward motion of the processional stops. The brass, wind, and string choirs alternate long sustained notes, just as choirs of voices would at the climax of a sacred ceremony. This closing passage is sublime, as is the manner by which Schumann manages to create a sense of lofty, echoing space on what is otherwise a concert-hall stage. [**Musical selection**: Schumann, Symphony No. 3 in E-flat Major, op. 97, movement 4.]

We would quote two contemporary reviews of this wonderful movement. Writing after the premiere performance of the symphony in February of 1851, a writer known to us only as J. C. H. called the fourth movement a "halo floating over the whole [symphony]."

In 1852, the German composer and writer Theodor Uhlig stated in the *Neue Zeitschrift für Musik* that in this fourth movement, Schumann had "entered the delicate sphere of aesthetic speculation." (I'm not sure what that's supposed to mean, but I like it, so I'm pretty sure I agree with it!)

Movement 5: Rondo

In his fifth movement, we transit from the explicit programmatic references of the fourth movement back to the more implicit, impressionistic character of movements 1 and 2. Let's hear the exuberant, energized rondo theme that begins the movement. [**Musical selection**: Schumann, Symphony No. 3 in E-flat Major, op. 97, movement 5.]

There's nothing explicitly programmatic in this music beyond a certain popular dance-type element. It's a purposeful populism on Schumann's part. Regarding this fifth movement, he told his wife Clara: "I wanted elements of popular music to predominate, and I think I have succeeded."

Frankly, if this were the final movement of a work known only as "Schumann's Symphony No. 3 in E-flat Major," we'd acknowledge its brilliant, dancing, up-beat quality (which had been typical of symphonic finales since the mid-18th century) without reading any particular programmatic content into it. But, of course, it is the finale of a symphony called the "Rhenish," so I—like every other commentator since Schumann's day—would like to ascribe to it some programmatic content consistent with the designation "Rhenish." OK. How about this? "The fifth movement is a dancing and sweeping return to the sunshine and bustle of life, on and by, the river Rhine."

Good enough.

It is a brilliant movement, made more so by a brass choir that now includes not just four horns and two trumpets but the three trombones that made their first appearance during the fourth movement. Typical of Schumann, he takes the opportunity, here in the final movement of the work, to subtly bring together musical elements from previous movements, most notably from the fourth movement and the first movement. For example, as this fifth movement approaches its conclusion, the brass and string instruments make a direct reference to the fourth movement processional. [**Musical selection**: Schumann, Symphony No. 3 in E-flat Major, op. 97, movement 5]) Roughly 40 seconds later, we hear this lick in the horns. [**Musical selection**: Schumann, Symphony No. 3 in E-flat Major, op. 97, movement 5.] My friends, let's hear that again. [**Musical selection**: Schumann, Symphony No. 3 in E-flat Major, op. 97, movement 5.] That should sound familiar. Here's that fifth movement horn lick once more, played on the piano. [**Piano demonstration.**] And now the beginning of theme 1, movement 1: [**Piano demonstration.**] Again, the fifth movement reference: [**Piano demonstration.**] The first movement theme: [**Piano demonstration.**]

The reference is subtle, but clear enough to evoke the memory of the first movement and thus create the sense of a journey complete. Let's hear the remainder of the fifth and final movement, starting with the blaring and magnificent reference to the fourth movement processional sampled just moments ago. [**Musical selection**: Schumann, Symphony No. 3 in E-flat Major, op. 97, movement 5.]

Conclusion

Schumann's "Rhenish" Symphony was the last, exuberant gasp of a doomed composer. On February 27, 1854, three years after its triumphant premiere, Schumann—his mind ravaged by bipolar disorder and melted by tertiary syphilis—tried to kill himself by jumping off a bridge into the Rhine. He was rescued and hustled off to a sanitarium, where he died—shrunken and quite insane—2½ years later, on July 29, 1856, at the age of 46.

Thank you.

Brahms—Symphony No. 4
Lecture 14

By the time Brahms composed his Symphony no. 4 in 1885—at the age of 52—he had begun to believe that he was written out. At the symphony's premier, the audience enthusiastically applauded every movement followed by an outstanding ovation at its conclusion. In retrospect, we can see that Brahms's fears regarding the symphony were just another manifestation of his monumental self-criticism, a lingering byproduct of the curse, and his existential inferiority complex vis-à-vis the music of Haydn, Mozart, Beethoven, and Schubert.

Johannes Brahms's four symphonies lie at the core of the symphonic repertoire. Incredibly, they are works that might never have been composed because of a so-called curse that descended upon him by way of an article that was published in October of 1853, when Brahms was just 20 years old. The article, written by Robert Schumann, announced Brahms as the new messiah of German music, the long-awaited successor to Beethoven. Schumann's article had brought him too much attention much too soon.

In May of 1857, Brahms finished his first major composition, his Piano Concerto no. 1 in D Minor. It had taken him four obsessive years of the most tortuous writing and rewriting to finish the piece—mostly because he was terrified that if his first major orchestral composition was not equal to the expectations created by Schumann's article, he would be laughed off the European musical stage. The concerto received its premiere—with Brahms at the piano—in 1859. The Leipzig audience, still mourning the death of their beloved Mendelssohn, sat silently after Brahms's final movement was played. As a result, Brahms decided not to compose music that would bring him into direct comparison with Beethoven—meaning, specifically, symphonies and **string quartets**.

However, in 1873, Brahms released not one, but two string quartets. Having done so, he was finally prepared to complete and release a symphony. Brahms's Symphony no. 1 in C Minor—21 years in the making—received its premiere in the fall of 1876, and it was respectfully received. It took

Brahms 21 years to complete his First Symphony, but it only took him four months to complete his Second Symphony. Years of pent-up orchestral ideas followed, as one major orchestral work after another emerged from his pen.

Symphony No. 4 in E Minor

Brahms was afraid that his Fourth Symphony was dry and pedantic, a fear reinforced by the tepid response of his friends when he played the symphony for them on the piano. In fact, it is a masterwork and was greeted as such from the moment of its premiere, which took place on October 25, 1885, in the German city of Meiningen under the baton of Hans von Bülow. The conductor immediately took the symphony on tour across Europe, and it became an instant favorite among audiences and musicians, which it remains to this day.

Johannes Brahms (1833–1897) composed his Symphony no. 4 at the age of 52—an age that some composers never reached.

Movement 1
This first movement—somber and noble in expressive tone – is a superb example of Brahms as compositional synthesizer. It is structured on the disciplined, 18th-century, classical-era lines of sonata form. However, in its continuous development of a single intervallic (pertaining to an **interval**) idea as well as its harmonic and expressive substance, the movement is most definitely a product of a late-19th-century German composer.

Theme 1 is based on a series of falling-then-rising thirds and is set in two phrases. The theme begins with a step ladder–like presentation of all the pitches in E minor and then all the pitches in C major. At this point, the essential melodic and harmonic grist of the movement is laid out: Thematic melodies will be based on the interval of a third with a particular harmonic relationship between two keys a third apart, E minor and C major.

Following the modulating bridge, a brief, fanfare-like passage scored for winds and then strings paves the way for theme 2. The passage is built almost entirely from strings of successive thirds. Theme 2, which now immediately follows, is a dark, powerful, march-like theme initially scored for the 'cellos and horns. Theme 2 is a further derivation of the opening of theme 1. The accompaniment beneath theme 2 is a series of descending thirds.

In just this way, this movement unfolds on parallel tracks. One track describes an ongoing metamorphic process, as Brahms spins his thematic materials into continuously new sounds. On the other track, he employs strings of thirds more or less verbatim, which gives this otherwise constantly developing music a sense of coherence and consistency.

Movement 2
The second movement is a solemn and impassioned andante of great gravity and power. It also employs musical elements first introduced at the beginning of the first movement—most notably, a shift between the tonalities of E and C. The opening theme is expressed quietly and with the measured step of a processional.

Movement 3
The suggestion of C major heard during the course of the second movement becomes explicit in the riveting third movement, which is set entirely in C major. In its large-scale A–B–A structure and brilliant spirit, the movement is a scherzo in all but name (Brahms entitles it *allegro giocoso*, meaning "fast and playful"). The hard, bright edge of this music owes much to the presence of a triangle and the piercing sound of the stratospheric piccolo part.

Movement 4
The fourth movement of Brahms's Fourth Symphony is generally considered his single greatest movement of orchestral music; it is a movement that emphasizes Brahms's compositional quintessence as a synthesizer. He employs a baroque-era procedure, passacaglia, to create a movement of

stunning romantic-era expressive impact. That Brahms would employ such an antiquated and potentially limiting musical procedure in a symphony composed in 1885 is the sort of thing that made the Wagnerian modernists think he was crazy. But Brahms knew—better than the romantic modernists—that without discipline, there can be no art.

It is generally believed that this fourth movement was the first to be conceived and might very well have inspired Brahms to want to compose his Fourth Symphony. The inspiration for this fourth movement came from two works by Johann Sebastian Bach. Brahms added one extra pitch to the passacaglia theme found in Bach's Cantata no. 150—an A-sharp—and thus was born the ground bass theme for the fourth movement of his Fourth Symphony. The opening of the fourth movement exhibits the first iteration of the ground bass theme, played with magisterial power by brass (including three trombones, which are playing for the first time in the symphony), winds, and timpani.

Brahms's four symphonies lie at the core of the symphonic repertoire.

There are 30 variations—that is, 30 repetitions of the ground bass theme with ever-changing materials around it—that can be organized into 3 distinct groups. Variations 1–11 are all set in E minor and are generally monumental in expressive impact and tone. In variations 4–7, the dramatic momentum really starts to build.

The second large grouping of variations consists of variations 12–15. These 4 variations are quieter, more lightly scored, and double the length of the first 11 variations. Variation 12 features an achingly melancholy solo flute. The mode switches to E major for the remainder of this second group of variations. Variation 14 is particularly spectacular—the 3 trombones intone a **hymn** of otherworldly beauty and majesty.

The lyric oasis represented by variations 12–15 ends with the beginning of variation 16, the first of the variations that comprises the third section of the movement. The mode returns to minor, the variations are once again shorter, and the monumental character of the first group of variations resumes.

Variation 16 sounds like a recapitulation—like a return from some contrasting place. However, the ground bass theme has been constant throughout, cycling back around every 8 measures. The lesson, which Brahms learned from Bach, is that the musical sameness and rigor of a passacaglia does not preclude a great composer from creating a sense of departure and return by providing groups of variations with certain shared characteristics.

The movement—and the symphony—conclude with a magisterial coda following variation 30. Most minor-mode symphonies—Beethoven's ninth, for example—mark a trajectory of darkness to light, of struggle capped by victory, and conclude, cathartically and triumphantly—in major. However, Brahms's fourth-movement coda brings this symphony to its conclusion in the tonal darkness of E minor. Brahms, who saw himself as the last exponent of the German symphonic tradition, does not surrender to convention at the end of his Fourth Symphony—his final symphony. ■

Important Terms

hymn: A religious song.

interval: Distance between two pitches, e.g., C–G (upward) equals a fifth.

string quartet: A performing ensemble consisting of two violins, a viola, and a 'cello. (2) A musical composition written for that ensemble.

Brahms—Symphony No. 4
Lecture 14—Transcript

We return to *The 30 Greatest Orchestral Works*. This is Lecture 14, and it is entitled "Brahms—Symphony No. 4."

Johannes Brahms was a maddening mass of contradictions. As prickly as a cactus in his day-to-day dealings with the world, he was, nevertheless, a man of great modesty with a heart of gold who loved children and working people. A story: Brahms spent the summer of 1885 composing in the Austrian resort town of *Mürzzuschlag*. One day, a fire broke out in a carpenter's workshop on the ground floor of the building in which Brahms was staying.

> [The 52 year-old] Brahms ran from his workroom in shirtsleeves to join the bucket brigade to fight the fire, shouting at well-dressed passersby to lend a hand. In the confusion someone pulled him aside and told him that his papers were threatened by the blaze. Brahms thought it over for a second, then returned to the buckets. [Brahms's friend] Richard Fellinger finally extracted from him the key to his room and ran to save the [manuscript] score of the [newly completed] Fourth Symphony. When the fire was out … Brahms shrugged off the threat to his manuscript with "Oh the poor people needed help more than I did."

Brahms then put his money where his mouth was and personally paid for rebuilding the carpenter's workshop where the fire had begun. Brahms's four symphonies lie at the core of the symphonic repertoire. Incredibly, they are works that might never have been composed because of events that took place in October of 1853, when Brahms was just 20 years old. It's a story that must be told!

The Curse

On the morning of October 1, 1853, Johannes Brahms, 20 years old, short, blond, blue-eyed, slim, and cute as the proverbial "dickens," entered the house of Robert and Clara Schumann at Number 15 Bilkerstrasse in Düsseldorf. He was expected: Robert and Clara's friend, the great and famous violinist Joseph Joachim, had told them to expect this little tow-headed miracle any day.

Robert Schumann opened the door. Brahms introduced himself; Schumann mumbled something and led Brahms to a piano. Brahms sat down and began to play his Sonata No. 1 in C Major. Brahms's biographer Jan Swafford describes what happened next:

> Brahms felt Schumann's touch on his shoulder. "Please wait a moment. I must call my wife." Schumann rushed from the room as Brahms sat staring at the keyboard, his heart pounding. He may never have heard Clara Schumann play, but he knew about her. Clara had performed only sporadically since her marriage in 1840, but her teenage years were still spoken of with awe.
>
> Clara greeted him with a smile that lit up her dark blue eyes.
>
> "Here, dear Clara," Schumann said, "you shall hear music such as you have never heard before. Now begin your sonata again, young man."

Brahms proceeded to play for the better part of two hours. That evening Clara wrote in her journal: "Here again is one who comes as if sent from God! … A great future lies before him, for when he comes to the point of writing for orchestra, then he will have found the true medium for his imagination." That same evening Robert wrote in his diary: "Visit from Brahms (a genius)."

Robert and Clara insisted that Brahms stay on with them for at least a month, an offer Brahms accepted. Within a few days, Schumann had contacted his publisher, the house of Breitkopf & Härtel, and arranged for Brahms's first publications. But for Schumann, this was not enough. He wanted—personally—to introduce Brahms to the German musical establishment. So Schumann wrote an article, his "Rhapsody on Brahms." The "article" appeared on October 28, 1853, in the prestigious *Neue Zeitschrift fur Musik*. In it, Schuman announced the coming of the new messiah of German music, the long awaited successor to Beethoven.

Oh, pooh.

Twenty years old and a virtual nobody, Johannes Brahms was declared by Robert Schumann to be the new messiah of German music. Brahms's eyes must have opened really wide when he read that. No one had to tell Brahms that the messiah was first greeted with laurels, and then he was crucified.

Brahms's biographer Karl Geiringer writes:

> Instantly, the name of Brahms became known, and the publication of his works was eagerly awaited. One thing already seemed clear: It was not going to be plain sailing for the young composer. The public and the critics expected the very best after this sensational introduction.

From that day on, Brahms had to work twice as hard as he might otherwise have had to work in order to justify Schumann's article. Did Schumann do Brahms a favor by writing the article? No, he did not; the article turned out to be—the curse!

Flying Leaps

At the time Brahms met Robert Schumann during the early fall of 1853, Schumann had been experiencing psychotic episodes for over 20 years. Brahms's arrival momentarily jolted Schumann back to reality, but not even Brahms could still the chorus of angels and demons whispering and screaming inside Schumann's head.

On February 27, 1854, dressed in only a bathrobe and slippers, Robert Schumann threw himself off the Rhine River Bridge in Düsseldorf into the river. He was rescued, but his mind had snapped. Clara, ordered away from her soaking wet husband, next saw him on his deathbed, 2½ years later. Brahms rushed back to Düsseldorf and pledged to stay with Clara (who was five months pregnant with child number seven) until the baby was born and Schumann had recovered.

Visitors came and went, but it was Brahms who stayed. And along the way, Johannes Brahms and Clara Schumann fell in love. In a letter to Joseph Joachim, Brahms made the following confession: "I love her and am under her spell. I often have to restrain myself forcibly from just quietly putting my arms around her and even … well, I don't know, it seems to me so natural that she could not misunderstand."

Brahms was 21; Clara was 34. She was the mother of seven children. Clara knew how Brahms felt about her, but these were feelings neither Clara nor Brahms could possibly act upon while Robert was still alive. By 1856, the now 23-year-old Brahms had come to realize that his role as Clara's surrogate husband was suffocating him. He needed to get on with his own life.

Fate intervened. On July 29, 1856, Robert Schumann died. The moment of truth for Clara and Johannes had arrived. Properly chaperoned, they took a vacation together to Switzerland. We do not know what they said to each other, but Brahms decided that he would not, could not marry Clara.

Clara's daughter Eugenie later wrote: "He broke away ruthlessly. My mother had suffered all the more as she could not understand the change in him. … She remained towards Brahms what she had always been; she loved him truly and wholeheartedly."

Postscript: Brahms never married. Clara was indeed the great love of his life, and they remained friends for the rest of their lives.

The Career Begins

And so Brahms began the process of building his career. In May of 1857, Brahms finished, more or less, his first "major" composition, his Piano Concerto No. 1 in D Minor. It had taken him four obsessive years of the most tortuous writing and rewriting to finish the piece.

Why? Well, chief among the reasons was the curse. Brahms was terrified that if the concerto—as his first major orchestral composition—was not equal to the expectations created by Schumann's article, he would be laughed of the European musical stage.

The concerto received its premiere, with Brahms at the piano, on January 22, 1859, in Hanover. Its second performance took place five days later, on January 27, 1859, at Leipzig's Gewandhaus, the single most important concert venue in all of Germany.

My friends, Brahms should have called in sick that night. The Leipzig audience—still grieving over their departed hero, Felix Mendelssohn—was not inclined to give Schumann's young "messiah" an even break. When the performance was over, nothing happened; the hall remained deathly silent. Brahms sat at the piano, waiting for some response. Finally, three people began to applaud, which provoked an explosion of hissing from the rest of the audience. Brahms stood up, bowed and, visibly shaking, walked off, accompanied at every step by the sound of hissing.

The review was brutal. I will spare you the reading.

Johannes Brahms was cut to his soul. Schumann's article—the curse—had brought him much too much attention much too soon. An immediate upshot was that Brahms decided not to compose—or at least, not to release to the public—music that would bring him into direct comparison with Beethoven, meaning, specifically, symphonies and string quartets.

Liar, Liar, Pants on Fire

It was during the early 1870s that Brahms, approaching 40 years of age, famously told the conductor Hermann Levi: "I'll never write a symphony! You have no idea how the likes of us feel when we're always hearing a giant like [Beethoven] behind us." Of course, Brahms was lying. In truth, he'd been working on a symphony for years.

In 1873, Brahms released not one, but two string quartets. And having done so, he was finally prepared to complete, and then release, a symphony!

Brahms's Symphony No. 1 in C Minor, 21 years in the making, received its premiere in the fall of 1876. Respectfully received, Brahms breathed a gigantic sigh of relief. It was done. Since 1853, he had lived with Schumann's curse: the assertion that he—Johannes Freaking Brahms—was the one and true heir to Beethoven, the messiah of German music. Since 1853, Brahms had been terrified to release a string quartet or a symphony.

Well, in 1873 he released two string quartets and no one chortled. Emboldened, he released his first Symphony in 1876; no one guffawed. In fact, Brahms's First Symphony prompted the pianist and conductor Hans von Bülow, to write: "I believe it is not without the intelligence of chance that Bach, Beethoven, and Brahms are in alliteration." Von Bülow's comment got out, and to Brahms's public dismay (and great secret pleasure) he became known as one of the "Three B's."

The Symphonic Brahms

It took Brahms 21 years to complete his first symphony. It took him four months to complete his second symphony, for which the Viennese public flipped when it was premiered on December 30 of 1877. In his review of the premiere, Eduard Hanslick declared the symphony an "Unqualified success!"

Well, that did it; Brahms orchestral imagination caught fire! Years of pent-up orchestral ideas came pouring out, as one major orchestral work after another emerged from his pen. Check it out: 1876, Symphony No. 1; 1877, Symphony No. 2; 1878, the Violin Concerto; 1880, *The Academic Festival Overture*; 1881, the Piano Concerto No. 2; 1883, the Symphony No. 3; 1885: the Symphony No. 4; and lastly, Brahms's final orchestral work, the Double Concerto for Violin and 'Cello of 1887.

Johannes Brahms at 52

Brahms composed his Fourth Symphony in 1885, at the age of 52. Fifty-two: It's an age that I, for one, have seen come and go. It's an age that we, today, consider youngish, during which we are in the prime of life, at the height of our powers. Today, our 50s are the new 30s, or so pop culture would have us believe.

These are sentiments that Johannes Brahms did not share. In early May of 1883, he wrote a note to his friend Dr. Theodor Billroth: "Hanslick [meaning Eduard Hanslick, the Viennese music critic] Hanslick and I, on Monday evening, want to have a little small sad festival together. Only you, [Artur] Faber, and we two."

The "sad festival" Brahms referred to was his 50th birthday on May 7, 1883. Brahms, despite his robust good health, was feeling his years. As a student of music history, no one had to tell him that Beethoven had died at 56, Robert Schumann at 46, Frederic Chopin at 39, Felix Mendelssohn at 38, Mozart at 35, and Franz Schubert at 31. It didn't help that Brahms's friend Dr. Theodor Billroth claimed that in his "scientific opinion," no artist could surpass himself after the age of 50. What it means is that by the time Brahms composed his Symphony No. 4 in 1885—at the age of 52—he had begun to believe that he was written out.

Johannes Brahms, Symphony No. 4 in E Minor, Op. 98 (1885)

Brahms was worried about his Fourth Symphony. He was afraid that it was dry and pedantic, a fear reinforced by the tepid response of his friends when he played the symphony through for them on the piano. Brahms's pal, the writer and critic Max Kalbeck, went so far as to advise Brahms to toss the third movement entirely, convert the fourth movement into a self-standing orchestral work, and then compose an entirely new third movement and an entirely fourth movements. That Brahms actually listened to such advice without tearing out Kalbeck's lungs testifies to his own doubts about the piece.

Brahms warned his publisher Fritz Simrock not to expect much from the symphony, writing: "I haven't the ghost of an idea whether I'll let the thing be printed. You'd be insane to invest a [penny] in it!"

What a waste of emotional energy. There was nothing "wrong" with Brahms's Symphony No. 4; it is a masterwork and was greeted as such from the moment of its premiere. That premiere—which took place on October 25, 1885, in the central-German city of Meiningen under the baton of Hans von Bülow—was a triumph. The audience enthusiastically applauded every movement followed by what one source calls a "delirious ovation" at its conclusion. The conductor, Hans von Bülow, immediately took the symphony on tour across Europe, and it became an instant favorite among audiences and musicians, which it remains to this day.

In retrospect, we can see that Brahms's fears regarding the symphony were just another manifestation of his monumental self-criticism, a lingering byproduct of the curse, and his existential inferiority complex vis-à-vis the music of Haydn, Mozart, Beethoven, and Schubert.

Movement 1: Sonata Form

This first movement, somber and noble in expressive tone, is a superb example of Brahms as compositional synthesist. It is structured on the disciplined 18th-century classical era lines of sonata form. However, in its continuous development of a single intervallic (an interval between two pitches) idea as well as its harmonic and expressive substance, the movement is most definitely a product of a late 19th-century German composer. Let's dive in.

Theme 1 is based on a series of falling-then-rising thirds. Let's listen to the theme, and then I'll demonstrate what I'm talking about. Here's theme 1 in its entirety, set in two phrases. [**Musical selection**: Brahms, Symphony No, 4 in E Minor, op. 98, movement 1.] Let's go back to the beginning and hear theme 1, phrase 1. [**Musical selection**: Brahms, Symphony No, 4 in E Minor, op. 98, movement 1.] Let's go back to the beginning and listen to just the opening of theme 1, phrase 1. [**Musical selection**: Brahms, Symphony No, 4 in E Minor, op. 98, movement 1.] OK. Back to the statement with which I introduced theme 1: "Theme 1 is based on a series of falling-then-rising thirds." The theme begins with a step ladder-like presentation of all the pitches in E minor and then all the pitches in C major. First E minor: [**Piano demonstration**.] Then C major: [**Piano demonstration**.] If we take out the leaps in the melody and simply line these pitches up, we get first a descending and then an ascending string of consecutive thirds. [**Piano demonstration**.] The descending string of thirds outlines the pitches of E minor. [**Piano demonstration**.] And the ascending string of thirds outlines the pitches of C major. [**Piano demonstration**.]

There you have it: the essential melodic and harmonic grist of the movement has just been laid out with absolute clarity: Thematic melodies will be based on the interval of a third, with a particular harmonic relationship between two keys a third apart, E minor and C major.

For example, following the modulating bridge—which, not incidentally, is woven almost entirely from materials derived from strings of thirds—following this modulating bridge, a brief, fanfare-like passage, scored for winds and then strings paves the way for theme 2. This fanfare-like passage is built, almost entirely, from strings of successive thirds. [**Musical selection**: Brahms, Symphony No, 4 in E Minor, op. 98, movement 1.]

Theme 2—which now immediately follows—is a dark, powerful, almost march-like theme initially scored for the 'cellos and horns. [**Musical selection**: Brahms, Symphony No, 4 in E Minor, op. 98, movement 1.] Theme 2 is a further derivation of the opening of theme 1, though a clear demonstration of that derivation goes frankly beyond the scope of this course. However! The accompaniment beneath theme 2 is easy to demonstrate and recognize. First, here's theme 2. [**Piano demonstration**.] And here's the accompaniment beneath theme 2: a series of descending thirds. [**Piano demonstration**.] Put them together. [**Piano demonstration**.] Theme 2, one more time! [**Musical selection**: Brahms, Symphony No, 4 in E Minor, op. 98, movement 1.]

In just this way this movement unfolds on parallel tracks. One track describes an ongoing metamorphic process, as Brahms spins his thematic materials into ever-new sounding stuff. The other track sees him employ strings of thirds more or less verbatim, which gives this otherwise constantly developing music a sense of coherence and consistency.

As an example of Brahms's ongoing metamorphic process, we turn to an episode in the development section at exactly the midpoint of the movement: a lilting and melancholy dance played by the clarinets, oboes and bassoons. It's a passage that grows out of a melodic idea drawn from the modulating bridge and a rhythmic idea drawn from the fanfare that introduced theme 2 (both of which originally grew out of theme 1). With its offbeat accompaniment provided by plucked strings, this shoulder-rocking music has the exotic feel of Eastern European dance music. Let's hear it! [**Musical selection**: Brahms, Symphony No, 4 in E Minor, op. 98, movement 1.]

As an example of Brahms's use of thematic materials in their more-or-less original form, let's hear the slashing, climactic version of theme 1 that concludes the movement. [**Musical selection**: Brahms, Symphony No, 4 in E Minor, op. 98, movement 1.]

Movement 2

The second movement is a solemn and impassioned andante of great gravity and power. It also employs musical elements first introduced at the beginning of the first movement, most notably a shift between the tonalities of E and C. Let's hear its opening theme, expressed quietly and with the measured step of a processional. [**Musical selection**: Brahms, Symphony No, 4 in E Minor, op. 98, movement 2.]

Movement 3

The suggestion of C major heard during the course of the second movement becomes explicit in the riveting third movement, which is set entirely in C major. In its large-scale A-B-A structure and brilliant spirit, the movement is a scherzo in all but name. (Brahms entitles it "Allegro Giocoso," meaning "fast and playful.")

Let's hear the opening of the movement, the A section of this erstwhile scherzo. Please note the hard, bright edge of this music owes much to the presence of a triangle and the piercing-as-a-hot-arrow-through-Jell-O sound of the stratospheric piccolo part. [**Musical selection**: Brahms, Symphony No, 4 in E Minor, op. 98, movement 3.]

Movement 4: Passacaglia

The fourth movement of Brahms's Fourth Symphony is generally considered Brahms's single greatest movement of orchestral music. It is a movement that puts an emphatic exclamation mark on Brahms's compositional quintessence as a synthesist, in which a baroque era procedure called a "passacaglia" is employed to create a movement of stunning romantic era expressive impact.

A passacaglia is musical form in which an entire movement is built upon the repetitions of a brief bass line called a ground bass theme. In a passacaglia, the parts above the ground bass theme change and metamorphose constantly, which provides no small compositional challenge given the repetitious sameness of the bass line.

That Brahms would employ such an antiquated and potentially limiting musical procedure in a symphony composed in 1885 is exactly the sort of thing that made the Wagnerian modernists think he was crazy. But Brahms, bless him, was crazy like a fox, and he knew—better than the Romantic modernists for whom anything went—that without discipline there could be no art! It is generally believed that this fourth movement was the first to be conceived and might very well have inspired Brahms to want to compose a fourth symphony in the first place.

The inspiration for this fourth movement came from two works by Johann Sebastian Bach. The first was Bach's Chaconne in D Minor for Solo Violin, a work that Brahms had arranged for piano left hand eight years before, in 1877. Brahms dedicated the arrangement to Clara Schumann, to whom he wrote:

> For me the Chaconne is one of the most incredible pieces of music. For a little instrument, the man writes a whole world of the deepest and most powerful expression. If I had written this piece—been able to conceive it—I know for certain the emotions excited would have driven me mad.

Let me play the opening of Brahms's arrangement. [**Piano demonstration.**] The immediate inspiration for the fourth movement of Brahms's Fourth Symphony was a passacaglia from Bach's Cantata No. 150, a work entitled *For Thee, O Lord, I Long*. Bach's passacaglia theme, his ground bass theme, goes like this. [**Piano demonstration.**]

Brahms played this very theme for the conductors Hans von Bülow and Siegfried Ochs sometime in 1880 at Ochs's house in Berlin, saying, in regards to Bach's theme: "What would you think of a symphonic movement written on this theme some day? But it is too [*klotzig*]; [too klutzy], too straightforward. … It would have to be chromatically altered in some way."

Well, that's exactly what Brahms did: He added one extra pitch to Bach's theme—an A-sharp—and thus was born his ground bass theme, the theme that underlies the fourth movement of his Fourth Symphony. [**Piano demonstration**.]

Here's the opening of the fourth movement of Brahms's Fourth: the first iteration of his ground bass theme, played with magisterial power by brass (including three trombones, which are playing for the first time in the symphony!), winds, and timpani. [**Musical selection**: Brahms, Symphony No, 4 in E Minor, op. 98, movement 4.]

Brahms's biographer Karl Geiringer writes:

> A simple theme of eight bars, which is [then] repeated 31 times, in the lower, middle, and upper voices, without a single modulation or transitional passage, provides the framework of this movement. How wonderfully the master's genius unfolded within this restricted form! … However, the technical mastery is as nothing compared with the power and magnificence, the wild defiance and astringent lucidity of thought. This movement leads, as [Hermann] Kretzschmar says in his fine analysis of the symphony, into the domain "where the human bends its knee to the eternal."

The 30 "variations"—that is, the 30 repetitions of the ground bass theme with ever changing materials around it—clump together into three distinct groups. Variations 1 through 11 are all set in E minor and are generally monumental in expressive impact and tone. Let's hear variations 4 through 7, during which the dramatic momentum really starts to build. [**Musical selection**: Brahms, Symphony No, 4 in E Minor, op. 98, movement 4.] The second large grouping of variations consists of variations 12 through 15. These four variations are quieter, more lightly scored, and double the length of the first 11 variations. Variation 12—the first of this second grouping of variations—features an achingly melancholy solo flute. [**Musical selection**: Brahms, Symphony No, 4 in E Minor, op. 98, movement 4.]

Taking a page from Bach's Chaconne in D Minor, Brahms now switches the mode to E major for the remainder of this second group of variations. Variation 14 is particularly spectacular, and we must hear it, as the three trombones intone a hymn of otherworldly beauty and majesty! [**Musical selection**: Brahms, Symphony No, 4 in E Minor, op. 98, movement 4.]

The lyric oasis represented by variations 12 through 15 ends with the beginning of variation 16, the first of the variations that comprises the third section of the movement. The mode returns to minor, the variations are once again shorter, and the monumental character of the first group of variations resumes. [**Musical selection**: Brahms, Symphony No, 4 in E Minor, op. 98, movement 4.]

What we just heard constitutes a small but significant miracle. You see, variation 16 sounds recapitulatory: It sounds like a return from some contrasting place. But from a purely thematic point of view, the music never went anywhere. The ground bass theme has been a constant throughout, cycling back around every eight measures, over and over again. This is a lesson Brahms learned from Johann Sebastian Bach. The lesson: that the "musical sameness" and rigor of a passacaglia does not preclude a great composer from creating a sense of departure and return by providing groups of variations with certain shared characteristics. The movement and the symphony concludes with a magisterial coda following variation 30.

My friends, most minor mode symphonies—Beethoven's Fifth and Ninth and Brahms's own First Symphony, for example —mark a trajectory of darkness-to-light, of struggle capped by victory, and conclude—cathartically and triumphantly—in major. Well, not Brahms's Fourth. The fourth movement coda brings this symphony to its conclusion in the tonal darkness of E minor. Brahms, who saw himself as the last exponent of the German symphonic tradition does not go gently into that good night here at the conclusion of his fourth and final symphony. Let's hear it! [**Musical selection**: Brahms, Symphony No, 4 in E Minor, op. 98, movement 4.]

Thank you.

Brahms—Violin Concerto
Lecture 15

> Johannes Brahms's great friend, the Hungarian-born violinist and conductor Joseph Joachim, is the one for whom Brahms composed his only Violin Concerto. Joachim went so far as to rewrite entire passages of the solo part in the concerto so that it became as idiomatic as possible. The concerto received its premiere in Leipzig on New Year's Day in 1879 with the concerto's dedicatee—Joseph Joachim—playing the solo part and Brahms conducting the Gewandhaus Orchestra.

Johannes Brahms was born on May 7, 1833, in Hamburg, the largest port city in Germany. Brahms's father Johann Jakob Brahms was a professional violinist who eked out a living playing in the waterfront dives and brothels of Hamburg's red-light district. Regardless, Brahms's remarkable talent as a pianist and composer manifested itself early, and to his great fortune, he was brought to the attention of a high-end local teacher named Eduard Marxsen, who took him on as a student and grounded him in the music of Johann Sebastian Bach, Haydn, Mozart, Beethoven, and Schubert.

When Europe was plagued by revolutions in 1848, and Hamburg—as a major port city—saw a huge influx of refugees in 1848 and 1849. Among these refugees were urban Hungarians, who brought with them their gypsy fiddle music: soulful, exotic, rhythmically striking music that inspired Brahms's Violin Concerto in D Major. In late May of 1853, while on a concert tour in Germany, Brahms met a Hungarian-born violinist named Joseph Joachim in Hanover. It was the 12-year-old Joachim who—under the baton of Felix Mendelssohn—had revived Beethoven's Violin Concerto, which had gone unperformed for 35 years. Within two days, Brahms and Joachim had forged a friendship that would last for the rest of their lives.

Violin Concerto in D Major

When Brahms decided to compose a violin concerto—in 1877, 24 years after he and Joachim met—it was clear that the concerto was going to be dedicated to Joseph Joachim. Besides, Brahms—as a piano player—

needed help with the solo violin part, and Joachim provided advice on how to properly compose for solo violin. Ultimately, Brahms acknowledged Joachim's irreplaceable role in helping to create the concerto by asking Joachim to compose the extended solo—the cadenza—that concludes the first movement.

Movement 1

During the classical era, sonata form was adapted to the particular needs of the concerto, which is today known as double exposition form (containing an orchestral exposition and a solo exposition). Because the orchestra gets to play the themes first in double exposition form, composers have come up with various strategies over the years in order to compensate the soloist for not being allowed to play the themes first. The strategy used by Brahms in the first movement of his Violin Concerto is brilliant. Our examination of the first movement in double exposition form will focus on this issue of thematic parity between the orchestra and the violin soloist.

Movement 1, Orchestral Exposition, Theme 1

The first movement begins with a lengthy first theme in four phrases, which can be schematized as a, b, c, and a^1. The theme begins quite simply and concludes quite majestically. However, for all its concluding majesty, there's still a sense of musical space unfilled. The reason is that the theme—as presented by the orchestra—is not so much a fully realized thematic melody as a harmonic framework that will not be melodically developed until the solo violin plays it in the solo exposition. The theme simply outlines a D major harmony.

Movement 1, Solo Exposition, Theme 1

In the solo exposition, the solo violin plays a ravishing, shimmering, extended, and highly embellished version of the theme. In doing so, the solo violin transforms the theme into something much more lyric and expressively complex than what it was in the orchestral exposition. In the solo exposition, theme 1 is set in three phrases: a^2, b^1, and c^1. This violin music is passionate, intensely lyric, and masculine—music that no doubt reflects Brahms's feelings about Joseph Joachim and Joachim's manner of playing the violin. This music is also an example of thematic parity: While the orchestra did indeed play theme 1 first, it is the solo violin that breathes life, light, and lyricism into what was otherwise a skeleton waiting for muscle and flesh.

Movement 1, Orchestral Exposition, Theme 2

Immediately following theme 1 of the orchestral exposition, a transitional passage dissipates the energy generated by the theme and paves the way for theme 2. The transition begins with a quiet bit of melody drawn from theme 1. Hushed strings eventually dawdle a bit on the last five notes of the transition melody. Like a gentle exhalation, descending winds anticipate the arrival of an important event, which is followed by a rising melodic idea—heard first in the winds and then in the strings—that seems to inhale in preparation for and anticipation of theme 2. However, theme 2 never materializes. Instead, the transitional music begins all over again, and we can't help but feel like we missed something—something that will materialize in the solo exposition.

The strategy used by Brahms in the first movement of his Violin Concerto is brilliant.

Movement 1, Solo Exposition, Theme 2

After the conclusion of theme 1 of the solo exposition, the transition music begins again, now with the solo violin in the lead. The orchestral strings and a solo flute quietly dawdle while the solo violin provides an arpeggioed accompaniment. Once again, like a gentle exhalation, descending winds anticipate the arrival of an important event, which is again followed by a rising melodic idea that seems to inhale in preparation for and anticipation of theme 2.

Brahms has saved his greatest treasure for the solo violin: theme 2. It is one of the most beautiful melodies ever composed, and it now emerges in the solo violin, filling the void we heard—and felt—back in the orchestral exposition. When it comes to the battle of the themes in this first movement, the solo violin wins triumphantly. Not only does the solo violin get to breathe life and substance into theme 1, but theme 2 was conceived entirely for the lyric capabilities of Joachim's violin and is played exclusively by the solo violin.

We conclude our examination of the first movement with the solo violin's entrance, which—as we would expect in a double exposition form movement—occurs immediately after the conclusion of the orchestral exposition. The entrance of the soloist is, perhaps, the most highly anticipated moment in any double exposition form movement. And for the first couple of minutes of the piece, the soloist has been just waiting to make an entrance.

The nature of the soloist's entrance tells us a lot about the personality of the solo part: The entrance is our first impression of the solo part, and it is nothing short of electrifying. The solo violin enters with an absolutely heroic version of the opening of theme 1. This is certainly not a typical, lyric, relatively quiet, violin-as-soprano entrance; this entry—in the dark key of D minor—practically exudes machismo and testosterone.

The orchestra is not pleased with this show of attitude from the solo violin. Defiant orchestral interjections challenge the solo violin, which ultimately manages to fight off the orchestra's challenge for musical supremacy. Eventually, the orchestra accepts the presence and attitude of the solo violin, after which the solo violin makes itself comfortable with a long series of arpeggios and scales accompanied by fragments of theme 1 in the winds and orchestral strings. It's a musical portrait that captures the full range of Joachim's personality as both a man and musician: From the most powerful to the gentlest, this is Brahms's tribute to his great friend—and an altogether awesome passage of music.

Movement 2

The second movement of Brahms's Violin Concerto is not the miserable adagio Brahms claimed it was but, rather, an intimate and delicate movement cast in three-part, A–B–A form. The opening and closing A sections feature the wind instruments and have the quality of a serenade. In the opening of the movement, the solo violin takes a well-deserved rest. The middle, or B, section of the movement has the character of an operatic aria, with the solo violin playing the role of an impassioned operatic diva.

Movement 3

In the third movement, Brahms exhibits a wonderful, dancing, Hungarian rondo theme. Brahms's penchant for continuous variation is well displayed in this movement, as the rondo theme is never heard the same way twice. After various contrasting episodes—including a marvelous Viennese-style **waltz** in the middle of the movement—Brahms concludes the movement with one last version of the rondo theme, sounding now like a jingling march. This march concludes the concerto. ■

Important Term

waltz: A dance of Austrian/Viennese origin in triple meter.

Brahms—Violin Concerto
Lecture 15—Transcript

We return to *The Greatest Orchestral Works*. This is Lecture 15. It is entitled, "Brahms—Violin Concerto."

Johannes Brahms was a passionate and problematic man whose personality might best be described as "the good, the bad, and the ugly." The product of a working-class family, Brahms was an inveterate rooter for the underdog. Rich and famous in his lifetime, he gave his money away by the handful. He was a friend and benefactor to young musicians and composers, including Antonín Dvořák, who came to consider Brahms among the greatest men who ever lived.

Brahms was a man of extraordinary wit and something of a practical joker. He adored children and generally preferred their company to that of adults; at gatherings he'd often be found down on his hands and knees, playing with the kids. He remained something of a child himself: Even as an adult he still loved to play with his toy soldiers. Unfortunately, with Brahms you had to take the bad with the good.

Brahms's great friend, the Hungarian-born violinist and conductor Joseph Joachim—for whom Johannes Brahms composed his one-and-only violin concerto—famously said that, "Sitting next to Brahms is like sitting next to a barrel of gunpowder!"

So true. Despite the fact that the adult Brahms barely topped out at five feet tall (various sources peg him as having been between 4-foot 11 and 5-foot 2), those who knew him tip-toed around him, as one would a wolverine or a growling pit bull. And wisely so, because Brahms had a personality as caustic as a vat of lye and a tongue sharper than a titanium scalpel. He had zero-tolerance for the pretensions and attitudes of the concert world in which he lived and worked and was known to mercilessly demolish fans (particularly ladies) who were foolish enough to approach him with compliments.

Brahms was famous for his rudeness. He was reputed to have left a soiree in Vienna by announcing from the door: "If there's anyone here I haven't insulted, I apologize!"

Sadly, Brahms was hardest on himself and his own music. He famously remarked, "It's not hard to compose, but it's wonderfully hard to let the superfluous notes fall under the table." By his own admission Brahms allowed countless works to thus "fall under the table," consigning some 20 string quartets to the furnace along with other works, manuscripts, sketches, his juvenile compositions, his personal papers, jottings, laundry lists, memorabilia, whatever; if it would burn, he burned it. Brahms, who avidly collected the sketches and manuscripts of other composers did his level best to wipe out his own paper trail.

Why? Well, for all of his fame and fortune, he believed that his music was unreservedly inferior to those of his idols, Bach, Mozart, and Beethoven. Brahms was terrified by the prospect of "posterity." He wanted only his very best work to survive him, and he believed that the scrutiny his unpublished works and sketches would eventually be subjected to could only diminish his reputation as a composer.

Understood this way, Brahms's thorniness was, as is so often the case, a cover for his own fear. Understanding this as we do only makes us like him more!

Childhood

Johannes Brahms was born on May 7, 1833, in the "Free City of Hamburg," the largest port city in Germany with a population, in 1833, of roughly 200,000. In 1783, a traveler wrote that the Hamburg's weather was "Damp and cold most days of the year, just like most of the people."—a not entirely inappropriate description of Brahms himself.

Brahms's father Johann Jakob Brahms was a professional violinist who eked out a living in the waterfront dives and brothels of Hamburg's red-light district. His mother, Johanna Henrike Christiane Nissen, was 17 years her husband's senior. She was 44 years old when Brahms was born, and that, my friends, was done analog, without fertility treatments.

It was within the squalid confines of Hamburg's notorious "Lane Quarter" that Brahms was born and grew up. His remarkable talent as a pianist and composer manifested itself early, and to Brahms's—and posterity's!—great fortune, he was brought to the attention of a high-end local teacher named Eduard Marxsen. Marxsen was stunned by the child's talent, and took him on as a student—with lessons four times a week—free of charge.

It was Marxsen who grounded Brahms in the music of Johann Sebastian Bach, Haydn, Mozart, Beethoven, and Schubert. And it was Marxsen—bless him—whose confidence and support allowed Brahms to blossom as a composer. Marxsen staked his reputation on Brahms. When Felix Mendelssohn died in 1847, Marxsen told his friends, "A great master of the musical art has gone hence, but an even greater one will bloom for us in Brahms."

If Brahms's relationship with Eduard Marxsen was the high-point of his childhood, then his early experiences as a professional pianist mark the lowest-of-low points.

Here's what happened. When Brahms was 12 years old, his father hired him out to play piano in the same waterfront dives in which he performed. It was a colossally stupid thing to do, something Brahms's parents would regret for the rest of their lives.

These waterfront dives were called *animierlokale*—"stimulation pubs"—and were combination restaurants, saloons, dancehalls, and brothels. The euphemistically-named "singing girls" who worked these pubs were combination waitresses, barmaids, dancers, and whores. A pianist who played in such a joint received "*twee Dahler un duhn*," two thalers and all you can drink.

Later in his life Brahms told a friend that he "saw things and received impressions which left a deep shadow on [my] mind."

Oh, yes. Brahms biographer Jan Swafford describes what Brahms was talking about:

> Johannes was surrounded by the stench of beer and unwashed sailors and bad food, the din of rough laughter and drunkenness and raving obscenity. He had to accompany the bawdy songs, he had to … look sometimes at the drunken sailors fondling the half-naked singing girls, and he had to participate sometimes too. Between dances the women would sit the prepubescent teenager on their laps and pour beer into him, and pull down his pants and hand him around to be played with, to general hilarity. There may have been worse from the sailors [as] Johannes was as fair and pretty as a girl.

It doesn't take a Freudian to figure out where and when Brahms's life-long fear of intimacy and preference for prostitutes began. By the time he was 14 years old, Brahms's schizoid life—gifted musician and hard-working student by day, saloon pianist at night—had taken its toll. He was anemic; he suffered from migraine headaches. He was underweight, under-rested, and emotionally overwrought. His parents finally figured it out and stopped sending him out at night to play. But for Brahms's psyche, the damage was done.

Two Hungarian Violinists

Who could have guessed that when revolution once again broke out in Paris on February 23, 1848, its impact on Brahms's music and career would be singular? But there you go; it's just another example of the sort of historical "butterfly effect" that we can identify in hindsight but never anticipate.

The revolutions spread across Europe, though by 1849, they had been crushed, each and every one. Hamburg, as a major port city, saw a huge influx of refugees in 1848 and 1849, and while most of them got on ships and left central Europe, many also stayed. Among these refugees were urban Hungarians, who brought with them their citified Hungarian gypsy music: a soulful, exotic, rhythmically striking music that hit the 15-year-old Brahms like a keg of *Dübelsbrücker Dunkel* dropped from a third-story window!

Brahms's love affair with this gypsy music lasted for the rest of his life. I would go so far as to say that based on such works as Brahms's Hungarian Dances; his Piano Quartet in G Minor; his Clarinet Quintet in B Minor; and his Violin Concerto in D Major; Johannes Brahms—a native of Hamburger— was the 19th-century's greatest composer of the Hungarian gypsy-flavored music. Sorry, Franz Liszt! I know the truth can hurt. Here's an example: the wonderful gypsy fiddle music that dominates the third movement of the Violin Concerto. [**Musical selection**: Brahms, Concerto for Violin and Orchestra in D Major, op. 77, movement 3.]

Hungarian Violinist No. 1: Eduard Reményi

Brahms's contact with the expat Hungarian musical community in Hamburg was snug. In August of 1850, the 17-year-old Brahms met and began performing with a 21-year-old Jewish-Hungarian violinist named Eduard Hoffman. A self-styled Hungarian patriot, Hoffman had renamed himself Eduard "Reményi," and it was as "Reményi" that Brahms came to know him.

In the spring of 1853, Brahms and "Reményi"—having worked on and off together for a couple of years—decided to do a concert tour Germany. About six weeks into the tour, late May 1853, the boys stopped in Hanover and dropped in on a classmate of Reményi's from the Vienna Conservatory, a violinist named Joseph Joachim.

Hungarian Violinist No. 2: Joseph Joachim

Joseph Joachim was famous. Though not quite 22 years old, he had been a regular on the Euro-concert scene for 10 years. It was the 12-year-old Joachim who—under the baton of Felix Mendelssohn—had revived Beethoven's Violin Concerto, which had gone unperformed for 35 years. He was appointed professor of violin at the Leipzig Conservatory at 17; concertmaster of the Weimar Court Orchestra at 19; and at 20, he joined the Hanover Court Orchestra as its concertmaster and violin soloist. High-end credentials.

Joachim asked this Brahms guy to play something he composed. Brahms did so, and Joachim's jaw hit the floor. Fifty years later he recalled, "Never in the course of my artist's life have I been more completely overwhelmed."

What Joachim heard was piano music with the expressive power of Beethoven, the compositional discipline of Bach, and the melodic grace of Mozart. It was, for Joachim, a revelation: This bit of blond lint appears from out of nowhere playing music the likes of which he had not heard before. Within two days Brahms and Joachim had forged a friendship that would last for the rest of their lives.

Before they departed Hanover, Joachim presented Brahms and Reményi with a gift: a letter of introduction to the "duce" of the avant garde, Franz Liszt, who was living and working in Weimar. Privately, Joachim told Brahms that should things not work out with Reményi, Brahms was always welcome to come on back and hang.

Well, things didn't work out in Weimar or with Reményi. Brahms was appalled by the whole "Liszt trip": his god-like manner and attitude; the obsequious acolytes and fawning women; and the politicized zealotry that claimed Liszt's particular brand of music composition was the one-and-only path for the music of the future. Brahms got surly; Liszt got annoyed; and Reményi—convinced that Brahms was about to ruin his career—upped and walked, leaving Brahms in Weimar. Brahms wrote to Joachim.

> Dear Herr Joachim:
>
> If I were not [an optimist] I should now have well-founded reasons to be somewhat dispirited, to curse my art and to retire as a clerk into [an office]. Reményi is leaving Weimar without me. I really did not need such another bitter experience; in this respect I had already quite enough material for a poet and composer.
>
> I cannot return to Hamburg without anything to show. I must at least see two or three of my compositions in print, so that I can look my parents in the face. May I visit you there? Perhaps I am presumptuous, but my position and my dejection force me to it.

Brahms did indeed re-visit Joachim, staying for roughly two months, during which time he composed, practiced, and performed with Joachim, with whom he bonded completely. Back in Hamburg, Brahms'S parents were dismayed that the "tour" had so abruptly ended and suspicious of Joachim's generosity. To allay their concerns, Joachim wrote to them.

July 25, 1853

Allow me, although I am unknown to you, to write and tell you how infinitely blessed I feel in the companionship of your Johannes; for who better than his parents know the joy their son can give. Your Johannes has stimulated my work as an artist to an extent beyond my hopes. ... His purity, his independence, and the singular wealth of his heart and intellect find sympathetic utterance in his music. How splendid it will be when his artistic powers are revealed [to everyone]! You will understand my wish to have him near me as long as his presence does not interfere with his duty to himself. How glad I should be if I could ever render my friend Johannes a real service, for it goes without saying that my friendship is always at his disposal. I can only hope that our new bond will find the blessing of your approval.

Truly yours,

Joseph Joachim

Brahms's parents kvelled. "The world famous Joseph Joachim said that about our little Johannes? What a nice man!" End of parental concern.

A Violin Concerto

When Brahms decided to compose a violin concerto, in 1877—24 years after he and Joachim met—it was the world's biggest no-brainer this side of "don't eat yellow snow" that the concerto was going to be for Joseph Joachim. Besides, Brahms, as a piano player, needed as much help with the solo violin part as he could get, and Joachim provided yeoman service in advising the not-always-receptive Brahms on how properly to compose for solo violin.

My friends, Brahms was a notorious slacker when it came to writing for strings. He almost never provided the sorts of slurs that would indicate in which direction a player's bow should move; more often than not, Joachim took it upon himself to add such indications to Brahms's scores before they were published. Joachim went so far as to rewrite entire passages of the solo part in Brahms's Violin Concerto so that the part be as idiomatic as possible. Depending on his mood, Brahms accepted, ignored, or outright rejected Joachim's advice.

To his eternal credit, Joachim persevered: He wanted the concerto to be a showpiece for both Brahms and himself. Ultimately, Brahms acknowledged Joachim's irreplaceable role in helping to create the concerto by asking Joachim to compose the extended solo—the cadenza—that concludes the first movement. It was an act of signal respect on Brahms's part and a smart move as well: Joachim's cadenza remains the standard for Brahms's concerto (as does the cadenza Joachim composed for Beethoven's Violin Concerto as well).

The concerto was originally a four-movement work. Two months before its premiere, Brahms wrote to Joachim, informing him that "The middle movements [movements 2 and 3] are a bust—naturally, they were the best ones! I'm writing a miserable adagio in their place." We'll decide if the second movement of the now three-movement concerto is indeed "miserable" when we get to it. One way or the other, we are reminded that no one was harder on Brahms than Brahms himself.

The concerto received its premiere in Leipzig on New Year's Day 1879, with the concerto's dedicatee—Joseph Joachim—playing the solo part and Brahms conducting the Gewandhaus Orchestra.

Movement 1: Double Exposition Form

During the classical era, sonata form was adapted to the particular needs of the concerto, and this adapted version is today known as double exposition form. Sonata form is one built around the presentation, interaction, and reconciliation of multiple principal themes, typically two in number. These themes are presented in an opening section called the exposition. The exposition of a sonata form movement will almost always be repeated verbatim, the better to plant the themes and their key areas firmly in our ears. The themes are then developed in a section called the development section; and brought back in their original order in a section called the recapitulation.

Unlike sonata form, in which the exposition is repeated, double exposition form features two separately composed expositions, neither of which is repeated, thus its name, double exposition form. The first exposition, called the orchestral exposition, sees the orchestra play the themes. The second exposition, called the solo exposition, sees the soloist play the themes.

My friends, there is something inherently unfair about double exposition form: Hey, the orchestra gets to play the themes first, leaving the soloist with what amounts to sloppy seconds. Consequently, over the years, composers have come up all sorts of strategies in order to compensate the soloist for not being allowed to play the themes first. Brahms's strategy in the first movement of his Violin Concerto is brilliant, and thus our examination of the first movement double exposition form will focus on this issue of thematic parity between the orchestra and the violin soloist.

Orchestral Exposition: Theme 1

The first movement begins with a lengthy first theme in four phrases, which can be schematicized as *a-b-c-a¹*. The theme begins quite simply and concludes quite majestically.

However, for all its concluding majesty, there's still a certain "bare-bones-ness," a sense of "musical space unfilled" to this theme. And this is why: The theme—as presented by the orchestra—is not so much a fully realized thematic melody as a harmonic framework, a framework that will not be melodically fleshed-out until the solo violin plays it in the solo exposition.

I demonstrate. Here's phrase *a*, the first of the four thematic phrases, as it appears in the orchestral exposition. Elegant though it is, there's a lot of empty space here, as this unaccompanied theme simply outlines a D major harmony. [**Piano demonstration**.] Let's hear the theme in its entirety, and let us be aware of its simplicity of utterance. I'll indicate the four phrases as the theme progresses. [**Musical selection**: Brahms, Concerto for Violin and Orchestra in D Major, op. 77, movement 1.]

Solo Exposition: Theme 1

In the solo exposition, the solo violin plays a ravishing, shimmering, extended and highly embellished version of the theme, and in doing so transforms it into something a thousand times more lyric and expressively complex than what it was in the orchestral exposition. In the solo exposition, theme 1 is set in three phrases: *a-b-c*. Let's hear this now fully realized version of the theme. [**Musical selection**: Brahms, Concerto for Violin and Orchestra in D Major, op. 77; movement 1.]

That's not just a violin! That's a one-person orchestra! That's big, passionate, intensely lyric and masculine violin music: music that no doubt reflects Brahms's feelings about Joseph Joachim and Joachim's manner of playing the violin! It's also an example of thematic parity: While the orchestra did indeed play theme 1 first, it is the solo violin that breaths life, light, and lyricism into what was otherwise a skeleton waiting for muscle and flesh!

Orchestral Exposition: Theme 2

Back to the orchestral exposition. Immediately following theme 1, a transitional passage dissipates the energy generated by the theme and paves the way for theme 2. The transition begins with a quiet bit of melody drawn from theme 1. [**Musical selection**: Brahms, Concerto for Violin and Orchestra in D Major, op. 77; movement 1.] Hushed strings eventually "doodle" a bit on the last five notes of that transition melody. [**Musical selection**: Brahms, Concerto for Violin and Orchestra in D Major, op. 77; movement 1.]

Like a gentle exhalation, descending winds anticipate the arrival of an important event, which is followed by a rising melodic idea—heard first in the winds and then the strings—that seems to inhale in preparation for and anticipation of theme 2. [**Musical selection**: Brahms, Concerto for Violin and Orchestra in D Major, op. 77; movement 1.] And then—nothing! The transitional music begins all over again, and we can't help but think we just missed something! And so we did, because here in the orchestral exposition, theme 2 never happens. But happen it will in the solo exposition!

Solo Exposition: Theme 2

We're back to the solo exposition. Theme 1 has just concluded. The transition music again begins, now with the solo violin in the lead. [**Musical selection**: Brahms, Concerto for Violin and Orchestra in D Major, op. 77; movement 1.] The orchestral strings and a solo flute now quietly "doodle" while the solo violin provides an arpeggiated accompaniment. [**Musical selection**: Brahms, Concerto for Violin and Orchestra in D Major, op. 77; movement 1.] Once again, like a gentle exhalation, descending winds anticipate the arrival of an important event, which is followed, again, by a rising melodic idea that seems to inhale in preparation for and anticipation of theme 2. [**Musical selection**: Brahms, Concerto for Violin and Orchestra in D Major, op. 77; movement 1.]

Yes? Yes? Yes?

Yes! Brahms has saved his greatest treasure for the solo violin. Theme 2 is one of the most beautiful melodies ever composed, and it now emerges in the solo violin, filling the void we heard (and felt!) back in the orchestral exposition. We listen from the rising idea that immediately precedes the theme. [**Musical selection**: Brahms, Concerto for Violin and Orchestra in D Major, op. 77; movement 1.]

When it comes to the "battle for the themes" here in the first movement of Brahms's Violin Concerto, game, set, and match go to the solo violin. Not only does the solo violin get to breathe life and substance into theme 1, but theme 2 was conceived entirely for the lyric capabilities of Joachim's violin and is played exclusively by the solo violin.

Moving On

There are so many other features and details we could (and should!) sample from this amazing first movement, but time marches on. Let us conclude our examination of the first movement with the solo violin's entrance, which—as we would expect in a double exposition form movement—occurs immediately after the conclusion of the orchestral exposition.

The entrance of the soloist is, perhaps, the most highly anticipated moment in any double exposition form movement. The solo instrument is the star, the concerto's reason to be. And for the first couple of minutes of the piece, the star has been hanging out on stage, waiting to make the entrance. The nature of the soloist's entrance tells us a lot about the personality of the solo part: Let's face it, the entrance is going to be our first impression of the solo part, and we all know about first impressions.

Well, Brahms's solo entrance is nothing short of electrifying! Here's what happens. The solo violin enters with an absolutely heroic version of the opening of theme 1. This is certainly not your typical, lyric, relatively quiet, violin-as-soprano entrance. Oh no! This entry—in the dark key of D minor—fairly stinks of machismo and testosterone! [**Musical selection**: Brahms, Concerto for Violin and Orchestra in D Major, op. 77; movement 1.]

The orchestra is not pleased—no, not at all—with this show of attitude from the solo violin. Defiant orchestral interjections challenge the solo violin, which ultimately manages to fight off the orchestra's challenge for musical supremacy! Eventually, the orchestra accepts the presence and attitude of the solo violin, after which the solo violin makes itself comfy with a long series of arpeggios and scales accompanied by fragments of theme 1 in the winds and orchestral strings.

Let's hear it: the thunderous, drum-accompanied violin entry, followed by theme 1 as it appears in the solo exposition. It's a musical portrait that captures the full range of Joachim's personality as both a man and musician: from the most powerful to the most gentle; Brahms's tribute to his great friend; and an altogether awesome passage of music. [**Musical selection**: Concerto for Violin and Orchestra in D Major, op. 77; movement 1.]

Movement 2

It sort of goes without saying that the second movement of Brahms's Violin Concerto is not the miserable adagio Brahms claimed it was but rather an

intimate and delicate movement cast in three-part A-B-A form. The opening
and closing A sections feature the wind instruments and have the quality of
a serenade. Let's hear the opening of the movement, during which the solo
violin takes a well-deserved rest. [**Musical selection**: Brahms, Concerto for
Violin and Orchestra in D Major, op. 77, movement 2.] The middle, or B
section, of the movement has the character of an operatic aria, with the solo
violin playing the role of an impassioned operatic diva. [**Musical selection**:
Brahms, Concerto for Violin and Orchestra in D Major, op. 77; movement 2.]

Movement 3: Rondo

We heard Brahms's wonderful, dancing, Hungarian gypsy-flavored rondo
theme earlier in this lecture. I will say that Brahms's penchant for continuous
variation is well displayed in this movement, as that marvelous rondo theme
is never heard the same way twice. After various contrasting episodes—
including a marvelous Viennese-styled waltz smack-dab at the center of
the movement—Brahms concludes the movement, and the concerto, with
one last version of the rondo theme, sounding now like a jingling/jangling
march. Let's hear that march, and with it, the conclusion of the concerto.
[**Musical selection**: Brahms, Concerto for Violin and Orchestra in D Major,
op. 77, movement 3.]

Conclusion

In January of 1896, 15 months before his death from liver cancer, Brahms
made his last appearance as a conductor, conducting his two piano concerti
with pianist Eugen d'Albert and the Berlin Philharmonic. Later that
evening, Joseph Joachim hosted a dinner in Brahms's honor. Joachim stood
up and, with his glass raised, proposed a toast, saying. " 'To the greatest
composer—'; before he could finish , Brahms called out 'Quite right, here's
to Mozart's health!' and insisted on walking round [and] clinking glasses
with the entire party."

Joachim—who had known Brahms for 43 years—must have laughed and
shaken his head. Brahms was Brahms: brilliantly disagreeable to the end.

Thank you.

Tchaikovsky—Symphony No. 4
Lecture 16

> After having composed three relatively small-scale symphonies, Tchaikovsky's Symphony no. 4 was a breakthrough work—a big, heroic symphony that synthesized many of the stylistic and expressive elements that were closest to his heart: his love for the music of Beethoven, for dance music and folk music, the atmosphere of the Russian countryside and people, and the extremes of joy and angst so basic to his expressive voice. Tchaikovsky's Fourth Symphony is dedicated to Nadezhda von Meck, his dear friend and benefactor.

Even by the frankly modest mental health standards of major composers, Pyotr (Peter) Tchaikovsky was a genuine neurotic. As a child, he was oversensitive to the point of mania. He was permanently scarred when he was shipped off to boarding school at the age of ten. As a musical late bloomer—he didn't commit himself to a career in music until his early 20s—he carried a sense of inadequacy his entire career.

As a cross-dressing homosexual living in one of the most homophobic societies of all time, Tsarist Russia, Tchaikovsky lived in constant terror that he would be exposed and punished. A sham marriage to a love-sick former student, Antonina Milyukova, lasted only 11 weeks and drove him to attempt suicide. With his life and fortunes at their lowest ebb, a fabulously rich widow miraculously, Nadezhda von Meck, stepped into Tchaikovsky's life and gave him the means to quit his teaching job and compose full time.

Far from being merely titillating, this information is entirely germane to the music of Tchaikovsky because he believed in the 19th-century, romantic-era view of music composition as an act of intimate self-confession. This means that many of his works—including his Symphony no. 4—are autobiographical in nature. Consequently, we must first know the life experiences that inspired the music to understand it.

Symphony No. 4 in F Minor

Tchaikovsky composed his Fourth Symphony (of an eventual six) between December of 1876 and the late fall of 1877. He began working on it at the same time he began corresponding with Nadezhda von Meck. He continued to work on it while he met and married Antonina Milyukova, and finished it a roughly two months after his emotional breakdown and escape from Antonina. Tchaikovsky dedicated the symphony to "My Great Friend," a veiled reference to Nadezhda, who had asked to remain anonymous.

The symphony received its premiere in Moscow on February 22, 1878, under the baton of Nikolay Rubinstein, the director of the Moscow Conservatory. Incredibly, Tchaikovsky was not there: With Nadezhda von Meck's money in his pocket, he was spending the winter with a few choice friends in Florence,

Pyotr Ilyich Tchaikovsky (1840–1893) composed his Fourth Symphony during a very emotional year in his life, 1877.

Italy. However, Nadezhda was at the premiere, and she reported to Tchaikovsky that the audience responded enthusiastically to the piece.

Movement 1

According to Tchaikovsky, his Fourth Symphony was a faithful echo of the trials and tribulations of the year 1877—about the implacability of fate, an idea that became something of a personal obsession during 1877. If Tchaikovsky's program sounds familiar, that's because it is familiar; Tchaikovsky's inspiration for his Fourth Symphony was Beethoven's Fifth Symphony, which is generally acknowledged to be about the human spirit overcoming the relentless hand of fate. The relationship between Beethoven's Fifth and Tchaikovsky's Fourth is not conjectural—Tchaikovsky openly admits that his is a reflection of Beethoven's.

Movement 2

Using a technique common to 19th-century symphonic and operatic literature, Tchaikovsky creates a lonely, melancholy sense by scoring the opening of the movement for a solo oboe with the sparest of accompaniments. The effect is pure opera: a lonely shepherd piping his lonely song on a lonely, wind-swept hill. Timeworn though the effect may be, it works to perfection, primarily because Tchaikovsky's wandering, vaguely pastoral melody in B-flat minor so perfectly evokes the complex combination of weariness and nostalgia that he intends.

The opening theme is played first by a solo oboe and then by the 'cellos. The violins then enter, and the music takes on a vaguely Slavic, vaguely processional character; there's a sense of ritual intermingled with regret. It's very difficult to put into words, but the effect is clear upon hearing it.

Tchaikovsky dedicated the symphony to "My Great Friend," a veiled reference to Nadezhda.

Movement 3

This third movement—a dance movement in the traditional symphonic template—reactivates the body after the lyric ruminations of the slow second movement. Like the second movement, this third movement is straightforward in musical form: a three-part, A–B–A form movement. Tchaikovsky has subtitled this third movement "pizzicato ostinato," meaning "continuously plucked." The opening A section is an absolutely fabulous chunk of music that is performed only by pizzicato strings.

A staggering little tune, played by various wind instruments, begins the middle B section of the movement. A distant military parade now appears—played, as we would expect, by brass and drums. Soon enough, plucked strings begin to alternate with the staggering tune and band music, and then the plucked strings effortlessly swing into the closing A section of the movement. All three elements—plucked strings, staggering dance, and marching band—come together to bring this wonderful movement to its conclusion.

Movement 4

With a lighthearted mood having been established at the conclusion of the third movement, the fourth movement finale is a sustained celebration of life and energy—and one of the glories of the orchestral repertoire. The movement begins with an explosive introduction and a chirping, skittering theme that rapidly builds up to a terrific climax. The quiet, minor-tinged music that follows might sound—to non-Russian ears—like a dark-toned contrasting theme, but in fact, it is a Russian folk song called *In the Fields There Stood a Birch Tree*. For the Russians, the birch is a symbol of strength, fertility, and renewal. Consequently, when heard with informed ears, Tchaikovsky's use of the folk song does not dramatically contrast with the joyful, dancing music that preceded it but, rather, reinforces the message of strength and renewal that this finale is all about.

Tchaikovsky presents the folk song in a series of increasingly louder, more powerful variations. The brilliant, dancing opening theme soon returns, followed by yet another set of variations of *In the Fields There Stood a Birch Tree.* This leads to the climax of the movement: a reappearance of the fanfare of fate that began the first movement. The ominous mood represented by the fateful fanfare doesn't last long, and the movement—and with it, the symphony—concludes in a blaze of glory.

Tchaikovsky's return to the fate fanfare during the course of this fourth movement has been roundly criticized by many commentators. In fact, Tchaikovsky referenced the first movement fate fanfare during the fourth movement because he wanted to put into high relief the emotional distance traversed over the course of the symphony: a symphony that, like Beethoven's Fifth, begins in darkness but ends in triumph. The presence in this fourth movement of the folk song *In the Fields There Stood a Birch Tree*—with its connotations of spring and rebirth—further reinforces the cathartic dramatic progression marked by the symphony. ∎

Tchaikovsky—Symphony No. 4
Lecture 16—Transcript

Welcome back to *The 30 Greatest Orchestral Works*. This is Lecture 16. It is entitled "Tchaikovsky—Symphony No. 4."

Even by the frankly modest mental health standards of major composers, Peter Tchaikovsky was a genuine neurotic. As a child, he was oversensitive to the point of mania; so easily chipped were his emotions that his governess referred to him as a "porcelain child." An obsessive momma's boy, he was permanently scarred when he was shipped off to boarding school at the age of 10. As a musical late-bloomer—he didn't commit himself to a career in music until his early 20s—he carried the late-bloomers' sense of inadequacy his entire career.

As a cross-dressing homosexual living in one of the most homophobic societies of all time—Tsarist Russia—Tchaikovsky lived in constant terror that he would be "outed" and punished for his "perversion." A sham marriage to a love-sick former student lasted all of 11 weeks and drove him to attempt suicide. With his life and fortunes thus at their lowest ebb, a fabulously rich widow miraculously stepped into Tchaikovsky's life and gave him the means to quit his teaching job, compose full-time, and indulge his tastes in traveling, fine hotels, tobacco, alcohol, and teenage boys.

Far from being merely titillating, this information is entirely germane to the music of Tchaikovsky, because Tchaikovsky believed entirely in the 19th-century romantic-era view of music composition as an act of intimate self-confession. This means that many of his works—his Symphony No. 4 included—are autobiographical in nature. Consequently, if we want to understand the music, we must first know the life experiences that inspired the music. Onward, then, to the two ladies whose attentions shaped Tchaikovsky's Fourth Symphony: his "wife" Antonina Milyukova and his benefactress, Nadezhda von Meck.

I Think I'll Get Married or Out of the Closet and Into the Fire

In the fall of 1876, Peter Tchaikovsky, 36 years old and a professor of music at the Moscow Conservatory, wrote his brother Modest, who was also homosexual:

> I've been doing a lot of thinking. I have made a firm decision, starting today, to enter into lawful matrimony with anyone prepared to have me. It seems to me that our inclinations are the biggest and most insurmountable obstacle to our happiness, and that we must fight against our natures with all our strength.

Tchaikovsky concludes his letter by explaining that only by marrying can he, "shut the mouths of various contemptible creatures whose opinions don't bother me at all, but can cause pain to my loved ones."

Poor Tchaikovsky. He wasn't the first nor would he be the last gay person to try to silence the gossip by marrying a member of the opposite sex. This was Tchaikovsky's mindset in early 1877. It was, then, an example of epically bad timing that in May of 1877 Tchaikovsky received—out of the blue—a love letter from someone claiming to be a former student of his, a 28-year-old one-time seamstress named Antonina Milyukova.

Tchaikovsky—who hadn't a clue as to who Antonina Milyukova was—should have burned the letter. But he didn't. Instead, he answered her. A correspondence followed. They met on June 1. A day or two later, at their second meeting, Tchaikovsky proposed. She accepted. That Antonina was unhinged is clear from the letters she wrote Tchaikovsky at the time. Yet Tchaikovsky didn't notice—or chose not to notice—that he had affianced himself to a depressed, sex-and-affection starved psychotic.

The wedding took place on July 18, 1877—just 6½ weeks after the lovebirds first met—at St. George's Church in Moscow. When invited by the priest to kiss the bride, Tchaikovsky, instead, began to weep. He fled home and hid after the ceremony, leaving Antonina to attend the wedding reception and banquet by herself.

From here, things got worse. Tchaikovsky spent the bulk of the honeymoon weeping. Confused and desperate-to-please, Antonina attempted to grasp the bull by the horn by putting on a negligee and seducing Tchaikovsky. What she got for her trouble was an outright rejection. A hysterical scene followed. And then things really got worse. Tchaikovsky discovered that Antonina didn't know a note of his music. According to Tchaikovsky biographer Anthony Holden: "This desperate revelation seems to have rendered Tchaikovsky speechless. It was certainly where the relationship, if it had ever begun, ended."

Less than three weeks after his marriage Tchaikovsky wrote to a friend, a very rich widow named Nadezhda von Meck.

> As I contemplate spending the rest of my life with this woman, I also realize that, far from feeling the slightest fondness for her, I hate her in every sense of the word. It seems to me that I am now irretrievably lost. ... The rest of my life stretches ahead as a long, slow, pathetic process of vegetation, an intolerable black comedy. I have begun to long fiercely and hungrily for death, which now seems to me the only solution.

A few weeks later, Tchaikovsky did indeed attempt to commit suicide, something we'll discuss in just a few minutes. But first, let's meet Tchaikovsky's new pen-pal, his benefactress from heaven, Nadezhda von Meck. Madame von Meck was the mother of 18 children and the widow of a Russian railroad tycoon. She was nine years older than Tchaikovsky and was fanatic about Tchaikovsky's music. In December of 1876—11 months after her husband's death, von Meck commissioned Tchaikovsky to arrange some music for violin and piano. In January of 1877, four months before Tchaikovsky received his first letter from crazy Antonina, Nadezhda wrote Tchaikovsky.

> Gracious Sir, Peter Ilyich,

> To tell you into what ecstasies your composition sent me would be unnecessary, because you are accustomed to the compliments and homage of those much better qualified to speak than a creature so

musically insignificant as me. I shall content myself with asking you to believe absolutely that your music makes my life easier and pleasanter to live.

Tchaikovsky penned a perfunctory reply. However, having gotten his attention, Nadezhda von Meck had no intention of ending her correspondence with Tchaikovsky. Her next letter made it clear that her interest in Tchaikovsky was more than just a passing fancy.

I should like very much to tell you of my thoughts about you, but I fear to [waste] your time. Let me say that my feeling for you is a thing of the spirit and very dear to me. So, if you will, Peter Ilyich, call me erratic, perhaps even crazy, but do not laugh. It could be funny if it were not so sincere and real.

That caught Tchaikovsky's attention. This was no stage-door Janie writing him. Oh no. This was Nadezhda Filaretovna von Meck, one of the richest and most generous patrons of the arts in all of Russia, the Melinda Gates of her time. Tchaikovsky wrote back the next day.

Why do you hesitate to tell me … your thoughts? I assure you I should have been most interested and pleased, as I—in turn—feel deeply sympathetic toward you. These are not mere words. Perhaps I know you better than you imagine. If … you will do me the honour of writing me what you have so far withheld, I shall be very grateful.

That was all Tchaikovsky needed to say. Nadezhda's next letter was a long, passionate paean to Tchaikovsky, in which she professed her adoration for his music and asserted, unequivocally, that only the most perfect of men could compose as he did.

My friends, by perceiving in Tchaikovsky's music a pure soul, free from sin, Nadezhda von Meck offered Tchaikovsky something he craved above all else: absolution. Tchaikovsky had found his soul mate. And the best part was that she wanted a relationship based only on music and correspondence.

She wrote:

> There was a time when I was desperate to meet you. But now, the more enamored I become of you, the more an acquaintanceship frightens me. In short, I prefer to think of you from a distance, to hear you in your music, and to feel at one with you in your work.

For Tchaikovsky, Nadezhda von Meck was a gift from heaven. She underwrote Tchaikovsky's life for the next 13 years to the tune of 6,000 rubles a year, at a time when a government official (or a music professor!) could expect to make between 300–400 rubles a year.

Between 1877 and 1890, Tchaikovsky and von Meck exchanged over 1,200 letters. Taken together, theirs is the most intimate and artistically revealing correspondence in the entire music literature.

Tchaikovsky dedicated his Fourth Symphony to Nadezhda, and among his letters to her is a lengthy explanation of the meaning of the symphony, which we will use as our guide in our examination. However, we have one last bit of business to discuss before moving on to the symphony, and that is: What happened to Antonina Milyukova?

Exit Antonina

In early October of 1877, after less than three months of marriage, Tchaikovsky decided to kill himself by soaking himself in the Moscow River, in the hopes that he would, in his own words, "die from pneumonia or some respiratory illness."

Tchaikovsky didn't so much as catch a cold. But he did suffer a nervous breakdown on October 7 and was hustled out of town by his brother Modest. When informed that Tchaikovsky had collapsed and would not be returning home any time soon, Antonina is reported to have smiled "and announced that she would be pleased to agree to whatever her 'darling Peti' wanted."

Whack job though she was, Antonina held tremendous power over Tchaikovsky; for the rest of his life he lived in fear that she would reveal the true nature of his sexuality. He paid her well for her silence. Meanwhile, Nadezhda von Meck was thrilled. Her rival eliminated, she began paying Tchaikovsky his 6,000 ruble "subsidy." Evidence now indicates that Nadezhda knew Tchaikovsky was homosexual and that she considered his homosexuality an asset: She correctly assumed that after the fiasco with Antonina, she'd never lose Tchaikovsky to "another woman."

Tchaikovsky, Symphony No. 4: Gestation, Premiere, and Meaning

Tchaikovsky composed his fourth symphony (of an eventual six) between December of 1876 and the late fall of 1877. He began working on it at exactly the time he began corresponding with Nadezhda von Meck. He continued to work on it while he met and married Antonina Milyukova, and finished it a roughly two months after his emotional breakdown and "escape" from Antonina.

All in all, it was an active year in Tchaikovsky's life. Tchaikovsky dedicated the symphony to "My Great Friend," a veiled reference to Nadezhda, who had asked to remain anonymous.

Tchaikovsky's progress on the symphony is revealed through his letters to Nadezhda. As he was finishing it up in December, Tchaikovsky wrote: "I am working hard on the orchestration of our symphony and am quite absorbed in the task. None of my earlier works ... has given me so much trouble, but on none have I lavished such love and devotion."

Having finished the symphony, Tchaikovsky wrote, "In my heart of hearts I feel sure it is the best thing I have done so far."

The symphony received its premiere in Moscow on February 22, 1878, under the baton of Nicolai Rubinstein, the director of the Moscow Conservatory. Incredibly, Tchaikovsky was not there: with Nadezhda von Meck's money in his pocket he was spending the winter with a few choice friends in Florence, Italy. Nadezhda was at the premiere, and she reported to Tchaikovsky that the audience responded enthusiastically to the piece. (Which was true, although the critics did not.)

In response to Nadezhda's information, Tchaikovsky described the story—the "message"—behind the symphony. We will allow Tchaikovsky's own words to guide our examination of the symphony.

Movement 1

Tchaikovsky described the opening of the first movement this way:

> The introduction is the seed of the whole symphony. This is fate, the fatal force which prevents our hopes of happiness from being realized, which watches jealously to see that our bliss and peace are not complete and which, like the Sword of Damocles, is suspended overhead and perpetually poisons the soul.

[**Musical selection**:Tchaikovsky, Symphony No. 4 in F Minor, op. 36, movement 1.] Tchaikovsky describes the first theme that immediately follows this way: "The gloomy, despairing feeling grows stronger and more burning." [**Musical selection**:Tchaikovsky, Symphony No. 4 in F Minor, op. 36, movement 1.]

Tchaikovsky continues:

> Would it not be better to turn away from reality and plunge into dreams? O, joy! At last a sweet and tender vision appears. How delightful! How remote now sounds the obsessive first theme . . . Little by little, dreams have completely enveloped the soul. All that was gloomy [and] joyless is forgotten. It is here: happiness!

We join theme 2—which represents the "dream of joy"—in progress. [**Musical selection**:Tchaikovsky, Symphony No. 4 in F Minor, op. 36, movement 1.]

"No!" (writes Tchaikovsky) "These were dreams, and fate awakens us harshly." [**Musical selection**: Tchaikovsky, Symphony No. 4 in F Minor, op. 36, movement 1.] Tchaikovsky concludes his description of the first movement this way: "Thus, life is a perpetual alternation between grim reality and transient dreams of happiness. There is no haven. Drift upon that sea until it engulfs and submerges you in its depths. That, approximately, is the program of the first movement."

According to Tchaikovsky, his Fourth Symphony was "a faithful echo" of the trials and tribulations of the year 1877, about the implacability of fate, an idea that became something of a personal obsession during the fateful year of 1877.

If Tchaikovsky's program sounds familiar, that's because it is familiar; Tchaikovsky's inspiration for his Fourth Symphony was Beethoven's Fifth Symphony, which is generally acknowledged to be about the human spirit overcoming the relentless hand of fate.

Compare, for example, the hammering, orchestral-unison "fate-knocking-at-the-door" opening gestures that begin each piece. First Beethoven: [**Piano Demonstration**.] And now Tchaikovsky: [**Piano Demonstration**.] The relationship between Beethoven's Fifth and Tchaikovsky's Fourth is not conjectural. Oh no. In a letter to his friend and fellow composer Sergei Taneyev, Tchaikovsky was quite explicit on this point:

> Of course my symphony is program music. I must tell you that I had imagined the plan of my symphony to be so obvious that everyone would understand its meaning.
>
> Please don't imagine that I want to swagger before you with profound motions and lofty ideas. Nowhere in the work have I made the least effort to express a new thought. In reality my work is a reflection of Beethoven's Fifth Symphony. I have not, of course, copied Beethoven's musical content, only ... the central idea. ... The same [central idea of fate and struggle] lies at the root of my symphony, and if you have failed to grasp that, it merely proves that I am no Beethoven—a point on which I have no doubt anyway.

Movement 2

We continue with Tchaikovsky's description of his Fourth Symphony as detailed to Nadezhda von Meck: "The second movement expresses another phase of depression: that melancholy feeling which comes in the evening when one sits alone. A whole host of memories appears. And one is sad because so much is gone, past. Life wearies one."

Tchaikovsky creates the sense of lonely melancholy he describes using one of the oldest tricks in the book: by scoring the opening of the movement for a solo oboe with the sparest of accompaniments. The effect is pure opera: a lonely shepherd piping his lonely song on a lonely, wind-swept hill. Examples of just such episodes abound in the 19th-century symphonic and operatic literature, from the first movement recapitulation of Beethoven's Fifth to the third movement of Hector Berlioz' *Symphonie Fantastique*, to the opening of the third act of Wagner's *Tristan and Isolde*.

Timeworn though the effect might be, it works to perfection here, primarily because Tchaikovsky's wandering, vaguely pastoral melody in B-flat Minor so perfectly evokes that complex combination of weariness and nostalgia he describes. Aside from Frédéric Chopin, we are hard-put to think of any other 19th-century composer who can create such complex emotional states with a single melody line as well as Tchaikovsky. Let's hear this opening theme, played first by a solo oboe and then by the 'cellos. [**Musical selection**: Tchaikovsky, Symphony No. 4 in F Minor, op. 36, movement 2.]

Tchaikovsky writes: "One remembers much. There were happy moments when young blood pulsed and life was good. There were gloomy moments, too, irreplaceable losses. ... And it is sad and somehow sweet to bury oneself in the past."

The violins now enter and the music takes on a vaguely Slavic, vaguely processional character; there is a sense of ritual here intermingled with regret. It's all very hard to put into words but clear as day when we hear it. [**Musical selection**: Tchaikovsky, Symphony No. 4 in F Minor, op. 36, movement 2.]

Movement 3

This third movement—the "dance movement" in the traditional symphonic template—reactivates the body after the lyric ruminations of the slow second movement. Like the second movement, this third movement is straightforward in musical form: a three-part A-B-A form movement. Tchaikovsky has subtitled this third movement *pizzicato ostinato*, meaning "continuously plucked." Let's hear the opening A section in its entirety, an absolutely whiz-bang fabulous chunk of music which is performed only by pizzicato strings. [**Musical selection**: Tchaikovsky, Symphony No. 4 in F Minor, op. 36, movement 3.]

Of this third movement Tchaikovsky writes:

> The third movement consists entirely of capricious arabesques, elusive apparitions that pass through the imagination when one has drunk a little wine and feels the first stage of intoxication. The soul is neither merry nor gloomy. One is thinking of nothing; the imagination is liberated, and for some reason sets off painting strange pictures. Among them one remembers the picture of a [drunken] peasant and a street song. Then somewhere in the distance a military parade passes … disconnected images, like those which flit through one's head as one is falling asleep.

That last sentence gives us permission to hear the remainder of the movement as a wonderful bit of burlesque. The "drunken peasant" is portrayed by a comic, "staggering" little tune, played by various wind instruments that begins the middle B section of the movement. [**Musical selection**: Tchaikovsky, Symphony No. 4 in F Minor, op. 36, movement 3.]

The distant military parade now appears, played—as we would expect—by brass and drums. Soon enough, the staggering peasant (as portrayed by solo winds) tries to dance along with the military band; plucked strings begin to alternate with the peasant music and band music, and then—effortlessly—the plucked strings swing into the closing A section of the movement. Let's hear all of that, starting with the distant appearance of the military band. [**Musical selection**: Tchaikovsky, Symphony No. 4 in F Minor, op. 36, movement 3.] All three elements—plucked strings, peasant dance, and marching band—come together to bring this wonderful movement to its conclusion. [**Musical selection**: Tchaikovsky, Symphony No. 4 in F Minor, op. 36, movement 3.]

Movement 4

With something of a party mood having been established at the conclusion of the third movement, the fourth movement finale is a sustained celebration of life and energy and one of the glories of the orchestral repertoire. Tchaikovsky's description reads as follows:

> Fourth movement. If you can find no joy within yourself, look for it in others. Go to the people. Look, they know how to enjoy themselves, giving themselves up to undivided feelings of pleasure. A picture of festive popular rejoicing. Oh, how happy they are! How lucky they are that all their feelings are simple and spontaneous. ... Simple joys do exist. To live is still bearable.

The movement begins with an explosive introduction and a chirping, skittering theme that rapidly builds up to a terrific climax. [**Musical selection**: Tchaikovsky, Symphony No. 4 in F Minor, op. 36, movement 3.]

The quiet, minor-tinged music that now follows might sound—to non-Russian ears—like a dark-toned contrasting theme, but from an expressive point of view, it is not a contrasting theme, no. No, not at all. It is a Russian folk song called *In the Fields There Stood a Birch Tree*, and it sounds like this. [**Piano demonstration**.]

In the Fields There Stood a Birch Tree. The typically white-barked birch is an incredibly hardy tree and one of the first trees to show new growth in springtime. It was worshipped as a springtime goddess in pagan Russia, and it remains the national tree of Russia (and is, as well, the state tree of New Hampshire, another place of long winters and sudden springs!).

For the Russians, the birch is a symbol of strength, fertility, and renewal. Consequently, when heard with informed ears, Tchaikovsky's use of the folk song *In the Fields There Stood a Birch Tree* does not dramatically contrast with the joyful, dancing music that preceded it but rather, reinforces the message of strength and renewal that this finale is all about! Tchaikovsky presents the folk song in a series of ever louder, more powerful variations.

[**Musical selection**: Tchaikovsky, Symphony No. 4 in F Minor, op. 36, movement 3.]

The brilliant, dancing opening theme soon returns, followed by yet another set of variations of *In the Fields There Stood a Birch Tree*. This leads to the climax of the movement: a reappearance (for reasons to be discussed) of the "fanfare of fate" that began the first movement. [**Musical selection**: Tchaikovsky, Symphony No. 4 in F Minor, op. 36, movement 3.] The ominous mood represented by the reappearance of this "fateful fanfare" doesn't last long, and the movement—and with it, the symphony—concludes in a blaze of glory. [**Musical selection**: Tchaikovsky, Symphony No. 4 in F Minor, op. 36, movement 3.]

Tchaikovsky's return to the "fate fanfare" during the course of this fourth movement has been roundly criticized by many commentators, who find it to be: "an artificial, even cynical act of compositional legerdemain, an attempt to tie the symphony together with a musical bow that has no organic reason to be."

With all due respect, to these critics we say, pooh on you. Tchaikovsky referenced the first movement fate fanfare during the fourth movement because he wanted to put into high relief the emotional distance traversed over the course of the symphony: a symphony that like Beethoven's Fifth, begins in darkness but ends in triumph. The presence in this fourth movement of the folk song *In the Fields There Stood a Birch Tree*—with its connotations of spring and rebirth—further reinforces the cathartic dramatic progression marked by the symphony, and by Tchaikovsky's own admittedly glum, Eeyore-like description of the finale: "Rejoice. To live is still bearable."

Conclusions

After having composed three relatively small-scale symphonies, Tchaikovsky's Fourth was a breakthrough work, a big, heroic symphony that synthesized many of the stylistic and expressive elements that lay closest to his heart: his love for the music of Beethoven, for dance music and folk music, the atmosphere of the Russian countryside and people, and the extremes of joy and angst so basic to his expressive voice.

Tchaikovsky might have "lost" a wife in 1877, but he gained a patron: and what a patron! Nadezhda von Meck was ecstatic over the Fourth Symphony. Following its premiere she wrote Tchaikovsky: "How delighted I was to read your description of our symphony, my dear, priceless Peter Ilyich!"

Tchaikovsky biographer Alexander Poznansky writes:

> By taking his personal anguish and transforming it into something sublime, Tchaikovsky had … fulfilled the romantic image of the artist [von Meck] held so dear. "How happy I am," she added, "to have found in you the perfect corroboration of my ideal of a composer."

Postscript

In October of 1890, Tchaikovsky received a packet from Nadezhda von Meck containing a year's subsidy in advance and a letter announcing the end of their relationship. He was cut to his core. In the letter, Nadezhda claimed she was bankrupt, and she begged Tchaikovsky not to forget her.

Nadezhda von Meck was indeed having financial problems, but her break with Tchaikovsky went beyond issues financial. Her children (remember? there were 18 of them) were embarrassed by her relationship with Tchaikovsky. There was gossip and innuendo, and the kiddies wanted to see the relationship brought to an end. Nadezhda was also ill with tuberculosis, and some authorities feel that her break with Tchaikovsky was part of an attempt to put her "affairs" in order.

Tchaikovsky died three years later, on November 6, 1893, never having gotten over the loss of Nadezhda's friendship. Nadezhda von Meck followed Tchaikovsky to the grave 68 days later, on January 13, 1894. When asked how her mother-in-law had endured Tchaikovsky's death, Anna Davidova von Meck replied, "She did not endure it."

And what of Antonia Milyukova, Tchaikovsky's one-and-only "wife"? She remained legally married to Tchaikovsky until his death. He supported her financially to the end of his life, and left her an annual pension of 1,200 rubles a year in his will. In 1896, three years after Tchaikovsky's death, Antonina was committed to a lunatic asylum outside of St. Petersburg, where she remained until her death, 21 years later, in 1917.

Thank you.

Timeline

1717 (circa) .... Johann Sebastian Bach, Violin
Concerto in E Major.

1720 (circa) .... Antonio Vivaldi, *The Four Seasons.*

1721 (circa) .... Johann Sebastian Bach,
Brandenburg Concerto No. 2.

1786 .... Wolfgang Mozart, Piano
Concerto No. 24 in C Minor.

1788 .... Wolfgang Mozart, *"Un bacio di mano."*

1788 .... Wolfgang Mozart, Symphony No. 41.

1795 .... Joseph Haydn, Symphony No. 104.

1801 .... Ludwig van Beethoven, *The
Creatures of Prometheus.*

1804 .... Ludwig van Beethoven,
Symphony No. 3.

1806 .... Ludwig van Beethoven,
Piano Concerto No. 4.

1824 .... Ludwig van Beethoven,
Symphony No. 9.

1826 .... Franz Schubert, Symphony No. 9.

1833... Felix Mendelssohn, Symphony
No. 4, "Italian."

1850... Robert Schumann, Symphony
No. 3, "Rhenish."

1855... Georges Bizet, Symphony in C Major.

1878... Johannes Brahms, Violin Concerto.

1878... Pyotr Tchaikovsky, Symphony No. 4.

1878... Pyotr Tchaikovsky, Violin Concerto.

1879... Bedřich Smetana, *Má Vlast.*

1885... Johannes Brahms, Symphony No. 4.

1888... Nikolay Rimsky-Korsakov,
Scheherazade.

1889... Antonín Dvořák, Symphony No. 8.

1895... Antonín Dvořák, 'Cello Concerto.

1896... Richard Strauss, *Thus
Spoke Zarathustra.*

1902... Gustav Mahler, Symphony No. 5.

1905... Claude Debussy, *La Mer.*

1907... Sergey Rachmaninoff, Symphony No. 2.

1912... Igor Stravinsky, *The Rite of Spring.*

1914...Charles Ives, *Three Places in New England.*

1916...Gustav Holst, *The Planets.*

1934...Paul Hindemith, Symphony *Mathis der Maler.*

1935...William Walton, Symphony No. 1.

1937...Dmitri Shostakovich, Symphony No. 5.

1943...Ralph Vaughan Williams, Symphony No. 5.

1944...Aaron Copland, *Appalachian Spring.*

1944...Sergey Prokofiev, Symphony No. 5.

1945...Dmitri Shostakovich, Symphony No. 9.

1953...Dmitri Shostakovich, Symphony No. 10.

Glossary

accent: The emphasis of certain notes over others.

accidental: A notational sign/symbol that modifies a pitch. *See also* **sharp**, **flat**, and **natural**.

adagio: Slow.

allegro: Fast.

andante: Moderately slow.

asymmetrical meter: Exhibits no particular repeated metric pattern.

atonal/atonality: Music lacking the sense of a central pitch, as opposed to tonal/tonality.

augmentation: The process of systematically extending the note values of a given melodic line.

bar: *See* **measure**.

bar lines: Notational device: two vertical lines that enclose a measure and are equivalent to one metric unit.

basso continuo: Those instruments in a baroque-era ensemble (typically a chord-producing instrument and a bass instrument) whose job it was to articulate with unerring clarity the bass line and play the harmonic progressions built atop the bass line.

beat: Smallest pulse to which we can comfortably move our bodies. *See also* **meter**.

cadence: A harmonic or melodic formula that occurs at the end of a phrase, section, or composition and conveys a momentary or permanent conclusion—in other words, a musical punctuation mark.

cadenza: Passage for solo instrument in an orchestral work, usually a concerto, designed to showcase the player's skills.

chord: Simultaneous sounding of three or more different pitches.

chromatic: A pitch that lies outside of whatever key area presently anchors a passage.

classical: Designation given to works of art of the 17th and 18th centuries, characterized by clear lines and balanced form.

closed cadence: Equivalent to a period or an exclamation mark; such a cadence ends on the tonic and gives a sense of rest and resolution.

coda: The closing few measures of a composition; usually not a part of the main theme groups of the standard form of a composition but a finishing theme added to the end to give the composition closure.

col legno: Striking the strings with the wood side of the bow.

compound meter: Any meter that features a triple subdivision within each beat.

concerto grosso: A multi-movement work in which multiple soloists are accompanied by, and sometimes pitted against, the orchestra.

conjunct: Melodic contour that generally features steps between pitches; such a melody will usually sound smooth and controlled.

consonance: A musical entity or state that can be perceived as a point of rest.

deceptive/false cadence: Equivalent to a colon or semicolon; such a cadence brings resolution but not to the expected tonic harmony.

development: The second large part of a sonata form movement, during which the themes are developed in a generally unstable harmonic environment.

diminution: The process of systematically shortening the note values of a given melodic line.

disjunct: Melodic contour that generally features leaps between pitches; such a melody will usually sound jagged and jumpy.

dissonance: A musical entity or state of instability that seeks resolution to consonance.

dominant: Pitch and chord five pitches above a given tonic pitch/chord. The dominant harmony is the chord most closely related to the tonic chord in a given key; the dominant chord will almost always immediately precede an appearance of the tonic chord.

double exposition form: Sonata form adapted to the needs of a concerto.

double scherzo: A five-part form in which there are two middle B sections separated by three A sections: A–B–A–B–A.

dynamics: Degrees of loudness—e.g., piano (quiet), forte (loud)—indicated in a musical score.

elegy: A song expressing sorrow for one who has died.

enharmonic: Pitches that are identical in sound but with different spellings, depending on the key context, e.g., C-sharp and D-flat.

exposition: The first part of a sonata form, during which the principal themes are introduced.

expressionism: The contemporary art movement that celebrated inner emotional states as the highest truth.

fermata: Pause.

flat: Accidental (sign/symbol) placed to the left of a note indicating that the pitch should be lowered by a semitone.

frequency: Rate of vibration of a string, column of air, or other sound-producing body.

fugato: A fugal exposition inserted into a movement that is not otherwise a fugue.

fugue: Important baroque musical procedure in which a theme (or subject) is developed by means of various contrapuntal techniques.

functional harmony: Harmonic usage that was standardized and codified into a fully coherent system during the baroque period. This method is still used by modern arrangers and orchestrators. The basic concept used in functional harmony is the fact that all harmonic sounds used in music may be classified into three large groups. These groups derive their names from the three important roots of the traditional harmonic system: the tonic, the dominant, and the subdominant.

fundamental frequency: Rate of vibration of the full length of a sound-producing body and the sound created by that full-length vibration.

graded dynamics: Markings used to indicate a progressive increase in loudness or softness, respectively, crescendo (getting louder) or decrescendo/diminuendo (getting softer/quieter).

half step: *See* **semitone**.

harmony: The musical art (and science) of manipulating simultaneous pitches.

home key: Main key of a movement or composition. *See also* **key**.

homophonic texture/homophony: Texture in which one melodic line predominates; all other melodic material is heard as being secondary or accompanimental.

hymn: A religious song.

inclusive art: An art in which distinctions between popular, sacred, and concert music are immaterial when compared to its universal power to move and enlighten.

intermezzo: An instrumental interlude between the acts of a performance.

interval: Distance between two pitches, e.g., C–G (upward) equals a fifth.

inversion: Loosely applied to indicate a reversal in melodic direction. Harmonic inversion is a situation in which a chord tone other than the root is in the bass.

key: Collection of pitches that relate to a specific major or minor mode.

largo/lento: Very slow.

major: Modern term for Ionian mode; characterized by an intervallic profile of whole tone–whole tone–semitone–whole tone–whole tone–whole tone–semitone (symbolized as: T–T–S | T–T T–S).

measure: Metric unit; space between two bar lines.

melody: Any succession of pitches.

meter: Group of beats organized in a regular rhythmic pattern and notated in music as a time signature.

minor: Modern term for Aeolian mode; characterized by an intervallic profile of whole tone–semitone–whole tone–whole tone–semitone–whole tone–whole tone (symbolized as T–S–T | T–S–T–T).

minuet: A dance of the 17th and 18th centuries, graceful and dignified, in moderately slow three-quarter time.

minuet and trio form: A three-part musical form consisting of a minuet ("A"), followed by a contrasting minuet ("B," called the trio), followed by a return to the original minuet ("A," called the da capo). Minuet and trio was the only baroque-era form to find its way into the instrumental music of the classical era.

modal ambiguity: Harmonic ambiguity, in which the main key is not clearly identified.

mode: A type of pitch collection (or scale).

modulation: The process of changing key during the course of a piece of music.

motive: Brief succession of pitches from which a melody grows through the processes of repetition, sequence, and transformation.

movement: Independent section within a larger work.

musical form: The manner in which a given movement of music is structured.

natural: Accidental (sign/symbol) placed to the left of a note, indicating that the note should not be sharpened or flattened; a white key on a keyboard.

note: A sound with three properties: a single, sing-able fundamental frequency; timbre; and duration.

open cadence: Equivalent to a comma; such a cadence pauses on the dominant harmony without resolving the tonic harmony, creating tension and the need to continue.

open form: A movement in which thematic ideas are introduced and immediately developed in a continuous sequence.

opus number: A number supplied by a publisher to indicate the order in which a composition (or set of compositions) is published.

orchestral unison: A technique by which multiple instruments simultaneously play the same pitch but in different registers (ranges).

ostinato: A brief melodic idea that is repeated over and over again.

overture: Music preceding an opera or play, often played as an independent concert piece.

pedal: A single pitch or harmony sustained or repeated for a period of time.

pitch: A sound with two properties: a single, sing-able fundamental frequency and timbre.

pizzicato: Plucking, rather than bowing, a stringed instrument.

polyphonic texture/polyphony: Texture consisting of two or more simultaneous melody lines of equal importance.

presto: Very fast.

recapitulation: The third large part of a sonata form movement, during which the themes return in their original order.

recitative: Operatic convention in which the lines are half sung, half spoken.

ritornello form: A refrain procedure in which a theme returns in part, called a fragmentary refrain, over the course of a movement. This form is among the most common of all baroque-era instrumental procedures.

rondo form: A classical-era form that sees a principal theme (the rondo theme) return like a refrain after various contrasting episodes.

scale: All the pitches inside a given octave, arranged stepwise so that there is no duplication. The names of the chords built on the scale steps are: tonic, supertonic, mediant, subdominant, dominant, sub-mediant, and leading tone.

scherzo form: Meaning literally "I'm joking," scherzo is the designation Beethoven gave to his modified use of minuet and trio form.

semitone: Smallest interval in Western music; on the keyboard, the distance between a black key and a white key, as well as B–C and E–F.

sequence: Successive repetitions of a motive at different pitches; compositional technique for extending melodic ideas.

sharp: Accidental (sign/symbol) placed to the left of a note, indicating that the pitch should be raised by a semitone.

solo concerto: A multi-movement work in which a single soloist is accompanied by, and sometimes pitted against, the orchestra.

sonata: Piece of music, typically in three or four movements, composed for a piano (piano sonata) or a piano plus one instrument (violin sonata, for instance).

sonata form: A classical-era formal process posited on the introduction, development, recapitulation, and reconciliation of multiple contrasting themes.

string quartet: A performing ensemble consisting of two violins, a viola, and a 'cello. (2) A musical composition written for that ensemble.

subject: The theme of a fugue.

suite: A concert work consisting of a collection of dances extracted from a longer ballet.

symphonic poem: Orchestral work in which the form is determined by the story being told.

symphony: A multi-movement work composed for an orchestra.

syncopation: Displacement of the expected accent from a strong beat to a weak beat and vice versa.

tempo: Relative speed of a passage of music.

texture: Number of melodies present and the relationship between those melodies in a given segment of music; they include monophony, polyphony (counterpoint), heterophony, and homophony.

theme: Primary musical subject matter in a given section of music.

theme and variations form: A classical-era formal process that exhibits a systematically varied theme in a series of variations.

timbre: Tone color.

tonal/tonality: Sense that one pitch is central to a section of music, as opposed to atonal/atonality.

tone poem: Also called a symphonic poem. A one-movement orchestral genre that develops a poetic idea, suggests a scene, or creates a mood. The tone poem is generally associated with the romantic era.

tonic: Home pitch and chord of a piece of tonal music. Think of the term as being derived from "tonal center" (tonic). For example, if a movement is in C, the pitch C is the tonic pitch, and the harmony built on C is the tonic chord.

tonicization: The process of creating a temporary tonic by articulating a dominant-to-tonic progression of a key other than the one currently in use.

triad: A chord consisting of three different pitches built from some combination of major and/or minor thirds.

trio sonata: Baroque-era genre of chamber music consisting of two soprano instruments, a bass instrument, and a chord-producing instrument (called the continuo). The most common trio sonata instrumentation was two violins, a 'cello, and a harpsichord.

triple meter: Metrical pattern having three beats to a measure.

tune: Generally sing-able, memorable melody with a clear sense of beginning, middle, and end.

waltz: A dance of Austrian/Viennese origin in triple meter.

whole-tone collection: Divides the octave into six equal segments; a whole-tone scale ascends and descends by major seconds, or whole tones.

Bibliography

Amis, Martin. *Koba the Dread: Laughter and the Twenty Million*. New York: Talk Miramax Books/Hyperion, 2002.

Bataille, Georges, and Annette Michelson. "Nietzsche's Madness." *October*, Vol. 36, Georges Bataille: Writings on Laughter, Sacrifice, Nietzsche, Un-Knowing (Spring 1986): 42–45.

Brown, A. Peter. *The Symphonic Repertoire, Volume II*. Bloomington: University of Indiana Press, 2002.

Bryson, Michael. *Reclaiming the Self: Transcending the Fragmentation of the Individual Subject*. http://www.brysons.net/academic/intro.html. Accessed June 17, 2011.

Bukofzer, Manfred. *Music in the Baroque Era: From Monteverdi to Bach*. New York: Norton, 1947.

Burk, John. *Clara Schumann: A Romantic Biography*. New York: Random House, 1940.

Chase, Gilbert. *America's Music*. 3rd rev. ed. Urbana: University of Illinois Press, 1987.

Dearling, Robert and Cecilia. *The Guinness Book of Music Facts and Feats*. Enfield, Middlesex: Guinness Superlatives, Ltd., 1976.

Downes, Edward. *Guide to Symphonic Music*. New York: Walker Publishing, 1981.

Downes, Olin. *Symphonic Masterpieces*. New York: Tudor Publishing, 1939.

Grout, Donald, Claude Palisca, and J. Peter Burkholder. *A History of Western Music*. 7th ed. New York: Norton, 2006.

Hildebrandt, Dieter. *Pianoforte: A Social History of the Piano*. Translated by Harriet Goodman. New York: George Braziller, 1985.

Holomon, D. Kern. *The Nineteenth Century Symphony*. New York: Schirmer Books, 1997.

Hopkins, Antony. *Talking About Music*. London: Pan Books, 1977.

Hutchings, Arthur. "Concerto." *The New Grove Dictionary of Music and Musicians*. London: Macmillan, 1980.

Kemp, Lindsay. "Bach, Violin Concerto in E Major." *The BBC Proms Pocket Guide to Great Concertos*. Edited by Nicholas Kenyon. London: Faber & Faber, 2003.

Kerman, Joseph. *Listen*. 3rd ed. New York: Worth Publishers, 1980.

Landon, H. C. Robbins, and John Julius Norwich. *Five Centuries of Music in Venice*. New York: Schirmer Books, 1991.

Layton, Robert, ed. *A Guide to the Symphony*. Oxford: Oxford University Press, 1995.

Lebrecht, Norman. *The Book of Musical Anecdotes*. New York: The Free Press, 1985.

Machlis, Joseph. *Introduction to Contemporary Music*. 2nd ed. New York: Norton, 1979.

Palmer, R. R., and Joel Colton. *A History of the Modern World*. 6th ed. New York: Knopf, 1984.

Plantinga, Leon. *Romantic Music: A History of Musical Style in Nineteenth-Century Europe*. New York: Norton, 1984.

Bibliography

Radzinsky, Edvard. *Stalin*. New York: Anchor Books, 1996.

Roeder, Michael Thomas. *A History of the Concerto*. Portland, OR: Amadeus Press, 1994.

Rubinstein, Anton. *Autobiography of Anton Rubinstein 1829–1889*. Translated by Aline Delano. New York: Haskell House Publishers, 1969.

Schonberg, Harold. *The Great Pianists*. Revised and updated. New York: Fireside, 1987.

———. *The Lives of the Great Composers*. New York: Norton, 1970.

Schorske, Carl. *Fin-de-Siècle Vienna: Politics and Culture*. New York: Knopf, 1980.

Shapiro, Harold. *An Encyclopedia of Quotations about Music*. New York: Da Capo Press, 1977.

Slonimsky, Nicolas. *Lexicon of Musical Invective*. Seattle: University of Washington Press, 1975.

———. *Perfect Pitch, an Autobiography*. London: Omnibus Press, 2002.

Steinberg, Michael. *The Concerto: A Listener's Guide*. Oxford: Oxford University Press, 1998.

———. *The Symphony: A Listener's Guide*. Oxford: Oxford University Press, 1995.

Stravinsky, Igor, and Robert Craft. *Memories and Commentaries*. Berkeley: University of California Press, 1981.

Taruskin, Richard. *The Oxford History of Western Music*. Oxford: Oxford University Press, 2005.

Weiss, Piero, and Richard Taruskin. *Music in the Western World: A History in Documents*. New York: Schirmer Books, 1984.

Bach

Boyd, Malcolm. *Bach: The Brandenburg Concertos*. Cambridge: Cambridge University Press, 1993.

Geck, Martin. *Johann Sebastian Bach: Life and Work*. Translated by John Hargraves. Orlando, FL: Harcourt, 2000.

Wolff, Christoph. *Johann Sebastian Bach: The Learned Musician*. New York: Norton, 2000.

Beethoven

Forbes, Elliot. *Thayer's Life of Beethoven*. rev. ed. Princeton, NJ: Princeton University Press, 1967.

Hopkins, Antony. *The Nine Symphonies of Beethoven*. London: Heineman, 1981.

Jones, Timothy. *Beethoven: The "Moonlight" and Other Sonatas, Op. 27 and Op. 31*. Cambridge: Cambridge University Press, 1999.

Kerman, Joseph. *The Beethoven Quartets*. New York: Knopf, 1971.

Landon, H. C. Robbins. *Beethoven: A Documentary Study*. New York: Macmillan, 1975.

Mellers, Wilfrid. *Beethoven and the Voice of God*. London: Faber & Faber, 1983.

Newman, William. *Beethoven on Beethoven: Playing His Piano Music His Way*. New York: Norton, 1988.

Plantinga, Leon. *Beethoven's Concertos*. New York: Norton, 1999.

Riezler, Walter. *Beethoven*. London: M. C. Forrester, 1938.

Simpson, Robert, ed. *The Symphony, Volume One, Haydn to Dvorak*. Baltimore: Penguin Books, 1966.

Solomon, Maynard. *Beethoven*. 2nd rev. ed. New York: Schirmer Books, 1998.

Brahms
Geiringer, Karl. *Brahms: His Life and Work*. Boston: Houghton Mifflin Company, 1936.

Holde, Artur. "Suppressed Passages in the Brahms-Joachim Correspondence, Published for the First Time." *The Musical Quarterly* 45, no. 3 (1959): 312–324.

MacDonald, Malcolm. *Brahms*. New York: Schirmer Books, 1990.

Niemann, Walter. *Brahms*. Translated by Catherine Phillips. New York: Tudor Publishing, 1945.

Swafford, Jan. *Johannes Brahms: A Biography*. New York: Knopf, 1997.

Copland
Copland, Aaron. *Copland on Music*. New York: Norton, 1960.

Copland, Aaron, and Vivian Perlis. *Copland: 1900 through 1942*. New York: St. Martin Press, 1984.

————. *Copland Since 1943*. New York: St. Martin Press, 1989.

Pollack, Howard. *Aaron Copland: The Life and Work of an Uncommon Man*. New York: Henry Holt, 1999.

Debussy
Cox, David. *Debussy Orchestral Music*. Seattle: University of Washington Press, 1974.

Debussy, Claude. *Monsieur Croche: The Dilettante Hater*. New York: Lear Publishers, 1948.

Trezise, Simon. *Debussy: La Mer*. Cambridge: Cambridge University Press, 1994.

Vallas, Léon. *Claude Debussy: His Life and Work*. New York: Dover, 1973.

Dvořák
Beckerman, Michael, ed. *Dvořák and His World*. Princeton, NJ: Princeton University Press, 1993.

————. *New Worlds of Dvořák*. New York: Norton, 2003.

Clapham, John. *Dvořák*. London: David & Charles, 1979.

Haydn
Geiringer, Karl. *Haydn, A Creative Life in Music*. Berkeley: University of California Press, 1982.

Larsen, Gens Peter. "Haydn." *The New Grove Dictionary of Music and Musicians*. London: Macmillan, 1980.

Holst
Greene, Richard. *Holst: The Planets*. Cambridge: Cambridge University Press, 1995.

Holst, Imogen. *Gustav Holst: A Biography*. New York: Oxford University Press, 1988.

————. "Gustav Holst." *The New Grove Dictionary of Music and Musicians*. London: Macmillan, 1980.

Ives
Cowell, Henry and Sidney. *Charles Ives and His Music*. New York: Oxford University Press, 1969.

Ives, Charles. *Essays Before a Sonata, The Majority, and Other Writings*. New York: Norton, 1970.

Rossiter, Frank. *Charles Ives and His America*. New York: Liverlight, 1975.

Swafford, Jan. *Charles Ives: A Life with Music*. New York: Norton, 1998.

Mahler
Cardus, Neville. *Gustav Mahler: His Mind and His Music, Volume I*. London: Victor Gollancz, 1965.

Carr, Jonathan. *Mahler: A Biography*. New York: Overlook Press, 1997.

Floros, Constantin. *Gustav Mahler: The Symphonies*. Portland, OR: Amadeus Press, 1994.

Greene, David B. *Mahler: Consciousness and Temporality*. New York: Gordon and Breach, 1984.

Mahler, Alma. *Gustav Mahler*. N.p.: Hesperides Press, 2006.

————. *Gustav Mahler: Memories and Letters*. 3rd ed. Seattle: University of Washington Press, 1975.

Raynor, Henry. *Mahler*. London: Macmillan, 1975.

Mendelssohn
Todd, R. Larry. *Mendelssohn: A Life in Music*. Oxford: Oxford University Press, 2003.

Mercer-Taylor, Peter, ed. *The Cambridge Companion to Mendelssohn*. Cambridge: Cambridge University Press, 2004.

Raphael, Teresa. Program booklet for *Mendelssohn, Symphony No. 4 in A Major, Op. 90*. NAXOS 8.553200, 1996.

Werner, Eric. *Mendelssohn*. New York: The Free Press, 1963.

Mozart

Abert, Hermann. *W. A. Mozart*. Translated by Stewart Spenser. New Haven, CT: Yale University Press, 2007.

Girdlestone, Cuthbert. *Mozart and His Piano Concertos*. New York: Dover, 1964.

Saint-Foix, Georges Poullain. *The Symphonies of Mozart*. Translated by Leslie Orrey. London: Dobson, 1947.

Rachmaninoff

Bertensson, Sergei, and Jay Leyda. *Sergei Rachmaninoff: A Lifetime in Music*. Bloomington: Indiana University Press, 2001.

Norris, Geoffrey. "Rakhmaninov." *The New Grove Dictionary of Music and Musicians*. London: Macmillan, 1980.

Rimsky-Korsakov

Rimsky-Korsakov, Nikolay Andreyevich. *My Musical Life*. Translated by Judah A. Joffe. New York: Tudor Publishing, 1936.

Schubert

Gibbs, Christopher H. *The Life of Schubert*. Cambridge: Cambridge University Press, 2000.

McKay, Elizabeth Norman. *Franz Schubert: A Biography*. Oxford: Clarendon Press, 1997.

Schumann

Daverio, John. *Robert Schumann: Herald of a New Poetic Age*. Oxford: Oxford University Press, 1997.

Taylor, Ronald. *Robert Schumann: His Life and Work*. New York: Universe Books, 1982.

Shostakovich

Fanning, David. *The Breath of the Symphonist: Shostakovich's Tenth.* London: Royal Music Association, 1988.

Fay, Laurel E. *Shostakovich: A Life.* New York: Oxford University Press, 2000.

Ho, Allan Benedict, and Dmitry Feofanov. *Shostakovich Reconsidered.* London: Toccata Press, 1998.

Litvinova, Flora. *Memoirs of Dmitri Shostakovich.* Article commissioned by Elizabeth Wilson.

MacDonald, Ian. *The New Shostakovich.* London: Fourth Estate, 1990.

Shaporina, Lyubov. *Intimacy and Terror: Soviet Diaries of the 1930s.* Edited by Veronique Garros, Natalia Korenevskaya, and Thomas Lahusen. New York: New Press, 1995.

Shostakovich, Dmitri. *Testimony.* Edited by Solomon Volkov. New York: Harper and Row, 1979.

Volkov, Solomon. *Shostakovich and Stalin.* New York: Knopf, 2004.

Wilson, Elizabeth. *Shostakovich: A Life Remembered.* Princeton, NJ: Princeton University Press, 1994.

Smetana

Clapham, John. "Bedřich Smetana." *The New Grove Dictionary of Music and Musicians.* London: Macmillan, 1980.

Large, Brian. *Smetana.* New York: Praeger Publishers, 1970.

Strauss

Del Mar, Norman. *Richard Strauss: A Critical Commentary on His Life and Works.* 3 vols. Ithaca, NY: Cornell University Press, 1986.

Williamson, John. *Strauss: Also Sprach Zarathustra.* Cambridge: Cambridge University Press, 1993.

Stravinsky
Eksteins, Modris. *The Rites of Spring.* New York: Anchor Books, 1989.

Stravinsky, Igor. *An Autobiography.* New York: Norton, 1962.

Stravinsky, Igor, and Robert Craft. *Conversation with Igor Stravinsky.* Berkeley: University of California Press, 1980.

————. *Expositions and Developments.* Berkeley: University of California Press, 1981.

Toorn, Pieter C. van den. *Stravinsky and* The Rite of Spring. Oxford: Oxford University Press, 1987.

Walsh, Stephen. *Stravinsky: A Creative Spring.* New York: Knopf, 1999.

White, Eric Walter. *Stravinsky: The Composer and His Works.* Berkeley: University of California Press, 1969.

Tchaikovsky
Holden, Anthony. *Tchaikovsky: A Biography.* New York: Random House, 1995.

Poznansky, Alexander. *Tchaikovsky: The Quest for the Inner Man.* New York: Schirmer Books, 1991.

Tchaikovsky, Modest. *The Life and Letters of Peter Ilyich Tchaikovsky.* Abridged and translated by Rosa Newmarch. London: John Lane, 1906.

Warrack, John. *Tchaikovsky.* New York: Scribners, 1973.

————. *Tchaikovsky Symphonies and Concertos.* Seattle: University of Washington Press, 1971.

Vivaldi

Everett, Paul. *Vivaldi: The Four Seasons and Other Concertos, Op. 8.* Cambridge: Cambridge University Press, 1996.

Heller, Karl. *Antonio Vivaldi: The Red Priest of Venice.* Portland, OR: Amadeus Press, 1991.

Landon, H. C. Robbins. *Vivaldi: The Voice of the Baroque.* London: Thames and Hudson, 1993.

Talbot, Michael. "Antonio Vivaldi." *The New Grove Dictionary of Music and Musicians.* London: Macmillan, 1980.

Walton

Cox, David. "William Walton." *The Symphony: Elgar to the Present Day.* Edited by Robert Simpson. London: Pelican Books, 1967.

Discography

Bach, Johann Sebastian
Brandenburg Concerto No. 2 (ca. 1721). NAXOS 8.520007. Bohdan Warschal conducting the Capella Istropolitana.

Violin Concerto in E Major (ca. 1717). NAXOS 8.550194. Takako Nishizaki (violin) and Olivier Dohnányi conducting the Capella Istropolitana.

Beethoven, Ludwig van
Piano Concerto No. 4 (1806). NAXOS 8.550122. Stefan Vladar (piano) and Barry Wordsworth conducting the Capella Istropolitana.

Symphony No. 3 (1804). NAXOS 8.553475. Béla Drahos conducting the Esterházy Sinfonia.

Symphony No. 9 (1824). NAXOS 8.553478. Béla Drahos conducting the Esterházy Sinfonia and Chorus.

Brahms, Johannes
Symphony No. 4 (1885). NAXOS 8.550281. Alexander Rahbari conducting the BRT Philharmonic Orchestra, Brussels.

Violin Concerto (1878). NAXOS 8.550195. Takako Nishizaki (violin) and Stephen Gunzenhauser conducting the Slovak Philharmonic Orchestra.

Copland, Aaron
Appalachian Spring (1944). NAXOS 8.550282. Stephen Gunzenhauser conducting the Czechoslovak Radio Symphony Orchestra.

Debussy, Claude
La Mer (1905). NAXOS 8.550262. Alexander Rahbari conducting the BRT Philharmonic Orchestra, Brussels.

Dvořák Antonín
Symphony No. 8 (1889). NAXOS 8.550269. Stephen Gunzenhauser conducting the Slovak Philharmonic Orchestra.

'Cello Concerto (1895). NAXOS 8.550503. Maria Kliegel ('cello) and Michael Halász conducting the Royal Philharmonic Orchestra.

Haydn, Joseph
Symphony No. 104 (1795). NAXOS 8.550287. Barry Wordsworth conducting the Capella Istropolitana.

Holst, Gustav
The Planets (1916). NAXOS 8.555776. David Lloyd-Jones conducting the Royal Scottish National Orchestra.

Ives, Charles
Three Places in New England (1914). NAXOS 8.559353. James Sinclair conducting the Malmö Symphony Orchestra.

Mahler, Gustav
Symphony No. 5 (1902). NAXOS 8.550528. Antal Wit conducting the Polish National Radio Symphony Orchestra.

Mendelssohn, Felix
Symphony No. 4, "Italian" (1833). NAXOS 8.553200 Reinhold Seifried conducting the National Symphony of Ireland.

Mozart, Wolfgang Amadeus
Piano Concerto No. 24 in C Minor (1786). NAXOS 8.550204. Jenö Jandó (piano) and Mátyás Antal conducting the Concentus Hungaricus.

Symphony No. 41 (1788). NAXOS 8.550299. Barry Wordsworth conducting the Capella Istropolitana.

Rachmaninoff, Sergey
Symphony No. 2 (1907). NAXOS 8.554230. Alexander Anissimov conducting the National Symphony Orchestra of Ireland.

Rimsky-Korsakov, Nikolai
Scheherazade (1888). NAXOS 8.550726. Enrique Bátiz conducting the Philharmonic Orchestra, London.

Schubert, Franz
Symphony No. 9 (1826). NAXOS 8.553096. Michael Halász conducting the Failoni Orchestra.

Schumann, Robert
Symphony No. 3 (1850). NAXOS 8.553082. Antal Wit conducting the Polish National Radio Symphony Orchestra.

Shostakovich, Dmitri
Symphony No. 5 (1937). NAXOS 8.550427. Alexander Rahbari conducting the BRT Philharmonic Orchestra, Brussels.

Symphony No. 10 (1953). NAXOS 8.550326. Alexander Rahbari conducting the BRT Philharmonic Orchestra, Brussels.

Smetana, Bedřich
Má Vlast (1879). NAXOS 8.550931. Antal Wit conducting the Polish National Radio Symphony Orchestra.

Strauss, Richard
Thus Spoke Zarathustra (1896). NAXOS **8.550182.** Zdenek Košler conducting the Slovak Philharmonic.

Stravinsky, Igor
The Rite of Spring (1912). NAXOS 8.553217. Alexander Rahbari conducting the BRT Philharmonic Orchestra, Brussels.

Tchaikovsky, Pyotr Ilyich
Symphony No. 4 (1878). NAXOS 8.550488. Adrian Leaper conducting the
Polish National Radio Symphony Orchestra.

Violin Concerto (1878). NAXOS 8.557690. Ilya Kaler (violin) and Dmitry
Yablonsky conducting the Russian Philharmonic Orchestra.

Vivaldi, Antonio
The Four Seasons (ca. 1720). NAXOS 8.553219. Takako Nishizaki (violin)
and Stephen Gunzenhauser conducting the Capella Istropolitana.

"The Ones That Got Away" and Extras

Beethoven, Ludwig van
The Creatures of Prometheus, Op. 43 (1801). NAXOS 8.553404. Michael
Halász conducting the Melbourne Symphony Orchestra.

Bizet, Georges
Symphony in C Major (1855). NAXOS 8.553027. Donald Johanos
conducting the New Zealand Symphony Orchestra.

Hindemith, Paul
Symphony *Mathis der Maler* (1934). NAXOS 8.553078. Franz-Paul Decker
conducting the New Zealand Symphony Orchestra.

Mozart, Wolfgang Amadeus
"Un bacio di mano," K. 513 (1788). Brilliant Classics 92632/5. Ezio Maria
Tisi (bass) and Wilhelm Keitel conducting the European Chamber Orchestra.

Prokofiev, Sergey
Symphony No. 5 (1944). NAXOS 8.554058. Theodore Kuchar conducting
the National Symphony Orchestra of Ukraine.

Shostakovich, Dmitri
Symphony No. 9 (1945). NAXOS 8.550427. Alexander Rahbari conducting
the BRT Philharmonic Orchestra, Brussels.

Vaughan Williams, Ralph
Symphony No. 5 (1943). NAXOS 8.550738. Kees Bakels conducting the Bournemouth Symphony Orchestra.

Walton, William
Symphony No. 1 (1935). NAXOS 8.553180. Paul Daniel conducting the English Northern Philharmonia.

Credits

Text Permission

Everett, Paul. *Vivaldi: The Four Seasons and Other Concertos, Op. 8.* Copyright © 1996 Cambridge University Press. Reprinted with the permission of Cambridge University Press.

Music Permissions

Featured Works

Bach, Johann Sebastian. Brandenburg Concerto No. 2 (ca. 1721). Performed by Bohdan Warschal conducting the Capella Istropolitana. Courtesy of Naxos of America.

Bach, Johann Sebastian. Violin Concerto in E Major (1717). Performed by Takako Nishizaki, violin; Olivier Dohnányi conducting the Capella Istropolitana. Courtesy of Naxos of America.

Beethoven, Ludwig van. Piano Concerto No. 4 (1806). Performed by Stefan Vladar, piano; Barry Wordsworth conducting the Capella Istropolitana. Courtesy of Naxos of America.

Beethoven, Ludwig van. Symphony No. 3 (1804). Performed by Béla Drahos conducting the Esterházy Sinfonia. Courtesy of Naxos of America.

Beethoven, Ludwig van. Symphony No. 9 (1824). Performed by Béla Drahos conducting the Esterházy Sinfonia and Chorus. Courtesy of Naxos of America.

Brahms, Johannes. Symphony No. 4 (1885). Performed by Alexander Rahbari conducting the BRT Philharmonic Orchestra, Brussels. Courtesy of Naxos of America.

Brahms, Johannes. Violin Concerto (1878). Performed by Takako Nishizaki, violin; Stephen Gunzenhauser conducting the Slovak Philharmonic Orchestra. Courtesy of Naxos of America.

Copland, Aaron. *Appalachian Spring* (Suite) (1944). Published by Boosey & Hawkes. Performed by Stephen Gunzenhauser conducting the Czechoslovak Radio Symphony Orchestra. Courtesy of Naxos of America.

Debussy, Claude. *La Mer* (1905). Performed by Alexander Rahbari conducting the BRT Philharmonic Orchestra, Brussels. Courtesy of Naxos of America.

Dvořák, Antonín. Symphony No. 8 (1889). Performed by Stephen Gunzenhauser conducting the Slovak Philharmonic Orchestra. Courtesy of Naxos of America.

Dvořák, Antonín. 'Cello Concerto (1895). Performed by Maria Kliegel, 'cello; Michael Halász conducting the Royal Philharmonic Orchestra. Courtesy of Naxos of America.

Haydn, Joseph. Symphony No. 104 (1795). Performed by Barry Wordsworth conducting the Capella Istropolitana. Courtesy of Naxos of America.

Holst, Gustav. *The Planets* (1916). Performed by David Lloyd-Jones conducting the Royal Scottish National Orchestra. Courtesy of Naxos of America.

Ives, Charles. *Three Places in New England* (1914). Published by Carl Fischer. Performed by James Sinclair conducting the Malmö Symphony Orchestra. Courtesy of Naxos of America.

Mahler, Gustav. Symphony No. 5 (1902). Performed by Antal Wit conducting the Polish National Radio Symphony Orchestra. Courtesy of Naxos of America.

Mendelssohn, Felix. Symphony No. 4, "Italian" (1833). Performed by Reinhold Seifried conducting the National Symphony of Ireland. Courtesy of Naxos of America.

Mozart, Wolfgang Amadeus. Piano Concerto No. 24 in C Minor (1786). Performed by Jenö Jandó, piano; Mátyás Antal conducting the Concentus Hungaricus. Courtesy of Naxos of America.

Mozart, Wolfgang Amadeus. Symphony No. 41 (1788). Performed by Barry Wordsworth conducting the Capella Istropolitana. Courtesy of Naxos of America.

Rachmaninoff, Sergey. Symphony No. 2 (1907). Published by Boosey & Hawkes. Performed by Alexander Anissimov conducting the National Symphony Orchestra of Ireland. Courtesy of Naxos of America.

Rimsky-Korsakov, Nikolai. *Scheherazade* (1888). Performed by Enrique Bátiz conducting the Philharmonic Orchestra, London. Courtesy of Naxos of America.

Schubert, Franz. Symphony No. 9 (1826). Performed by Michael Halász conducting the Failoni Orchestra. Courtesy of Naxos of America.

Schumann, Robert. Symphony No. 3 (1850). Performed by Antal Wit conducting the Polish National Radio Symphony Orchestra. Courtesy of Naxos of America.

Shostakovich, Dmitri. Symphony No. 5 (1937). Published by G. Schirmer, Inc. Performed by Alexander Rahbari conducting the BRT Philharmonic Orchestra, Brussels. Courtesy of Naxos of America.

Shostakovich, Dmitri. Symphony No. 10 (1953). Published by G. Schirmer, Inc. Performed by Alexander Rahbari conducting the BRT Philharmonic Orchestra, Brussels. Courtesy of Naxos of America.

Smetana, Bedřich. *Má Vlast* (1879). Performed by Antal Wit conducting the Polish National Radio Symphony Orchestra. Courtesy of Naxos of America.

Strauss, Richard. *Thus Spoke Zarathustra* (1896). Published by C.F. Peter Corporation. Performed by Zdenek Košler conducting the Slovak Philharmonic. Courtesy of Naxos of America.

Stravinsky, Igor. *The Rite of Spring* (1912). Published by Boosey & Hawkes. Performed by Alexander Rahbari conducting the BRT Philharmonic Orchestra, Brussels. Courtesy of Naxos of America.

Tchaikovsky, Pyotr Ilyich. Symphony No. 4 (1878). Performed by Adrian Leaper conducting the Polish National Radio Symphony Orchestra. Courtesy of Naxos of America.

Tchaikovsky, Pyotr Ilyich. Violin Concerto (1878). Performed by Ilya Kaler, violin; Dmitry Yablonsky conducting the Russian Philharmonic Orchestra. Courtesy of Naxos of America.

Vivaldi, Antonio. *The Four Seasons* (ca. 1720). Performed by Takako Nishizaki, violin; Stephen Gunzenhauser conducting the Capella Istropolitana. Courtesy of Naxos of America.

Additional Works

Beethoven, Ludwig van. *The Creatures of Prometheus*, Op. 43. Performed by Michael Halász conducting the Melbourne Symphony Orchestra. Courtesy of Naxos of America.

Bizet, Georges. Symphony in C Major (1855). Performed by Donald Johanos conducting the New Zealand Symphony Orchestra. Courtesy of Naxos of America.

Hindemith, Paul. Symphony *Mathis de Maler* (1934). Published by Schott Music GmbH & Co. KG. Performed by Franz-Paul Decker conducting the New Zealand Symphony Orchestra. Courtesy of Naxos of America.

Mozart, Wolfgang Amadeus. *"Un bacio di mano,"* K. 513 (1788). Performed by Ezio Maria Tisi, bass; Wilhelm Keitel conducting the European Chamber Orchestra. Courtesy of Brilliant Classics.

Prokofiev, Sergey. Symphony No. 5 (1944). Published by G. Schirmer, Inc. Performed by Theodore Kuchar conducting the National Symphony Orchestra of Ukraine. Courtesy of Naxos of America.

Shostakovich, Dmitri. Symphony No. 9 (1945). Published by G. Schirmer, Inc. Performed by Alexander Rahbari conducting the BRT Philharmonic Orchestra, Brussels. Courtesy of Naxos of America.

Vaughan-Williams, Ralph. Symphony No. 5 (1943). © Oxford University Press 1946. Licensed by Oxford University Press. All Rights Reserved. Performed by Kees Bakels conducting the Bournemouth Symphony Orchestra. Courtesy of Naxos of America.

Walton, William. Symphony No. 1 (1935). © Oxford University Press 1936. Licensed by Oxford University Press. All Rights Reserved. Performed by Paul Daniel conducting the English Northern Philharmonia. Courtesy of Naxos of America.

Notes

Notes

Notes

Notes

Notes